Albert Gallatin Riddle

A Romance of the Cuyahoga Valley

Albert Gallatin Riddle

A Romance of the Cuyahoga Valley

ISBN/EAN: 9783744664967

Printed in Europe, USA, Canada, Australia, Japan

Cover: Foto ©Thomas Meinert / pixelio.de

More available books at **www.hansebooks.com**

A ROMANCE OF THE CUYAHOGA VALLEY.

By A. G. RIDDLE,

AUTHOR OF "BART RIDGELEY."

———

CLEVELAND:

COBB, ANDREWS & CO.

BOSTON: NICHOLS & HALL.

1874.

Stereotyped by John C. Regan, 19 Spring Lane, Boston.

CONTENTS.

THE PORTRAIT.

CHAPTER I.

THE PROPHECY.

ALL the short rainy autumn day, with his bare brown feet, and scant,worn and soiled roundabout and pants, had he been walking and runing through the muddy roads and by-ways, down through Shalersville to Ravenna, and finally back to Freedom, and so across the woods home. His poor faded mother had been suddenly taken worse toward morning of that day, and he had hastily cut and carried in some wood, and, after a scant breakfast, had hurried off for the doctor. He had gone by way of one of the neighbors, and asked that some one would go and stay until he returned, and was off. He would give the doctor his five mink-skins, that he had caught that fall, along the Cuyahoga, and would do without a new preceptor and spelling-book. Now, weary, famished and disheartened, as the early night deepened in the leafless trees, he hurried towards home, with an unusual depression and foreboding. He nad failed to meet the doctor, and had only left word

(5)

for him at his residence, and the places where his patients lived. All the day he had carried over his long and lonely road a sad, undefined presentiment.

It was already quite dark as he hastened on. He was familiar with all the forest paths, and could traverse the woods anywhere without a trail, and with a sense of absolute security. As he approached the little clearing, he ran forward and climbed upon the decaying brush-fence that marked its uncertain limits, and paused a moment to look at the log hovel but a few rods distant — the only home he could remember — with its leaky roof, and decaying walls, slowly lapsing to ruin.

No window was on the side of his approach, and he could detect no smoke escaping from the blackened opening at one end of the low roof. As he passed around to the front, he stopped to listen at the low door of rough boards that hung on rude wooden hinges. No sound reached him; and with a trembling hand he pulled the string and pushed the door open, into the single, dark, silent room.

"Ma," he called out in an eager, distressed voice, with the tears unconsciously escaping from his eyes. A moan answered him from one corner.

"Oh, ma, I didn't find the doctor at Hines's, and I went clear to Ravenna, and they told me he had gone up to see old Mis Roper at the centre of Nelson; and I went there, and he had gone home by way of Randolph, and I missed him, — I hurried fast as I could. Has pa been home?" Another moan was his answer.

"Oh, ma! are you worse?" An undistinguishable murmur was all he heard in reply.

"Where's John? Has nobody been here?" faintly. He went to the broken stone hearth of the jambless fireplace, and found the shortened wooden poker, and stirred open the ashes, which disclosed the glowing remains of the charred back-log. Upon the coals he put some pieces of hickory bark, and soon a crackling flame leaped up and revealed the wretched room, with its two or three broken chairs and wooden stools, — its rickety, rough table standing by the poor thin bed, upon which lay the weak and suffering woman.

The boy again approached the bed, and was frightened by the change in the face, disclosed by the ruddy light of the fire.

"Ma! ma!" said he, in hushed and awed voice. The heavy eyes opened, and the face was with an effort turned towards him. "Fred, is it you? — I feared you wouldn't come — I wanted — to tell ye — ye — I— I— ain't yer mother, Fred — I —"

"Ma!" with a low cry of anguish. and a look in his great innocent eyes like that with which a young fawn would receive a death-blow from its dam.

"No matter," said the exhausted woman, "yer an angel to me."

"May I love you, ma? May I love little Johnny?" in a low, plaintive voice. The poor woman moaned again, and tears ran over her faded face, and broken murmurs died on her drawn and shrivelled lips. At last she said:

"Fred, put yer fingers on my eyes for a little — so —," and he stood with his fingers lightly resting on the closed lids, and listening to the slow, low breathing. Slower it came, and then, — it did not come again.

The child listened with a great awe, and a great pallor came into his face, and what next occurred he never knew.

A plaintive cry from John, lying by the side of the silent, unbreathing form, aroused him, as a little soiled face, and head with tangled flaxen hair, started up.

"Hush! hush, John!" said Fred, taking him from the ragged bed-clothes. "Hush! don't cry." Something in his manner seemed to awe the child, who stood half naked in the strong light, looking frightened at the elder, and then turning towards the bed, cried out: "Ma, ma; Don wants micky — Don wants micky."

"Hush, hush, John! she won't hear you." And going to a shelf he found a pewter basin, from which he poured some milk into a battered cup, and gave the hungry child; to whom he also gave the remains of a johnny-cake. He then drew from under the bed a small truckle-bed, and placed the appeased and sleepy John carefully among its tattered coverings, where he subsided into quiet sleep.

The boy, used to these offices for the younger, and doing the scanty chores about their wretched home, mechanically replenished the fire, and put two or three things in their places, all the time with a dumb, benumbed feeling, aroused by the words: "I'm not yer mother." He was too young to reason, or reflect, or think; he could only feel that the world was torn from him; that his mother was not his, that "little Johnny" did not belong to him, and that he must go away, — but not to-night; for they would want him. Then he went on his tip-toes towards the bed, and began to realize, in his childish way, the awful thing that had happened.

He was not afraid of the rigid form, that was dear and tender to him; but it was the shadowy, unknown thing, Death, and it was there, and he shrunk away a little from it; and going out, he brought in more wood and placed it about the fire to dry. Then with a gourd shell he brought fresh water from the spring; and remembering that he was very hungry, drank the remainder of the milk, and thought he would bake a johnny-cake; but when he found that there would not be more than meal enough for a cake for breakfast, he gathered up a few dry crumbs, and contented himself with them.

He remembered that when his sister died, two years ago, they placed a clean wet cloth over her face; and ransacking a small chest, from which the lid had been broken, he found a white rag, which having moistened, he carefully and reverently spread over the face of the dead. Then replenishing the fire, he removed his clothes, and lying down by little John, twice or thrice uttered, with folded hands, the little prayer his mother had taught him; and with a hazy numbness of heart, he went to sleep; while the strong fire-light, leaping up the open chimney-way, for a time lit up the wretched room, glinted the white covering on the face of the dead, and played lovingly upon the features of the sleeping boys, — one round and chubby, with the flaxen locks of infancy, and the other dark and beautiful, with long black eyelashes fringing his brown cheek, and his striking, but prematurely old, face framed in tangled masses of dark damp hair. The rain subsided into sprinkles, and the fitful wind was sinking to little gusts that played among the few

belated leaves which still clung to the trees without.
Within, the fire burned out and the brands fell apart,
throwing, from time to time, a sudden flame which filled
the room with ghostly shadows, and then subsided to a
red glow, that gave color and warmth to everything,
until that, too, faded out.   An eye that could look beyond the gross and material world, might have seen the
sordid room luminous with a beautifying radiance, in
the light of which soft and tender fingers were removing the harsh and bitter lines of earth and suffering
from the face of the dead, and bestowing upon the
mouth the sweet, indescribable smile of serene and
beautiful death ; while loving forms were bending over
and kissing the eyelids of the sleeping children, and
leaving on the brow of the dark one a wreath of mingled light and shadow.   Had this sight met the eyes
of a seer, he would have prophesied of suffering and
final triumph.   Was it martyrdom in this world, and
crowning in the next?   The wreath was very like a
garland, and its roses had the hue of earth.

CHAPTER II.

MORNING came, and its sunshine lay rich and warm through all the narrow but beautiful valley of the Cuyahoga, whose scarcely tinged waters, escaping from the Welchfield marshes, plunged through the rocky barrier known as "the Rapids," and sweeping southerly along the eastern border of Mantua, turned its vehement current, swollen with the autumn rains, south-westerly. Below the bend of the river, on its southerly bank, and a few rods distant, stood the solitary cabin mentioned above.

Silent and lonely under the gilding sun, with its rude door and patched and botched window, and all its wretchedness brought out from the night, in strong relief, as the level rays illuminated it. Two or three acres of cleared ground, with little signs of cultivation, and bearing a thrifty eclectic crop of thistles, mullen, dock and burdock, surrounded it, with a little imperfectly paled patch, in which were a few weed-choked vegetables, ripened and shrivelled by the late autumn, without a pig or hen, cow, or even a dog to relieve the squalid desolation of the place. A pathway led down to the river, where, attached to a little tree, with a bark painter, floated Fred's half-filled little dug-

(11)

out. Another path led up from a clearing a little below, along which, with an unsteady step, a slouched, rough-looking man, with bloated face, blood-shot eyes, half-covered with tatters, and the wreck of an old straw hat, broken down on one side of his matted hair, was straggling up. The face may have been good once, but no traces of youthful freshness or purity remained. An unsuccessful effort to troll the refrain of a low drinking song, employed the small surplus of faculties not used in keeping his feet, as he came through the belt of woods into the field surrounding the hut, but was hopelessly abandoned, as, with a seemingly infirm purpose, he approached — not his home — but the place where he sometimes got sober. He was evidently recovering from a long and exhausting debauch, and his eye still had the dull, uncertain swimming of inebriation. He reached and steadied himself on the rotting wooden step, in front of the door, at which for a moment he stared with an earnest intensity, as if to remove any lingering doubt of its identity; then, with a muttered ejaculation, he dashed the door open, and partially stumbling, stepped and reeled over the decayed door-sill. Recovering himself, and resting with one hand on the door, he sent his stupid stare about the now well-lighted hovel. His swimming eyes stopped on the covered face at one end of the wretched bed. "What the hell! — hullo, old woman! — I say; ye sleep with yer — yer — night-cap over yer eyes, eh?" Making a step forward, he snatched the cloth from the dead white face, which for a moment struck even his obscured and staggering faculties. The noisy entrance of the drunken man awakened the children;

when Fred, with his eyes staring wide, like those of a
timid wild animal, into which in a moment came
something of the instinctive courage of the brute,
sprang between the man and the bed, and, with all his
force, pushed him back. "You shall not touch her!
you shall not touch her!" he cried; "she said she was
not my mother, and you shall not touch her!" As if,
somehow, this declaration released him from all respect
for the person of the intruder. The man turned and
gazed at the defiant boy with uncomprehending amazement, while John, who was aroused to the crying stage,
put up a dolorous wail. Beginning to be sobered by
the unwontedness around him, the still dazed man
looked wonderingly about, — even a drunken man could
not fail to identify the place. Presently he again approached Fred, and in a low confidential tone, as if to
assure him that he was somehow on his side, if he only
knew where that was, — "I say, Fred, eh; old feller,
yer know, what is't?" The boy's only answer was a
dumb gesture toward the bed.

"Eh! come now, tell a feller; can't ye?"

"She is dead!" with his lip quivering and tears well-
ing into his eyes.

"No; yer don't come that on me!" when his eye
again fell on the ghastly, changeless face. Something in
its immovable rigidity, its stark pallor, seemed to
strike his returning senses, and he dashed his soiled
hand over his bleared, rheumy eyes, and slowly,
and with a doubting reverence, approached the bed,
when the wasted and sharp outline of the features,
with the unopening eyes and still bosom, impressed
upon the wretched man that he stood in the presence

of his dead wife. When that idea had fully mastered him, — "I say, Fred, when d' this yer 'appen?" in a low, hollow whisper.

"Last night," said Fred, giving way, in sobs of boyish agony, for the first time.

John, who had tumbled out of his nest of reeking rags, came toddling to the bedside. "Ma! ma! ma!" in his piping wail. So the three miserable beings — the unknowing John, the just comprehending, sobering father, ready to fight or cry, as a feather might incline, and the utterly overcome older child, severed from the world by their poverty, squalor and wretchedness — united in their abandoned and desolate cries over the finally extinguished spark that had shed a ray of warmth upon them, — the broken band that had feebly united them to home and a bare existence.

Their grief was interrupted by the entrance of the neighbor below, who, although poor, had occasionally looked upon them with a cheery face and a little help, and who remembered that he had seen none of them for two or three days. Surprised and shocked, he aroused the now nearly sobered man, and hurried him off to call the neighbors to his assistance, while he helped to huddle the scanty clothes upon the children, intending to take them to his house, a half mile below. Fred refused to leave his mother alone, and when induced to go, he wet and replaced the cloth over her face; and the wondering neighbor, acting upon the suggestion, drew the soiled sheet over the woman's head, and hurried the children away.

CHAPTER III.

ALONE.

ON the second day after her death, the remains of
the poor woman were put away, with decent and
tender respect. In that far-off time, of log-cabins,
scattered along the rough highways, of small, rude,
stumpy fields, of ox-sleds and heavy carts, of coarse
fare, of flax breaks, hatchels, spinning-wheels, hand-
looms, and fulling mills ; of tow cloth for summer, and
butternut fulled cloth for winter ; of cow-hide boots
and fox-skin caps, — the "forehanded" were not much
better off than the poor. A community of fortune and
interest, a common struggle for subsistence with the
rugged stubbornness of even a kindly nature in the
wilderness, when the coming of a new settler was an
event of public importance, and the raising of a log-
house a sort of holiday, forbade much real suffering,
and toil-roughened hands were ready to do the needed
kindness to the unfortunate and afflicted.

The actual condition of the Wardens, made known
at the death of the poor woman, was a surprise, and
created almost a horror. What could now be done,
was done for them. A coffin was prepared, a preacher
was procured, and a large concourse assembled from

(15)

the nearest settlements ; a very respectable procession
followed the remains, borne by the men, to their quiet
resting-place.

Warden, sobered and decent, Fred, with an extemporized suit and cow-hide shoes, and little Johnny, with
his clarified face and combed hair, led between his
father and elder brother, as the sole mourners, were
the objects of much comment and commiseration.

Fred, who went about in a benumbed and dazed sort
of a way, came in for the largest share of notice.
Living in the woods with his mother, and seldom asso-
ciating with other boys, and tall for his age, his manner was shy ; and, accustomed to the solitude of the
forest, and loneliness of the river, he was growing up
thoughtful and taciturn.   As well as he was capable, he
had turned over in his mind the words of the dying
woman, that she was not his mother.   He remembered
to have heard it said that persons, when dying, were
often out of their heads, and he thought that these
disturbing words might have been spoken in that condition ; so he went over and over with this subject,
and then tried to think of what was going on around
him.

As a group of women stood a little apart, looking at
the filling of the grave, — " Did you ever hear o' such
a thing?   Old Mis Pettibone said that he went mor'n
twenty mile for the doctor, and got back jest 'afore his
mother died, and he'n the baby's there all livin' alone
at the time ; an' that he must a closed 'er eyes, an' put
a wet cloth on 'er face, and him not mor'n 'levin year
old ! "

" Not mor'n nine," was the answer.   " His folks

came here 'bout six year ago; and Mis Warden told
Mis Jones that Fred was three year old, then."

"Du tell!" and the low-voiced women relapsed into
admiring silence, as they intently watched the unconscious boy, now as impassive in his grief as a young
Indian.

"What a time she must a' had, all her life. Sam
allers away, an' when to hum never sober, and never
doin' nothin', and Mis Blair said there warn't a blessed
thing in the house, but a little musty meal; an' how on
airth them children lived, mortal sakes only knows."

The grave was filled, and the broken turf replaced,
the simple ceremony ended, and the saddened neighbors dispersed homeward. At the entrance to the
burying-place, a kind woman, who had taken charge
of little Johnny, resumed possession of him, and
placing him in the box of a lumber wagon, drove
away; while Fred, who relinquished his hand, stood
with his great, innocent, tender eyes, full of mute sadness, staring after him, and thought, for the moment,
that he must turn back in the twilight, and go alone to
the deserted hut by the river; then he turned again, as
if undecided, to the fresh mound of broken earth that
hid his mother. At this moment, a man who had
attentively and kindly observed him approached, and
holding out his hand, — "You are going home with
me to-night," he said, speaking in a voice so gentle
and tender, that the poor child looked up in wonder.
The face was a good, strong, homely, manly face, now
all aglow with a tender smile, and with moisture in the
kindly gray eyes.

Fred had never met such a look before, and at once

2

held out both his hands to his new friend. As they turned into the highway, another younger, slender, thin-faced, but kindly man, joined them, and took Fred's other hand, which he held with a grasp almost painful. Thus between them they led him eastward. to the Maryfield Corners, and so north on the state road, along which they proceeded for a half mile, and then turned off to the east.

"I understand," said the younger man, as they walked along, "that this young man is quite a trapper, and I don't know but a hunter also."

"Indeed! Is this the boy that caught the otter? How was that? Is your name Jake?" asked the elder.

"Fred," was the answer.

"How was it about the otter?" No answer.

"Uncle Bill asks you about catching an otter," said the younger, kindly.

"The otter? Oh!" as if awakening, "he broke the trap and got away." It was evident that his thoughts were elsewhere.

"Poor boy!" said Uncle Bill; "he is overcome and worn out; sha'n't I carry you?" very kindly. "You are not so heavy as a buck."

"Oh, I can walk!" cried the boy, aroused partly by the unwonted kindness of their voices, and as much by a wish to appear manly. Not many rods east of the state road, they reached Uncle Bill's residence, one of the few framed houses that then indicated one of the better-to-do. The younger of the two men left them at the gate, and Fred was tenderly received by a kind, matronly woman, who, with a young man and a boy, about Fred's age, constituted the household. Fred seemed to have been expected, and he was soon seated with his kind host at a table covered by a clean white cloth, and with more and better dishes than he could remember ever to have seen. A tender, smoking venison steak was placed before him; and when his supper was finished, with a bowl of milk, he was taken into the best room, more sumptuously furnished than he had dreamed of, and sank, wonderingly, into the bed, and into a slumber deeper than dreams, and longer than the night.

CHAPTER IV.

WHAT WAS SAID ABOUT IT.

LATE in the evening, at the new yellow store at the Corners, several men dropped in,— Uncle Bill Skinner and Fenton, just mentioned; Sim Shelden, from the Carman neighborhood, and others; and naturally the talk turned upon the funeral and the Wardens.

"Brother James had rather a tight fit to bring 'er in, eh — Uncle Bill?" asked one.

"Rather. He left it a leetle in doubt, whether the water had been efficaciously applied, — so that if Elder Rider should happen to be there when she arrives, he will make a point against the poor thing. You see they don't hold just alike, on all the vital points."

"I think," said Fenton, with the broad accent of his Irish origin, "that if brother James should put in Sam by way of mitigation of damages, as the lawyers call it, he'd carry his case."

"Sam's not a bad fellow nat'rally," said another.

"He was anything but a good husband," rejoined Fenton, with warmth, "to leave that poor woman to die alone with those starving children Free as grace is during a revival, none was ever wasted on him. Why, in that old hovel there warn't enough to draw a mouse, — the flies had deserted it."

(20)

"Where do ye s'pose Sam is to-night?" asked one.

"Down at Green's, drinking that stuff, — one drop of which will kill sixteen old rats," answered Fenton. "He loafed off that way, from his wife's grave."

"There ought to be something done to break up that place," said Shelden.

"What can be done?" asked Uncle Bill. "He's rich and cunnin', and sly and shrewd, and deep and still."

"Yes, he 'stils and brews too, and has a devil of a gang about him, and will meet you all the time as smooth, and plausible, and polite, and soft as a basket of chips," said another.

"Where did he come from?" asked Shelden, "and how did he make his money?"

"The devil only knows," answered Fenton. "He came from the South somewhere. He brought up a good team, looked coarse and rough, can't read or write, as you know, rented the old tavern stand over there, and then bought it, and bought other land; brought a deed for a good deal with him, and has slipt and slid, and worried and wriggled along, nobody can tell how, till I heard Squire Foster say he was the richest man in Portage County."

"Did Warden come with him?"

"No, I think he came a few months later," said Uncle Bill. "There must be some sort of relation or connection between them; for Sam built that shanty over across the river on Green's land, and Green's sister used to go over there once in a while. I never knew much about 'em."

"No wonder Green's wife died," remarked Fenton;

" such a husband, or such a son as Jake, would either be too much for any woman, and no one could stand both."

" I never heard anything specific against Green," said Shelden, " except that he has a gang about him."

" No, nor I," said Uncle Bill; " but the atmosphere is bad about him; you don't feel easy in his presence; and if he laughs, nobody laughs with him; such men ain't healthy."

" What will become of the children?" asked Shelden. " There's two or three, ain't there?"

" One died a year or two ago," said Fenton. " Mrs. Jones has taken the youngest, and the oldest is at Mr. Skinner's."

"Do you know, Fenton," said the latter, " that as I sat lookin' at 'em this afternoon, Sam, with his florid, bloated face, and red eyes, and the freckled, round-faced, tow-headed little one, and remembered the pale, flaxen-haired mother, and then looked at Fred, tall and dark, with his splendid eyes and well-cut features, it 'peared to me that he belonged to another race?"

"Of course he does," said Fenton, decidedly; " there's blood and race in that boy, you may depend upon that; you can see it in his motions. Row Lewis said that he treed a wild cat, off in back of Sam's house, about a month ago, and got a ball stuck in his rifle, and that this boy came to him, and staid, and watched the cat till he went down to Giles's shop, and fixed the gun, and went back and shot it. He said the boy never thought of being afraid of it."

" How old is he?" asked Shelden.

"I can't tell," said Uncle Bill; "nine or ten or 'leven — maybe twelve."

"What will become of him?" asked the practical Shelden.

"I don't know; I was so taken with him this afternoon, that I told Sam I would take him home with me, till he could see what he could do."

"You'd better keep him," said Fenton, decidedly.

"I would, willingly," said Uncle Bill, "if his father would let me have him. The notion has somehow got into my head," lowering his voice, "that Green is in some way interested in this boy."

The three men looked silently at each other for a moment, and Shelden gave a low whistle.

"The devil!" exclaimed Fenton; "the boy is no more like Green than a young eagle is like a thieving old owl."

"There are other things besides blood. We shall see," quietly replied Uncle Bill.

CHAPTER V.

GREEN'S TAVERN AND ITS LANDLORD.

JUST below, on the south-east corner, fronting on the State Road, stood Green's Hotel, an extensive rambling collection of buildings, composed partly of hewed or squared logs, partly of round logs, and to which had been added, within three or four years, a new, and, for the time, spacious two story framed building, neatly finished and painted. Near these were extensive sheds, and partly in the rear, roomy, well-built barns and stables. The whole place bore the appearance of being much frequented. The bar-room was in the block part,—a large, low, and unattractive room ; and on the night after the funeral it was dimly lighted, and deserted by its usual frequenters.

In an inner room, also dimly lighted, was the proprietor, a tall, muscular, heavy built, heavy shouldered, heavy headed, heavy browed, rough featured man, his small, quick, deep set, hard, round blue eyes peering stealthily out from his overhanging eyebrows, with florid face, and scanty light hair. Although a heavy man, he was walking up and down the room with a light feline step, and occasionally dropping his head on one side, as if to listen for his own foot-fall, or to see if he could hear what his thoughts were.

(24)

He was not alone; near a table at one end of the room sat Sam Warden. silent, dogged and defiant;— sober now, the wretched man seemed to have been surveying the abyss. at whose bottom he found himself, under conditions that enabled him to comprehend its depth and hopelessness. His eyes were on the floor, with the sullen look of a man broken. exhausted. and hunted down. who hoped nothing, looked for nothing, and feared nothing.

The men had evidently conferred and disagreed.

" Sam," said Green, gliding up to him like a serpent, and laying his hand upon him like a feather, and breathing his name in a voice that he intended not to hear himself, while his quick eye stole stealthily about to detect any listening shadow, — " Sam ! "

" What ? " said Sam, in a rough, hoarse voice.

" 'Ush-h-h-h ! " with a deprecating wave of his hand, as if urging the shadows to withdraw, " they'll hear ye."

" Who the devil cares ! "

" Sam ! " with seduction in his breath ; " Sam, take a little sothin'," holding up to the light a bottle of spirits. " It's brandy— rale fourth-proof— try a little?"

" Not a dam drop ! " sulkily.

" Sam, what d'ye want? tell a feller."

" Not a dam thing."

" Remember, Sam —"

" I do remember."

" What d'ye remember?" with a voice of thunder, and a stamp that shook the house ; " what d'ye remember, ye mis'able whiskey-suckin' cuss ! ye poor bloated porpant ! "

" Porpant ! who made me a porpant?" springing up,

and confronting the enraged landlord with a stolid look of defiance.

With a gasp, half a hoarse bark, lost in an angry growl, the furious Green, with livid face and eyes burning with murder, grasped the miserable and helpless Sam by the throat, with the strangling hands of speedy death, and literally lifting him from his feet, shook him as if he had been a figure of cork, and threw him helplessly several feet upon the floor.

"Uncle — Uncle Jarvis," feebly moaned the subdued wretch. With a single step Green stood over him, and hissed, "Say Uncle Jarvis again while ye live, an' I'll murder ye!" And turned to confront the shadows.

The cowering wretch lay dumb and trembling on the floor, when Green, bringing a glass of brandy from the table, lifted his head up.

"'Ere, drink this!" The poor wretch swallowed a little, which his stomach immediately rejected. Again and again the dose was repeated, until the liquor was retained.

"Get up," said Green, "and sit down like a reason-'ble man."

"Why're ye so 'ard on a feller!" whined the somewhat recovered Sam. "What d'ye want, anyway? What'll ye do with 'im?"

"What business's that o' yourn? as his father. ye s'll bind 'im to me. 'E s'll work in the stable, pick up chips. black boots, an' mebby drive stage. What's that to ye?"

"Ye know that she that's dead, poor Betsey, liked 'im, an' 'e put a wet cloth on 'er dead face,—I seed 'im," and the poor creature broke down.

" Come, come, Sam ! " with his old gammoning way,
and waving off a shadow, " don't be a fool ; take
another drink. an' be a man ; put a wet tow'l 'round
that neck o' yers, so that yer licker 'll do ye good in the
mornin'."

" There's sothin' in that boy oncommon," said Sam,
preparing to go. " The mornin' after Betsey died, he
pushed me from the bed, an' thar was sothin' in 'is eyes,
that — that —"

" That what, you fool ? " looking about, a little fearful
of eavesdroppers.

" That made me kind o' —."

" Shet up, will ye ! " with a backward, deprecating
motion of his hand ; and then, with the old wheedle,
" Come, come, Sam. ye ain't yerself to-night ; ye 'll be
better in the mornin'," looking around to see that the
way was clear.

As Sam was about to go, " Say ! " said Green, and
coming up with the old noisless tread, with the wave
at the shadows, and putting his lips to Sam's ear,
" D' ye s'pose she tole 'im anythin' ? "

" Who tole — what ?

With another look around, " Betsey — Fred ? "

" 'Ow could she ? "

" If she did, I 'll —"

CHAPTER VI.

LAUNCHED UPON THE STREAM.

THE day after the funeral Fred went down by the grave of his mother, and out across to Jones's, to see Johnny, and then down across the river at Atwater's; then, turning up the southern bank, went back to the little desolate hut, — the only home he had any memory of. It was very lonely and silent in the Indian summer sunshine. The door stood open, and, as he entered, he was surprised to find it stripped and empty of the poor and scanty things it had once contained. The hearth was cold, with the extinguished brands and dead ashes lying upon it. A few tattered rags, a broken chair and stool, and a few fractured earthen vessels, amid straw and dust, were all that remained within. How coldly and dumbly it all smote upon the childish heart of the boy who had been so sorely tried, and was so incapable of understanding his own emotions! The air and silence oppressed, almost suffocated him. He turned out, and, as he went, he closed the door and latched it instinctively, as if to shut in the impressions that had so smitten him. How still and lonely everything lay in the warm sun outside! Fred looked about him, and went with a saddened face to the side of the river where his little canoe still floated;

(28)

he thought of his two or three traps, set above, but somehow he did not care for them : and carefully baling the water from his boat, he loosed its fastening, and with his little paddle pulled himself across to the other bank. Here he landed ; and pushing his boat out again into the rapid current, bow down stream, he abandoned it to its fate. As the mid-current took it, it shot around a turn, and Fred sprang up the bank just in time to catch a glimpse of it, through an opening, as it was swept forever from his sight. He looked where it had disappeared, and turned for a moment to the deserted cabin ; then, with sobs of pain, he passed into the woods with an instinctive but incomprehensive feeling that he was entering upon a new phase of life.

His new friends, in their kindness, were concerned at his day's absence, and greatly relieved upon his return. They found him a pleasant, cheerful boy, apparently observing, and much interested in books, who modestly answered all questions, though disinclined to talk much, and especially about his father and mother.

The next morning his father called for him, and said that he was to go with him down to Green's. Without reply or question, Fred took his hat to accompany him. With a word to his wife, Uncle Bill said to Sam that he would go with him.

On their arrival at the hotel they found the proprietor in the bar-room, whom Uncle Bill approached at once.

"Good morning, Mr. Green."

"Good mornin', good mornin', Misto Skinner," in soft voice, and with a very polite and not ungraceful bow. "I hope yer well; and how's yer lady — an' the young gents, this mornin'?"

"Very well," indifferently. "Mr. Green —" At the business address, the landlord stepped quickly and stealthily forward, with a wave of his hand to a group in a remote part of the room, as well as the world generally, by way of warning not to interfere.

"You wish to speak to me?" in a low voice.

"A moment, if you please." Without further words he was conducted politely and obsequiously into the room where the interview with Sam Warden had occurred.

"Be seated; take a cheer, I beg ye."

"No matter — about this boy, this Fred ?—"

"What about him?" with a glance and a warning sweep of the hand. He bent low, and his voice sunk to an anxious whisper, as he asked:

"I feel an interest in him, and want to know what is to become of him," with a straightforward look into the keen and tremulous eyes of the landlord.

A quick flash out to the right and left, with a slight twitch of the muscles at the corners of the eyes, and a backward wave.

"Wery kind o' ye; wery, wery kind o' ye; the poor boy needs frins," with a tremor in his voice, and a movement of the eyelids, as if to suppress a sudden revolt of the feelings. "'Ad I knowd, I'd a' talked with ye; but Sam cum to me and wanted me to take 'im, an' though 'taint the best place for 'im, I consented, an' he made this paper," drawing a folded writing from a capacious leather pocket-book, carried in an inside pocket, which he handed to his visitor.

"I thought best to 'ave it in black an' white."

Mr. Skinner saw endorsed on the back of it the ominous word "Indenture," and below it, "Recorded in the records of Mantua Township, this 10th day of November, 1829." Opening it, he found it pursued the prescribed formula of binding a minor. He ran his eye on down, — "until he is of the age of twenty-one years"; "not less than three months' schooling each year until the age of eighteen"; "to be taught so much of arithmetic as includes the Rule of Three,"— which requirement had been placed in the Ohio Statutes by the Yankees of the Reserve. The indenture also provided, that on his reaching said age of twenty-one years, "that Green should pay him, the said Frederick Warden, the full sum of one hundred dollars current money, and furnish him with one good freedom suit of fulled cloth." Signed, Samuel Warden (his x mark), and acknowledged and witnessed as the law directs. Uncle Bill's eye ran back to the descriptive parts,— "Frederick Warden, aged about ten years, born near Danville, Ky., May 15th, 1819."

While Uncle Bill was carefully studying this paper, Green, at times, threw his whole force into a look and attitude of the most intense interest, with an occasional glance and gesture to imaginary spectators not to interfere; that it should be all right; and occasionally he would incline an ear, as if trying to hear what the silent reader and cogitator thought about it.

"Three months' schooling each year," said Uncle Bill, with his full voice, "until the age of eighteen years," and thus repeated several other provisions of the paper.

" Square Lyman — Lawyer Lyman of Ravenna — drawn it," remarked Green, by way of assurance of its correctness.

" The paper's all right," said Uncle Bill, coldly, handing it back.

" Does the boy know of it?" he demanded.

" I s'pose Sam's told 'im ; no matter, 'e'll find it out as — "

" Soon's he'll want to know it," interrupted Uncle Bill, regardlesss of the deprecating gesture of the landlord.

" Call 'im in," said Uncle Bill.

With a deprecatory gesture to the imaginary spectators, as if to say, " I'll do it, and save all hard feeling," the landlord stole out of the room, and a moment after stole in, followed by the wide-eyed. wondering boy.

" Ef I may be so bold " — with great suavity, that had a little ring of self-assertion in the tone — said Green, " I'm the boy's master. You'll rec'lect, pleas'."

" Master ain't a good word up here," said Uncle Bill, " and you'll recollect that I'm one of the ' Selectmen ' of Mantua Township, and live about a mile from here," with a look that took nothing from the remark.

" Freddy," he continued to the boy, " your father has placed you with Mr. Green to live. You'll be a good boy, do whatever he tells you, and he'll be kind to you. You'll let him come and see us occasionally," — to Green. " Good-by, Freddy. Good morning, Mr. Green." Turning hastily away, Uncle Bill walked rapidly out of the house, and, with a saddened face, away from it.

" Freddy," said Green to the boy, who stood with his

eyes staring hard at the door, through which his friend had departed, with an expression like that with which he saw his canoe disappear; "Freddy"— and the voice was soft and winning —"ye was alone with yer ma when she died?"

The boy looked wonderingly at his questioner, and moved a little from him. "Yer's alone with 'er, yer fayther says."

"Yes sir, — Johnny and I."

"Did she say anythin' to yer? leave any word, anythin' about yerself, or Johnny, or yer pa?" Fred still stared at him with wonder in his wide, innocent eyes, and without winking, until tears came into them, and ran over their lids. "Nothin', nothin', Freddy? We'll go out now, and look about." An impatient gesture might have notified the observant shadows that it was not altogether right.

The place was not new to Fred. He had been there, but not often. Once or twice he had come to look for his father, and a few times to get a small wooden bottle replenished.

As he went out through the bar-room, he hurried and made a sweep around a group at the bar, behind which stood Jake, with his hard, freckled, repulsive face. "'Ere, Fred, take this pitcher, an' bring some fresh water; ye'll 'ave ter work 'ere. I'll put ye through. Do ye 'ear?" As the boy wonderingly took the pitcher, and went out, Jake added: "If the ole man means ter 'ave that little cuss lazin' round, fishin' an' trappin', he'll find himself damly mistaken. I'll make him 'ump." Just then Fred came in, and placed the heavy pitcher

3

on the bar. "There now," cried Jake, "go'n bring in
some wood, an' I'll tell ye what ter do next."

"You'd, better take care." said Israel Patterson,
just drunk enough to be independent, "he won't stand
much."

"What dam business 's that o' yourn? Drink yer
licker, an shet up, or I'll —"

The landlord had stolen in, and his quick glance de-
tecting none but the ordinary tipplers, — "Jake!" with
a voice which made the decanters start on the shelves,
and under which that youth sunk to sullen silence.
When Fred came in with the wood he gave him a
quarter, and told him to go over to the store and buy a
paper of tobacco, and when he returned with the change,
told him to keep it. The boy looked up wonderingly,
but laid the money down on the bar, and walked
away in silence.

"Wal, if that don't beat the devil!" exclaimed
Jake, and all turned in surprise at him. As he walked
away the landlord repeated his gesture of uncertainty
and warning. "'E'll larn better'n that," he said.

From the solitary life of his childhood, in the woods
by the river, to that of boy of all work in the stable
and kitchen of a much frequented country tavern, was a
great change ; and Fred made it, and adapted himself to
his new situation, with the plastic readiness of the young
backwoods boy. Whatever ulterior views Green may
have had in seeking the control of the boy, he evidently,
at first, sought to gain his confidence and good-will ;
and although he did not spare him from the ceaseless
round of chores, his manner was not unkind, and he
often, in his stealthy, confidential way, seemed anxious

to penetrate and mould the boy's inner thought and nature. At such times Fred would turn upon him with his wide, open eyes, in seeming wonder, altogether puzzling to the wily nature of the man, who occasionally made a beckoning motion, as if asking attention, till he finally saw, or fancied that he saw, in those eyes distrust, and something like defiance.

When Green moved into Mantua seven or eight years before, from the south part of the State, as he said, he was understood to be a widower, and was accompanied by a middle-aged sister, a stout, coarse, dark woman, and his only child, the unpromising Jake : the rest of his household consisted of hired men, and a young woman or two, as the exigencies of business required. Save these, few knew of the inside of his household and family, and they knew but little of it. His relations with outsiders were of a purely business character, which he conducted with a marked politeness of manner, and generally fairly. His ways were said to be Southern — at any rate of a type different from the Yankee — and the marked success that attended his operations, conducted with much cautious enterprise, gained him the reputation of being long-headed and deep ; which qualities, viewed together with his success, inspired men with a certain respect for him, while his sly, stealthy ways, and suavity, led his cool and calculating neighbors to regard him with a wholesome distrust. His tools were of a style and fashion unknown in Yankee land, — immense hoes, and clumsy axes with straight handles, instead of helves ; and, harnesses sewed with leather thongs, he used to drive with one line, mounted on a wheel-horse, and used words, and pronounced them, in a way unknown to down-country dialect. Men talked about him, yet nobody knew any thing positively discreditable to him, beyond the drinking and tippling he permitted upon his premises.

CHAPTER VII.

ON the morning after the advent of Fred, another interview took place, in the domain of Sally, between that personage and her brother John.

"Goin' ter change yer sign, I s'pose," said the lady, indifferently. "I see ye've taken a pardner. It'll be Green an'—"

"Shi-shi!" hissed John, in alarm, and turning to beat off intruders. "What's the good o' names, when ye don't know 'em."

"What's the good o' 'avin' this young catamount, to tear yer eyes out? I know mor'n ye think I do;" snappishly, like a woman.

"Ye do, do yer? What d'ye know — come? Didn't the feller die, an' warn't 'e buried with 'is father? An didn't 'is mother dig 'im up, an carry 'im off — come?" With a triumphant glance at the shadows.

"Yah-h-h; an' didn't Betsey break 'er 'art for 'im; an' warn't the money drownded in the river? — if I warn't thar." During the utterance of this sentence, the efforts of Green to prevent interlopers were quite frantic.

"Sally! will ye never 'old yer tongue?" looking dangerous.

(37)

"Will ye give me the deed? Warn't ye satisfied lien' 'bout me?"

"That's long ago. Av course ye knowd ye'd 'ave it. Wut sho'd I do with the boy?"

"Send 'im adrift wi' Sam, if yer afeard o' 'im;—its nothin' to me."

"Yis, to float 'roun an' turn up nobody knows when 'er whar."

"Better turn up any whar than yere. Can't ye see that 'e's goin' ter look like men o' blood?"

"Who's goin' to see 'im yere? if they do, can't 'e be a come-by-chance o' yers? Think o' Bill Conyers."

"More lies about yer sister." in a wearied, despairing tone. "An' Jake says yer to edicate 'im; an 'e reads a heap now. Yer 'd better chuck 'im inter a 'devil's 'ole' som'ers 'bout yere."

"Sally! Sally!" with a ghastly look round at the shadows, "what der ye kno? That's only a nigger, anyway. An' then I 'as Sam on my 'an's."

"Sam won't trouble nobody long; only let 'im keep on."

"An' if this chap sho'd take to ways, bein' 'bout the bar, who co'd 'elp it, yer know?"

"Jest let 'im go ter school, and be made of by the sneakin' Yankees roun' yere, an' ye'll see. Besides, who kno's what Betsey may tole 'im."

"Do yer s'pose?—" with a scared look around, "but Betsey knowd nothin'—."

"She didn't, eh? No wonder yer 'feard; ye'd be wus cust if yer—"

"'Ush!" with the voice and manner with which he strangled Sam, and silenced Jake.

"Wal," said the persistent but cowed woman, "ye allus 'ad yer way, an' what do I keer? But ye'll see what'll come o' it."

Food, shelter, a place to sleep, safety to life and limb, with air to breathe, and room to exercise and grow in, are conditions in which young life will thrive and physical development progress. Nothing that breathes has such marvellous adaptability to all possible conditions as the human, and the young human.

Fred — in his little loft, his hard pallet, coarse but abundant food, and scant clothes ; in the stable, watering horses, riding them bareback with a halter, chopping and splitting wood, building fires, feeding the young cattle at a stack, rising early, working hard, and going to bed late — had the needed conditions of physical life, and his principal business, next after living, is to grow. Thus with immense vitality and almost wonderful physical capabilities, inherited from a fine strain of men, or cropping out anew, as is sometimes the wont of seemingly capricious Nature, this isolated boy is to grow and thrive, be hardy and strong.

And what of his heart, his soul, his affections, his moral nature? Love is not so essential to the young. The realm of affection, of morals and spirit, develop later. He is not precocious. He will regretfully and tenderly remember his poor faded and dying mother, and once in a while start off and see little Johnny. Between him and his father the feeling was that which subsists between a man and young boy, thrown much together, but not the liking of a son for a father on Fred's part.

The two nights and the day at Mr. Skinner's had given him a new and strange glimpse of life, — of a home full of warmth and love and plenty ; and how his heart hungered, at times, for it ! But it was not for him, and he did not think of murmuring. even to himself ; and finally, when he began to go to school, when he could snatch himself away, and saw the little troops of brothers and sisters come and go, glad and happy, he thought how very, very sweet it must be, and that some time, when he grew up, he would live in some pleasant place with little Johnny. But these things were not for him. Still he could not help looking hungrily into the faces of those happy children, going back alone to his round of chores, and his cold, dark, and solitary little room, with a feeling which he could not explain or comprehend.

At first he stood around and looked on, wistfully, at the sports of the other boys ; but, when invited, readily and gladly joined with them. It is marvellous how soon children get acquainted. In ten minutes they are the oldest of acquaintances, and in an hour the fastest of friends. The children at first thought him shy and distant, and there was something in his high looks like pride and coldness ; so that they were astonished to find how ready and glad he was to mix in their sports, and what a bright, cheery, and joyous nature he had. His teacher found him very docile, and eager to learn, but rather slow, very attentive to his books, and observant of all the rules. In a week he became quite a favorite both with teacher and scholars. To Fred, his school and its associations were the opening up of a new life, — whole new realms of activity and enjoyment, which lit up his hard, dreary surroundings, imparting to them new and varying interest. and developing the buoyant and impulsive hopefulness of his nature ; he was even heard to whistle and sing, and sometimes laugh. about the tavern.

The fresh life of his face and manner were a new source of anxiety to John Green, who studied him with keener scrutiny than before.

" There, what did I tell ye ! " exclaimed the triumphant Sally to the discouraged landlord, as the boyish notes came to him ; " ye'll see ! " and John thought that he was getting glimpses. Fred was active and attentive to his many calls, and there was no cause for complaint ; yet complaints there were. It cannot be said that Fred felt anything like attachment for any of the family. nor did he spend much time, save compulsorily, in their presence.

Sally he avoided on the general principles that had always, perhaps. governed most of his sex in reference to her. Jake he avoided on his own account, from a feeling of aversion. There was a difference of five or six years in their ages, and an irreconcilable difference in their natures. Jake disliked Fred from the beginning, and in a month grew to hate him, while Fred returned a hearty disfavor.

It would be difficult to determine what were the feelings of the elder Green towards the boy. He would have concealed them from himself had he known them, and that from the secretiveness of his nature. So accustomed was he to deceive and mislead others, to conceal his purposes and intentions, that he sometimes spoke in an undertone so profound that he was himself in doubt as to what he said, while his real intention was often a matter of uncertainty in his own mind.

He seemed at times to be fascinated by Fred, and would furtively follow him about, taking all kinds of opportunities to steal upon and watch him. He usually addressed him in his soft and bland manner, and sometimes, without apparent cause, in a rough, coarse, almost brutal voice, in accordance with his nature; and occasionally he seemed actually to fear him. He saw, or fancied he saw, in the boy's eyes a singular and strange expression, as if he thought of something, or remembered something, or knew of something; but sometimes it was fearless and defiant, and then it was arch and knowing again; Green would look again, and the expression would be gone, nothing appearing in Fred's face but the frank, innocent, open outlook of young boyhood. That did not please him much better.

CHAPTER VIII.

SIR WALTER.

THE winter wore on, and was like a dawn of sunshine streaked with black to Fred. He was often kept out of school, usually reached it late, and always had to hurry home, — or to the place where he worked and ate and slept; but he did not much mind the hardships. So the winter passed, and the spring came, and the snows melted. and the days grew long. and the roads muddy and deep, and travellers' horses had to be groomed. The last day of school came, and the noisy urchins and little maidens divided up into groups for the last time. and went home : and Fred, looking regretfully at each as they passed off, went sadly to the tavern alone. It was not an attractive place, and few boys ever went there unless on errands, all being afraid of the landlord, and none of them liking Jake. Fred felt himself left to unrelieved work and endless chores. without pleasant companionship. Once in a while Uncle Bill called. or gave him a passing word, and a boy friendship had sprung up between him and young Bill. Sometimes Fred saw Fenton at the store, but his position at the tavern was almost complete isolation from the neighborhood.

One friend and companion had come to him in the

(43)

winter, between whom and himself had sprung up a tenderness and devotion beautiful in itself, and precious to the famished heart of the boy.

A gentleman had put up at the hotel, attended by a beautiful Newfoundland dog, a magnificent fellow, with great intelligent human eyes, and knowing, sagacious ways. The toes of his forefeet were slightly marked with white, and a singular oblong white circle on the upper part of his head, surrounding a spot of black, and a delicate white ring about his neck, united on the back in a knot of white, like a white ribbon tied in a flat, graceful way. He wore a collar, on which was engraved his name, — Sir Walter.

By accident, a day or two before reaching Green's, a carriage had been driven over one of his forefeet, and crushed it, so as to render him a cripple. His master took him into his carriage and brought him forward. At Green's, Fred had devoted himself unremittingly to Sir Walter, on whose account the gentleman remained over a day or two; and when he felt obliged to go on, the foot seemed to be too bad to admit of Walter's attending him. So, after asking the permission of Green, the gentleman made a present of Sir Walter to Fred. Had he given him a princedom he could not have made him more proud and happy. Tears came into his eyes; and kneeling down by Sir Walter, he put his boy arms about the dog's neck, and hugged him in mute joy, while the grateful and affectionate animal looked up dumbly into the boy's lifted face, as if he comprehended and returned his love, and with the half sad, pitying expression which is sometimes seen in the eyes of the nobler of that race. What a possession he was! What a world of love and care and human interest came to him! Save his little canoe, and two or three traps, this was the sole thing he had ever possessed, and this was alive, — a dog, of all things that he had most longed for. With a moistened eye, the gentleman renewed his injunction to Green, accompanied with a five-dollar bill for the extra care and room which Sir Walter might need until well again, and a kindly squeeze of Fred's hand, and " good-by old fellow " to the dog, — drove away.

Walter, whose race and form had never before been seen in that region, was an object of great curiosity in the neighborhood, and under the care and nursing which he received, in the course of three or four weeks he fully recovered. At first he was much petted by Jake, who often asserted his ownership over him, but the sagacious Sir Walter took a very hearty and natural dislike to him ; indeed, he exhibited no warmer attachment for the elder Green, whom, however, he treated with the sort of deference which intelligent dogs usually bestow upon the master of a house. His devotion to Fred was something marvellous, and was manifested in a grave human way. He so far recovered as to be permitted to go at large before the school closed, and always insisted on attending his young master to school. Taking the books in his mouth, he walked gravely by his side to the school-house, and turning back from the door where he usually presented himself when school was out, with a chip, or stick, or straw in his mouth, and his head curbed in, as Fred came out to attend him home again. After several

battles royal with Sally, Sir Walter was permitted to
sleep in the room with his master.

When school closed, Fred had this one priceless
friend and possession to brighten his world, and bless
his otherwise lonely and loveless life. The end of the
school brought an increase of work to him, and placed
him in a more constant contact with Jake, who seemed
to regard him with growing malevolence, and began to
find opportunities to do him acts of unkindness and
spite. As the youngest about the premises, Fred was
the servant and menial of all ; and it was in Jake's power
not only to increase and multiply his chores, but to put
various personal slights and indignities upon him, and
the presence of Sir Walter seemed to present an
incitement, as well as occasions for augmenting the
poor boy's annoyances. It was not quite prudent to
kick or strike Sir Walter, but it was easy to shut him
up, drive him out of the house or stable, and subject him
and his master to many annoyances and indignities.
The position of a friend to Fred would have been very
humiliating to a human being at Green's : for a dog,
it was quite intolerable.

This state of things continued, and daily became
more aggravated and sore. If Green saw or knew of
it, as of course he did, he did not interfere, nor did
Fred complain of it to him. Jake had never ventured
upon any decided personal violence towards Fred,
beyond rough, profane words, or an occasional push.
That, too, would have been dangerous in the presence of
Sir Walter.

Some time in May, when the threshers had finished
the oats in the upper barn, and the boys were set to

clean them up, they were there alone, the younger turning the fanning-mill, and the elder with a scoop shovel feeding it. Jake, as usual, was growling and fretting and swearing at Fred and Walter, who was never far from his friend. The door being open from the barn floor into a granary, Walter went in there, which Jake observing, closed the door. This made Walter uneasy, and he whined to come out. When Fred heard him he sprang to open the door, but found that Jake had locked it, and withdrawn the key.

"There, dam ye!" exclaimed Jake, approaching him, with burning eyes and clenched hands. "I've owed ye a dam lickin' a long time, an' now I'm goin' to give it to ye."

Though taken utterly by surprise, the bold and defiant attitude of his young enemy caused Jake to pause an instant; and when he finally made a rush for the boy, he was met half way in a desperate grapple. He had underrated both the courage and strength of Fred, and found himself called upon to put forth all his force to overcome the suddenness and fury of the onset. The struggle was fierce, and superior weight and strength began to tell, when there was a crash of shattered wood and glass, which the combatants heard without heeding, a fierce growl, a black plunge, and a great muzzle fastened upon Jake's neck; the bully was torn from the sinking Fred as if he had been a rag baby, and lay writhing in the strangling jaws of Sir Walter.

"Walter! Walter!" exclaimed Fred, springing to his enemy's relief, and seizing the dog by his collar. At his voice, the docile animal released his hold, when

Jake sprang up and dashed out of the barn, not seriously injured.

Unaccustomed to scenes of violence, the whole thing had come and passed so suddenly, that Fred stood amazed and excited, not only not knowing what to think, but incapable of thinking at all. He finally remembered to have heard the crash of the window of the granary, through which Walter had leaped when he came to his rescue, and he stepped out to examine it, followed by Sir Walter. He had just turned the corner of the barn when a gun was discharged near him; and springing back, he came upon the fallen dog, within two paces of whom stood his infuriated murderer, with a devilish exultation on his face.

" There, God dam ye! y'll never 'elp 'im agin."

Heedless of Jake, with a cry of anguish, as the earth darkened, the poor boy threw himself upon his wounded friend. Not outright was the noble Walter slain. Without a moan or whine, by a great effort he raised himself upon his forefeet, with his hinder parts, which had received the charge, lying helplessly on the ground, and looked with his great, tender, loving human eyes, full of mute compassion, upon the now unfriended boy, as if he was the only one to be mourned for, and tenderly licked his face, as if to show his undying attachment.

" Oh, Walter! Walter! Walter! Oh, Walter! Walter! Walter!" in broken, sobbing gasps, was all the poor boy could say, as, with his arms around his dying friend's neck, he sank with him upon the ground, wishing only to die with him.

Anger and indignation throbbed back in the blood

of the passionate boy, and he sprang up to take ven-
geance on the slayer; but it was silent and empty about
him, with nothing but sunshine and the chippering cry
of the returned swallows in the air. How hateful everything was! Turning to his dying friend, with a great
exertion he lifted him tenderly in his arms, and partly
carrying and partly drawing him, got him within the
barn, and placed him on a bed of straw. The grateful
fellow seemed to understand the kindness, and looking
tenderly in his master's face, licked his hands. He
made a low plaint, a sound such as that he used to
make when he wanted to drink; and springing for a
bucket, Fred brought him fresh water from the pump,
of which the poor animal drank eagerly.

The weapon used was a shot-gun; and so near was
the miscreant, that the charge made a single ragged
wound, which bled but little externally, but had shattered the spine, and destroyed the possibility of more
than two or three hours of life to the noble dog, who
lay with his sad eyes upon his young master, with a
shadow deepening in them, as if conscious of approaching death. The poor boy felt that he must die, and, in
his desolation, he knew of no mortal to whom he could
turn; his only instinctive thought was to remain with
his brave defender, who had sacrificed his life for him.
Feeling a sort of shiver in poor Walter's frame, the boy
brought a horse blanket from the stable, and lying
down by his dying friend, drew the blanket over both;
and clasping him about the neck with both arms, and
drawing his head up to him, the wretched boy, burying
his face in the long silky hair of Walter's neck, abandoned himself utterly to grief. Never before had the

4

complete isolation and desolation of his life so come to him, as he lay in this rude barn, clasping the murdered form of the only thing that loved him, with the darkness of night falling over the earth, that now held no heart, nor home, nor hope for him.

Green had been away; and when he returned at a late hour, Fred was not there to take his horse. He had not milked the cows or fed the pigs, or brought in the wood, and Sally had not seen him at his supper; nor was Walter about. Jake was hulking around the bar-room, more sulky than usual; and, on inquiry, said that he had left Fred at the upper barn with Walter. Thither the now alarmed and misgiving elders repaired, — Sally with a sick sensation at the heart, for she remembered to have seen Jake bringing his gun from that direction.

A few rods brought them to the north door, which they found open; and on pausing for a moment, they were startled by low, distressed sobs, that came from the dark mass which lay upon the floor near them.

"Bring a lantern, Sally," said the alarmed brother, who stood at the entrance. A lighted candle was brought, the two entered the barn, and lifting the blanket, discovered the sobbing boy, with his arms clasped about the neck of the dying dog.

"Fred! what is it?" cried the somewhat excited Green, while Sally shook with apprehension.

"He shot him!" cried the boy, starting up; "Jake shot him. He sneaked up behind him, and shot him like a coward."

The brother and sister exchanged glances.

"Are you 'urt?" asked Sally, doubtingly.

"No. He didn't have time to hurt me, when Walter took 'im. Oh, Walter! Walter! Walter!" with a voice so pathetic that it even reached the hearts of his auditors, and throwing himself again upon the dog's neck. The presence of the intruders seemed to disturb the dying creature, and he made ineffective efforts to rise. "Better put 'im out o' misery," said Green, in a not ungentle voice, looking about the barn, as if for a bludgeon with which to despatch the dog.

"You shall not touch him! You shall not touch him!" exclaimed the boy, starting up, with desperate defiance.

"Don't 'urt 'im, John; it'll soon be over," said the softened woman; and whispering something to him, John went out of the barn, when Fred again laid the mass of his shining hair down, and it mingled with the silky mane of Walter.

With unwonted tenderness the cold and blighted woman approached and knelt by them, and laying a hard, wrinkled, toil-worn hand on the head of either,— "Pore, pore Freddy! pore Walter!" and for a moment bowed her head to the great wave of womanly tenderness that smote upon and overwhelmed her. The voice reached the hearts of the boy and Walter; the first gave a cry of relieving anguish, and the latter, turning his tender eyes upward to her, feebly licked the hand that caressingly slid down over his muzzle.

Green just then returned to the barn, bringing a lantern and a basin of milk, which he offered to Fred's lips. The boy took it, and attempted to attract Walter's attention to it, placing it near his mouth; the grateful brute looked at it, and turned his eyes back to the face of the boy near his own.   A slight rigor passed through his frame, and the love and light died in his eyes.

A few minutes later, the womanized Sally unclasped the relaxed hands of Fred from his defender's neck, and lifting him in her strong arms, bore him nearly insensible to the house ; while her brother, wondering at his own weakness, spread the blanket carefully over the lifeless form of Sir Walter, and closing up the barn, followed her.

CHAPTER IX.

MR. GREEN EXPLAINS.

THERE happened to be no guests at Green's that night, and an unwonted quiet reigned over the premises. The next morning there were low words and whispers exchanged between the hired men and the young women. They had observed that Walter was missing, and the girl had heard a gun, and late in the night, she knew that Fred had been brought in from the barn.

A rumor made its way to Delano's store, and spread through the neighborhood, that Jake had the night before shot Walter, and wounded Fred ; and at a pretty early hour Fenton, Uncle Bill Skinner, Chapman, Delano, and others, with a constable, proceeded to the hotel together.

Green received them with more than wonted suavity and deference, and seemed quite anxious about their several healths. He was interrupted by Uncle Bill, who inquired where Jake was, and also what had happened the night before. At that moment Jake came in, when the constable approached and arrested him.

"'Ow! What, gentleman? what is't? asked Green, in alarm.

(53)

"That's what we came to find out," said Fenton, decidedly.

"Jake'll not be hurt," said Uncle Bill, "if he has hurt nobody. Where's Fred and his dog?"

"Fred? Somebody call Freddy," with his assuring wave that it was all right. "You see I's away, an' the boys had a little trouble, an' Jake shot the dog; that's all."

"That's all, is it?" said Fenton, quite excitedly. "How was it, Jake?"

"Ye see," said that young gentleman, sulkily, "ye see, I'n Fred 'ad a little scuffle, an' Fred told Walter to take me, an' he kitched me by the throat; ye can see the marks now;" pulling away a neckcloth, when quite decided marks were apparent.

"Look at 'em! look at 'em! gen'lem'," said the delighted Green; "look at 'em, all round, gen'lem'!"

"I shook 'im off," continued Jake, "an' shot 'im."

"It's a lie! It's a lie!" cried Fred, springing into the room in his shirt and trousers, and confronting Jake. "It's all a lie! We were at work in the upper barn, and he locked Walter into the granary, and then he said he owed me a dam lickin, an' came at me, an' I went at him, an' he hit me here," showing a mark near the shoulder, "an' we clinched, an' he was getting me down, when Walter jumped through the window, an' just as I was falling under, he jumped an' took Jake by the throat, an' dashed him down like nothin', an' would a' killed him in a moment; an' I sprang an' took 'im by the collar, an' called 'im out, an' Jake ran out the barn; an' then I remembered I heard the window smash, an' soon, as I thought, I started out to see what 'twas, an' just as I got round the corner, I heard the gun, an' I turned back, an' there lay Walter."

A moment's pause, in which Fred drew nearer to the sulky and cowed youth, and raising his hand, — " You came up behind him without a word, and shot him, like a sneaking coward as you are." Had a sculptor wanted a model of boyish indignation, denunciation, contempt and defiance, it stood before him, with his splendid form drawn up and quivering, his fine head thrown proudly back, and the whole figure posed with all the muscles and veins starting in his bared neck, his sharply cut nostril dilating, and his great black eyes flashing. The last words came hissing, and were closed with a superb blow downward, with his right hand. There could be no question of his blood, however he came by it.

A look of amazed admiration greeted this rapid narration, and splendid burst.

" What do you say to that?" demanded Fenton of the silent youth.

" What does he say? " exclaimed Fred. " Bill said that he had asked him to help him skin him! " His lips trembled and quivered now ; and laying his finger on the arm of Jake, — " You touch him! you touch him! "

" Freddy, Freddy," exclaimed Green, interposing between the boys, " he sha'n't touch 'im! he s'll be buried like a human bein'."

Uncle Bill proposed to examine the barn, to which Green at once led the way, followed now by the somewhat numerous party, Jake attended by the constable. The granary was found locked, and Jake reluctantly produced the key from his pocket, when it was found that the window, some six feet from the floor, had been carried out, as if by a flying leap, and there, near the corner, was the blood, where Walter had fallen.

The eager and compassionate men gathered around poor Walter, from whom the blanket was removed, and wondered over and admired his splendid proportions, and again and again went over with the astonishing sagacity of the imprisoned dog, which led him to divine the danger of his master, and the agility, strength, and courage with which he came to his rescue. "It's a pity that Fred called him off," said Fenton, in a decided voice.

"What if Walter had not been here?" asked Uncle Bill. "And he won't be here any more," remarked Chapman.

These comments were made in the presence of the Greens. On their return to the house, —

"I know what ye think, gen'lem'," said the elder, "it's nat'ral, but you needn't be afeard; Jake's to blame, an' ye may prosecute 'im, and send 'im to jail if ye wish. We's raised different, we's 'ad no larnin', and Jake's mother died amost as soon's 'e was bornd;" and a quiver of real feeling shook the man's voice, and played on his lips.

"No wonder she died, when she saw what she'd done," remarked the unmoved Fenton to Uncle Bill.

"Gen'lem'," said Green, "let me see Misto Skinner, Misto Fenton, Misto Delano, and Misto Chapman for a moment;" and followed by these parties, he led the way to the room where we have seen him before. After closing the door, and dropping the curtains, and with many protesting glances and gestures against all interference or listeners, he began in words that he could not himself hear, and finally, when heard, in language so ambiguous that no meaning was conveyed, to communicate some secret touching the birth of Fred. What it really was, it would be impossible to say. The impression finally produced was, that that young gentleman was a near relative of his own, and a nephew. It was a secret confided to their honor. The father was of high blood, in the South, and no questions must be asked. He made this explanation that they might see how safe Fred, who was ignorant of this fact, must be with his nearest of kin. " His own flesh an' blood, gen'lem'," said Green, with an assuring look, and gesture to outsiders, that it was of course, now, all right. A few words among the gentlemen themselves, and their minds concurred that there could be no occasion for further interference. No complaint had been made, and no warrant issued, and the matter had better drop where it was.

On their way back to the bar-room they passed Sally, whose tall, robust frame and dark marked and masculine features seemed to confirm the story they had just heard, not improbable in itself, and which so fully explained some things which before seemed mysterious to them.

On their return to the bar-room Uncle Bill remarked that the matter had been fully talked over, and that Mr. Green had given them the most satisfactory assurances that Fred should be well used, and that they thought nothing could be gained by any action in the premises.

Mr. Green then placed some choice liquors and cigars upon the bar, and in the most gracious way invited all to participate. Jake was released from cus-

tody, and the next hour was very convivial. It was
observed that Sam Warden, though present, contented
himself with chewing the end of an unlit cigar.

Late in the afternoon, by a bunch of barberry bushes,
under which a deep and shapely grave had been dug,
stood Fred and Sally and John Green. Sam Warden,
and Bill, the hired man, brought a rough box, in which
was the body of the murdered Sir Walter, which they
lowered into the grave. Fred dropped some locks of
hay carefully upon the box, and stood intently watching them as they filled it. When the work was finished,
it seemed to him as if the warmth and light of life had
passed from the earth.

That night a long, earnest, and at times bitter, defiant, and threatening interview occurred between John
and Sally, ending in a seeming acquiescence of the
latter with her brother's wishes.

CHAPTER X.

A WOMAN AFTER ALL.

MANY long, bitter, tossing, burning, delirious days, which ran into weeks, lay poor Freddy in the grasp of a brain fever. Young Doctor Moore attended him with persistent determination, and the tenderness and unwearying devotion with which Sally watched and nursed him gave fatal confirmation to the confidential communication of her brother on the morning referred to in the last chapter. She permitted nothing to reach him, save from her own hand, or that of Dr. Moore. His great vitality and strong constitution brought him through; and, as he came throbbing back to life, he was conscious only of long blanks, with here and there a snatch of old-time memory, — the hut by the river, his pale mother, his little boat shooting out of sight, with wondrous visions of a beautiful woman bending over and kissing him, and calling him names that he had never heard before.

When he grew strong, and went down, Jake had gone. So odious had his conduct made him, that his politic father had found it wise to send him away from the tavern, — to Kentucky, Fred was told.

The pony had been brought up from the farm, and was waiting until Fred was well enough to ride; better

(59)

clothes were put on him, and somehow he found that a
change had come to him. So sweet and exquisite were
the sensations of returning health and coming strength,
and so childish and weak did he find himself, in his
wants and whims, as well as in his limbs and body,
that he almost felt as if he was growing up anew, and
too fast to be strong and lasting.

When he went out it was midsummer. He heard the
mowers whetting their scythes, and saw the harvesters
with their grain cradles going about for jobs. He rode
out, and got the fragrance of the new hay, and saw the
dark, rustling corn ; and the grass was drying on his
poor mother's grave. He rode down to the river, and
over to the Centre, and up to Mr. Skinner's ; and somehow, everywhere, there was a change. People seemed
curious to see him, and looked at his pony, but also
seemed changed to him. Even at Mr. Skinner's, they
did not ask him to stay, or to come again. People
seemed to look at him, and turn and exchange looks,
as if they meant something. So, as the consciousness
of the change grew on him day by day, he finally asked
Sally, whom he had come to love very much. She
seemed shocked and hurt, and finally told him that he
must not mind it, that he was growing older, and was
changing, and that he would change more. These
people were cold and curious, she said, and not like
their people ; some time they would go South ; and he
wanted to know about that country, and she told him
stories of it.

CHAPTER XI.

A FRESHENING in the religious sensibilities
in that far-off time, among a people whose
sojourn in the Ohio wilderness had freed them somewhat from the mere conventional trammels of habit
and thought, had taken place, and was still agitating
the common mind.

Strong, earnest, and somewhat rude men, with the
zeal of the apostolic day, had stood forth among the
people, and reproclaimed the message of Peter at Pentecost: "Repent, and be baptized, every one of you,
in the name of Jesus Christ, for the remission of sins,
and ye shall receive the gift of the Holy Ghost."

Men heard it with amazement. It struck them with
the force of a new revelation, and they could hardly
believe that it was quoted aright. Many doubted, and
shook their heads; it was heretical and schismatic,
this unclothed word, preached with the fervor of a new
doctrine. Many gladly received it, and were baptized;
and new associations were organized, without other word
or formula than the New Testament. Much of the old
spirit of sweetness and love and charity prevailed
among them, calling themselves, as they did, "dis-

(61)

ciples," and with one accord they were much given to
assembling themselves together, seeking to practise the
rites and follow the usages of the first disciples, so far
as the wide difference in the conditions of the ages
and peoples permitted.   Feeling certain that they had
. embraced the full gospel in its simplicity and purity,
this people could not doubt that they had one and all
received the fruition of the promise.   It was gravely
discussed and hoped that, with a genuine Christian
growth, all the promises and privileges of the primitive Christians might be realized, — the gift of tongues,
prophecy, and healing the sick ; and many looked, as
well they might, to a full and complete restoration of
all these gifts and graces, and high communings.

The accepters of these restored views included many
men of consideration through the country generally ;
and among them, in Mantua, the younger Atwater, the
Snows, Seth Carman, and others, with the Reudolphs
of Hiram, and many persons of consideration in the
various towns.   While the movement which produced
this awakening revived the zeal and fervor of the other
sects, and led to feebler revivals among them, singularly enough, it was thought that they did not look
complacently upon the uprising of the disciples, whom
they rather contemptuously called " Campbellites," and,
in Portage County, " Rigdonites."

Among all the preachers whose fervor and zeal had
re-lighted some of the dim or extinguished torches and
tapers of Christian faith in Northern Ohio, Rigdon
stood preëminent.   Then thirty-two or three years of
age, he was in the first maturity of his remarkable
powers as a popular preacher.   Of stout, compact, and

vigorous frame, endowed with wonderful vitality, with a short neck, large, well-formed head, and good face, Nature had given him a wonderful command of the powers to persuade and move men. He had learning enough to save him from the charge of being illiterate, with a fervid imagination, and copious language; with large veneration, and a love of worship, he was stinted in the moral make-up. Bold, skilful, and adroit, had he been capable of a lofty purpose, he might have become a religious reformer, like Savonarola; as it was, he became the apostle of a new delusion, that so grotesquely caricatured Christianity, that even the reverent regard it as a fit theme for sarcasm and ridicule; and which, without the aid of Rigdon's powers of eloquence, and persuasion, and mastery of the weaknesses of human nature, would have perished in its miserable infancy. Rigdon had boldly preached that the early gifts to the churches would again be restored to it.

In the autumn of 1830, rumors had already reached the Mantua settlements of the new revelation that had been made to an obscure young man in Manchester, Ontario County, N. Y.; stories of the angel, the golden plates, the opening of the side hill, of miracles and marvels, were rife among them. Suddenly it was announced that the Prophet, with his brother and the three witnesses, had arrived in Hiram, and were at the Johnsons, near where the college building now stands; that a miracle had been wrought on the person of Mrs. Johnson, whose withered arm had been restored, in the presence of the Rev. Sidney Rigdon and others, and that Rigdon had become a convert.

It was said that, in a meeting of a few, it had been

announced that a wonderful manifestation would be vouchsafed, and that, at the time, the Prophet, who was usually silent, and spoke only upon spiritual compulsion, had broken forth in a prophetic rhapsody, at the end of which he turned to Mrs. Johnson, who, as was well known, had for years suffered with a withered arm, usually carried in a sling, and bade her stand forth; that she arose, and thereupon he commanded her to stretch forth her arm, and she did, and behold it was fully restored! It was further reported that others spoke in tongues, and that their words were rendered by others; that Rigdon declared himself convinced, and gave in his adhesion to the Prophet.

It is difficult to comprehend the intense excitement and commotion produced by the tales of these marvels. Especially were the New Disciple churches shaken by the course of Rigdon; and all the more so, when it was known that he in no way changed or varied from his old faith and preaching, and that the new revelation was but a supplement of the old, — a realization of the pouring out of the spirit in these last days. It was also said that the text of the new and marvellous book explicitly sustained the special views and dogmas of their churches.

Those outside of all church organizations, as well as the members of established sects, were under a degree of excitement which cannot be appreciated at this remote time. Indeed, for the most philosophical reasons, the non-professors, the negatives, are often the more easily taken, and are in some sort predisposed to become the victims of new religious dogma.

Very soon it was announced that the Prophet and his

proselytes and witnesses would hold a meeting at the South School-house, in Mantua, afternoon and evening. The room was large; but, long before the hour appointed, it was packed, while hundreds stood outside, notwithstanding the cold of a late November day.

The Prophet and his party came over from Hiram, and, muffled in cloaks, made their way through the yielding crowd into the building, and occupied an elevated platform, specially prepared. Nothing could exceed the eagerness of the crowd to obtain a sight of the Prophet. What a temptation to turn aside from my little tale to philosophize upon the strange nightside of human nature, that allies it so helplessly to marvels and quackery in medicine, and hopelessly to clouds and mists in religion! The Prophet, stepping upon the platform, uncovered, turned, and, stretching his hand over the hushed crowd, said, "Peace be with you!" and sat down. These words were uttered, not without dignity, in a deep and not unpleasant voice; and, in the wrought and unhealthy condition of mind of the excited multitude, the words and action produced a deep impression.

The Prophet was then about twenty-five years of age, and nearly six feet in height; rather loosely but powerfully built, with a perceptible stoop in his shoulders. The face was longish, not badly featured, marked with blue eyes, fair blond complexion, and very light yellowish flaxen hair. His head was not ignoble, and carried with some dignity; and on the whole, his person, air, and manner would have been noticeable in a gathering of average men. He was attired in a neat-fitting suit of blue, over which he wore an ample cloak

5

of blue broadcloth, which he threw back, exposing his neck and bosom, — all with a simple and natural manner.

At his left, sat his fair-haired younger and slighter brother Hiram, the one redeeming strand in the dark web then fabricating; his face was almost beautiful, with the rapt adoration with which he regarded the Prophet. On his right sat Rigdon, and behind them the three witnesses of the presence of the golden plates, of their delivery, with the silver-framed crystals, the ancient " Urim and Thummim," the spectacles through which alone could the characters be read — to the shining Messenger Moroni, and his flight with them from earth — the youthful, handsome. and dainty Cowdry, the rough, homely, and honest looking Harris, and the stolid, meaningless face of Whitmer.

The awful presence of the Prophet had of itself imposed upon even the most sceptical; and when Rigdon arose as the spokesman, it was in a hush of the profoundest expectation and awe. His effort, masterly for its seeming want of art and simplicity of language, was devoted to a summary of the new revelation, its reasonableness and proofs. In his citations and application of Scripture texts, he was ingenious and plausible. When he came to the living witnesses, he called first Oliver Cowdry, whose statement was clear and explicit, and fully confirmed by the others. When they sat down, he challenged any man to produce the same quantity, and as high quality, of evidence to support the authenticity of the received Scriptures. He closed with the assertion of the miracle wrought on the person of Mrs. Johnson, in his presence, in confirmation of which, at his call, that lady stepped upon the platform. Many present recognized her, and knew the crippled condition of her arm. At his bidding, she removed her shawl, and extended and moved, in various ways, it and its fellow, both seeming to be in a perfectly healthy condition. At this exhibition an intense sensation ran through the crowd, that several times threatened to break out in irrepressible excitement. But the deep voice of the Prophet was heard rebukingly, " Peace, be still ! " at which the eager, pressing crowd bent backward like summer grain before a wind. Then Rigdon, with a loud voice, proclaimed :

" Go your way, and tell what things ye have seen and heard, how that the blind see, the deaf hear, the lepers are cleansed, the lame walk, the dead *shall be raised;* to the poor the gospel is preached ; " and sat down in a profound silence, which remained unbroken for a moment, when it was announced that in an hour Mr. Rigdon would preach at the same place, after which the rite of baptism would be administered to believers who had not been immersed according to the gospel, as always preached by him. Then the Prophet and his party passed out amid the most respectful silence of the audience, many of whom retained their places during the interval before the promised services.

At the hour, the house was, if possible, more crowded than during the afternoon. When the Prophet and his party resumed their places, Rigdon arose, and reading a simple revival hymn, uttered a fervent prayer, read one of his favorite and well-known texts, and, as was his wont, dashed headlong into his subject. It was the old awful story of the lost and ruined without light or hope, and the old and grand expiation, the offer of rest and bliss on the simplest and easiest condition ; the sweeping downward of time, the devious courses of men, the mingling of traditions with the golden strands of truth, the need of a new vindication of the truth, and the vindication of the ways of God to men.

He was never more thoroughly master of himself, never held his subject with a firmer grasp, and never had his audience more completely in his power. His mastery of the passions and sympathies was perfect ; and the almost awful stillness with which he was heard, was at times interrupted by low moans and heart-broken sobs. He uttered the old message of Peter, and closed with a fervid and passionate appeal to the lost and ruined, to acknowledge and obey the gospel.

When he ceased, men still bent eagerly forward to catch the next accents, — when the deep voice of the Prophet broke over the expectant throng :

" The Spirit and the Bride say, Come. And let him. that heareth say, Come. And let him that is athirst, come. And whosoever will, let him take the water of life freely."

At once, spontaneously, a large number of men and women from all parts of the room arose, and made a movement forward in response to the demand, when Ridgon, as had been announced, and was his custom, passed out with his party, and collecting the new converts, extemporized flambeaux and torches, conducted them to the margin of the neighboring creek often resorted to for such a purpose, followed by a procession of several hundreds. As they reached the dark, wintry stream, suddenly a brilliant flame burst up from the opposite bank, burning with a strong, clear, steady light over the scene. Unexpected as this was, it hardly excited surprise ; and had the dead arisen, many would have regarded such a marvel as quite in the order of events.

Among the many who pressed forward to receive the rite, were John and Sally Green ; and so the new evangel was preached, and so was it received.

CHAPTER XII.

IT IS A PITY.

THE next morning a group at the store were talking over the events of the night before. The Prophet, his person, powers and designs were discussed, as also the relation of Rigdon with him, and the probable results.

"If this new gospel can convert and hold old Green," said Uncle Bill, "I'll admit it has claims over the old dispensation."

"That would prove nothing," contemptuously remarked Fenton; "genuine grace, like good liquor, would be wasted on him. Universal salvation wouldn't reach him."

"I think," said Chapman, "it would 'a been well to have let him soak awhile."

"There'd been no danger of his drowning," continued Fenton, "for if there was ever a man born to be hanged, it's him."

"I suspect," observed Uncle Bill, "that old Sally had something to do with it. I'll believe in her conversion. They say, in fact, she's been a changed woman ever since Fred's fight with Jake."

"So I've heard," said Fenton, "and I don't understand it at all, if what Green said was true. If she's

(70)

Fred's mother, she of course knew it before that, and they say that she always hated him before."

" 'There's no knowin' by what Green says," replied Chapman : " he's like Delano's watch, here, — the only certain thing you ever can tell by that is, that it is not the time that his turnip says 'tis."

" Don't compare my watch with Green," said Delano, laughing with the others, " for it will point at something directly, while one really never can tell what Green does point at."

" I wonder if they put Jake in ? " asked Fenton. " I see he's back again. The washing would have done him good, anyway. He don't look as if he had been washed since the flood."

"And then he carried an umbrella," added Chapman.

" I should 'a thought old Sally would 'a taken Fred in," remarked another.

" Fred wouldn't go," said Uncle Bill. " Though a queer, strange boy, he knows mor'n the whole on 'em."

" What a pity ! " said Fenton. " These chaps are always as smart as steel ; there's never but one mistake about them. In a year or two he'll take care of Jake, and all the rest on 'em. — What a pity ! "

" It is a pity," commiseratingly remarked Uncle Bill ; " of what use is strength, and good looks, and learning, and even money, to this poor boy ? He feels it now, though he don't know, and could not understand it. Even these Green's were so sensitive that they left the South an' came away here among us Yankees, that they hate as — as — "

" Sam Warden does water," suggested Chapman.

"Yes," continued Uncle Bill, "and only to escape this shame, and it followed 'em, as it always will; and this boy'll grow up under its shadow, and be dwarfed and warped and made crooked by it. None but the naturals of kings and nobles, in countries where their vices have made such things common, ever escape, and the fame and greatness of such men always disappear when we learn that fact; we see nothing but the ugly blot."

"It's in the nature of things," said Fenton. "When we don't know how to explain a thing, we always refer it to the inexplicable ' nature of things.' But think how unjust it is! We don't think the less of the man the most guilty; we condemn the woman, though we always feel an interest in her, who is often scarcely to blame; while the child, the only innocent one, and who can by no possibility be in fault, we at once loathe, abhor, and outlaw. What a hero this boy was! We would have fought for him in a moment; and yet, at a word from that dam'd, lying old scoundrel, we went and drank his liquor, and passed off without a word or thought of the boy. Not a man of us would 'a touched him; and I swear," growing excited, "I believe he lied about it all the time. There's some infernal mystery about it after all."

"Does the suspicion of this change your feelings towards this boy?" asked Delano.

"Not as I know of, although I am ashamed of the feeling."

"While I think the feeling is natural," said Uncle Bill, "I think it is unworthy and unmanly. It never came home to me before, and I am ashamed to admit that it has influenced me, in common with the rest of you."

"How did it get out?" asked Fenton.

"I don't know," replied Chapman; "I told my wife, because she ought to know."

"Exactly," answered Fenton; "and if she ought to, everybody else ought to, and what ought to be for once was, and is. I had no wife to tell, and before I had a chance to tell anybody else, everybody knew it. It's a great pity —"

"That you did not get a chance to tell it?" asked Uncle Bill.

"William Skinner," replied Fenton, a little decidedly, "we humans are a low, depraved, malicious, uncharitable set, and I would be glad to believe in the fall and original sin."

"And have a devil to lay things to, which would be a handy get-off. David Fenton, I prefer to think that we wretched humans began very low, and are certainly and surely very slowly working our way upward, and we bring with us the stains of our savage wallow. For one, I'm sorry that we have not reached a level where this poor boy could have found rest and friends and home, and where his misfortune, redeemed from its odium, would have so appealed to our sympathies and sense of justice, that he would in some sort have found compensation, — and that's the pity."

"Uncle Bill," said Fenton warmly, "you're a Christian philosopher. notwithstanding what you sometimes say. For though you reject Christianity, it has not rejected you; — its beautiful spirit, — for, mock as you will, it is beautiful. I, who sometimes swear — right-

eously, of course — say this : its beautiful spirit penetrated and fashioned the sources of your nature, however unregenerated theologically speaking, that may
be, and changed the atmosphere you breathe, till you
have a desire to be higher and better than we were
born, and work for that.   The regard in which we hold
this poor boy is a prejudice ; it is unworthy, but it is
powerful.   It is below the level of intelligent discussion, and cannot be reasoned with.   It is universal, and
cannot be escaped from.   It is, as we say, natural, and
cannot be overcome ; and, once again, it is a pity, and
that is all that can be said."

It was a pity, and pitiable now as then.

CHAPTER XIII.

A PRINCE OF THE HOUSE OF JUDAH.

IN that inner room of Green's, for all the afternoon, sat the Prophet and Rigdon, and John Green, who seemed to have been at the confessional; and now pale, abject, and cowering, on his knees, with his hands clasped, and not daring to raise his eyes, with his blanched and tear-stained face ghastly in its wretchedness, he tremblingly awaited sentence, — whether it was to consign his body to a jail and death, and his soul to perdition, or both to earthly penance and contrition.

· " Arise," said the Prophet; " it doth not yet appear what the spirit shall command. Withdraw." The poor wretch proceeded towards the door.

" One moment, — does she your sister know? "

" Not all. She 'spicions a 'cap."

" Go and bring in Oliver, the scribe."

Green returned with that worthy, who served the Prophet as a secretary, and who now, in the presence of Green from his chief's dictation, reduced a lengthy statement to writing; a magistrate was brought in, and in his presence Green prefixed his mark to it, and acknowledged it to be his free act and deed. The justice subscribed it as witness, when it was sealed up, receiving

(75)

an impression from a seal ring, worn by the Prophet, who handed it to Cowdry, and all withdrew but Smith and Rigdon.

"And so the Mammon of unrighteousness is made to redound to the glory of the Most High," said Smith, with mock solemnity, his blue eyes twinkling with immense satisfaction. "Sid, this's a devilish good strike. We'll take this poor cuss and relieve him of his sins, that is, his money, so that he'll have nothing to do but to lay up treasures in heaven, — eh, Sid? you see, he can't complain, his tongue's tied. He shall be our servant, our ox, our ass, and see his hoards put to goodly, if not godly, uses, and this shall be to him instead of the law of the Lamanites. He shall be doomed to ten years' penance and hard labor."

"And his sister, Jo?"

"She's a knowing one. She must go with us, too. It'll do to keep our eye on her."

"And the boy? What of him? It will not do to let him go, — something might come of it if he does."

The Prophet, who had dropped, as was his wont, his prophetic mantle when with his confidential ministers, was really kind at heart, and this question posed him.

"This boy," continued Rigdon, who was not then prepared to depart utterly from all recognition of natural law, "would seem to have some claims, at least, on his father's money."

"That's so, though we can't admit them very fully," answered Jo; "let's have him in, and John and Sally, and settle it at once, Sid."

At Rigdon's summons, the parties were soon before them, — John cowering and fawning, Sally sad-faced, collected, and with a restful look ; and Fred wondering, open-eyed, and diffident, but without a particle of fear. He had fully recovered ; his face was bright, and his long, wavy black hair hung negligently about his face, and down his neck, with a carelessness that would have taken the eye of a painter.

The eye of the Prophet rested kindly upon him. He placed his hand on his shining hair, and shook him by his firm shoulder, regarding his promising figure, and frank, handsome face, and open, fearless brow, with approving admiration.

"It is a goodly youth," he said at length, "a child of the lords of the Lamanites. He shall become a prince of the house of Judah. Clothe him in fine raiment, and let him be skilled in all the knowledge of his fathers, and come in and go out before the Lord. And he shall wax, and become a mighty man, and a great captain, and in the great day will lead the hosts of the Lord to battle against the Lamanites and the Gentiles, and shall prevail. So let it be."

"And for you, man of guile"—turning to John, who cowered before him—"into whose heart temptation came, that in the end God might be glorified, go forth, to toil diligently with thy hands. Thou shalt care for the herds and swine. Be discreet with thy tongue, penitent and patient in thy heart, constant in prayer, and diligent in works of repentance ; if, haply," and rising to his full height and extending his arm, "if, haply, in the fulness of thy years, God shall pardon and give thee rest. So let it be."

The last sentences were pronounced with a solemnity and awe that impressed even Rigdon, who looked for a moment as if he believed that a real coal from the high altar had touched the Prophet.   John shrank murmuring, and coweringly towards the door ; Sally reverently dropped her head, and tears streamed from her eyes ; while Fred, with a half amused, half puzzled expression, stood where the Prophet had left him.

"Man," said the Prophet, "go and be diligent, rendering accounts to the steward of the Lord.   Woman, remain with him, and care for the goodly youth." And laying his hand for a moment on the head of the latter, as if in benediction, they went out.

"Ha! Sid! old fellow!" slapping the still astonished Rigdon on the shoulder, "what do you say to that, — rather goodish, eh?"

"It will do, I think," replied the latter, laughing faintly.   "But I'll tell you what," gravely, "that light on the other side of the creek was rather shallow, and won't bear repeating."

"Oh, well, it won't be necessary to claim anything for that if there's anything said about it ; cotton wicking and turpentine don't cost much.   But I was devilish afraid that Olny would give tongue with his unknown jargon, — 'Shalang, Shala, Shale, Shalo.' God! I'd give something for an interpreter of that.   No wonder brother Paul discouraged this sort of thing."

"Let us have none of that here," said Rigdon, decidedly.   "Nor will it do to attempt such another performance in this neighborhood.   There are cool, shrewd heads all about us here."

"What's the prospect with the Atwaters, and the Snows, and Deacon Carmon?" asked Smith.

"I've some hopes of the Snows ; Uncle Oliver is

long-headed, but then he's wrong-headed, and we'll catch him in that. If we do, the family will follow. As for young Atwater, he and the younger Campbell married sisters, you know."

"I'd like to try Alexander himself," said Jo, a little assertively.

"You'd wither under his glance like a plucked pumpkin-blossom in August," said Rigdon, contemptuously. "His eye is like an eagle's; and he is as firm and clear as rock crystal."

"'Urim and Thummim' in one," retorted Jo, derisively.

"I think," said Rigdon, quite decidedly, "that we'd better not remain here long. If we stir up these churches too much, we shall have Campbell after us. I don't care for old Tom, but I'd rather not have Alexander after me, just now."

"Well, what's to hinder? Johnson will buy land anywhere, only he must have the title to himself, which is pretty dam'd shrewd for a new convert. No matter; we'll take this swag, and make a plant, wherever you say. I wonder if supper's about ready? and tell Oliver to have some of that brandy on hand."

The outside world knew that something was going on. All day long a crowd had been about the tavern watching for a glimpse of the Prophet, and wondering. Towards evening, they knew that Squire Ladd had been sent for, and had been in; but he knew nothing, and chose to say less. Late in the evening, the Prophet and Rigdon, with Cowdry, returned to their more permanent quarters, at Hiram.

John Green did not appear again in the bar-room,

over which Jake, who had been back for some time, sulkily presided, while Fred came and went as usual.

People had latterly regarded him and treated him in such a queer way, that he had avoided them, and seemed not very communicative.

CHAPTER XIV.

THE CITY OF THE SAINTS. — BRIGHAM YOUNG.

TWENTY-THREE or four miles east of Cleveland, and six or seven south from Lake Erie, and within the township of Kirtland, lie Kirtland Flats, traversed north and south by the Chillicothe road, running over the old trail from the old Indian town of that name, to the lake.

Through the flats, or rather valley, and one of the loveliest of its tame character, in a northwesternly direction, runs Kirtland Creek, on each side of which spreads out a rich alluvial at this point, nearly two miles in width, and of unsurpassed fertility.

The latter part of the winter and early spring of 1831, saw strange sights of the gathering of strange people on the flats, — houses and shops, and huts and shanties and boxes, rudely extemporized, dropping and squatting here and there, and teams of horses and oxen, with every variety of strong or rude vehicle, and a motley assemblage of men, women, and children, in which the rude, rough, ignorant, squalid and poor were the prevailing type, until one wondered where they could have come from, with here and there a manly, intelligent face, and well-clad form, and occasionally a beautiful and refined woman, strangely out of place.

6 (81)

And all this various assemblage of the odds and ends, with this sprinkling of the higher element of humanity, had one thing in common, — a cord of fanaticism that vibrated in all alike, and some evidences of which a thoughtful observer would have seen in their countenances.

Such a zeal, having nothing to do with knowledge, a reckless abandonment of all the sober considerations of human life; such an exultant, headlong casting of self upon the ecstasies of the wildest faith, to drift and be borne by the resistless currents of fanaticism gone mad, the earth had hardly seen, since Peter the Hermit, and Walter the Penniless, assembled their hordes for the recovery of the Holy Sepulchre. Hymns and preachings by day, and prayers and shoutings and prophecies, and the jargon of unknown tongues, with visions and trances, ruled the night.

It was the first gathering of the Latter Day Saints, at the beginning of their marvellous pilgrimage. The voice of the Prophet had gone forth, calling the new elect to come out from the world, and they came. Lord, what a sight!

Marvellous success attended the preaching of Rigdon and his associates. Not many of his earlier faith followed him, but two remarkable conversions had already taken place: Mr. Boothe, a leading Methodist preacher of learning and decided ability, and Elder Ryder of the disciples. The adhesion of these two to the Prophet gave him a real moral power in Northern Ohio, and he had already ordained the twelve apostles, and sent them forth; the fruits of their ministry were gath-

ering to the New Zion, and, by the first of May, some
hundreds had assembled.

Johnson, of Hiram, had sold out his property, and
invested the proceeds in the purchase of the flats, several hundreds of acres, the title to which he had taken
to himself, as the Prophet had predicted he would.

A spacious dwelling, already on the property, was
the head-quarters of the Prophet and his immediate
suite, counsellers and advisers. A hotel was immediately opened, new buildings of a better class were commenced, and, with the exactions and contributions of his
rapidly-increasing followers, he found himself in a condition to subsidize the material, labor, and skill of the
surrounding country, which was profoundly excited by
the sudden springing up of this outgrowth of religious
delusion.

In June, among others, there arrived from the East
a young man by the name of Young, son of a farmer,
with a fair English education,— a young man of fine
person, genial, handsome face, and pleasing manners
and address. He soon manifested an unusually shrewd
managing mind, with a great capacity to win confidence, and grow upon men. He had a natural aptitude
for affairs, and things on his hands instinctively went
right: obstacles disappeared in his presence, and order
and method waited upon his footsteps. He contented
himself with modestly doing what came to hand, unconscious of his own powers, perhaps, and was educated by
circumstances and opportunity, which always attend
the lives of the naturally shrewd. Not long was the
modest young brother Brigham among the saints, as
they meekly styled themselves, before he attracted the

notice of the Prophet, who was quick to discern the qualities of men, and who was not slow to avail himself of the executive talents of the young convert. Brigham was no zealot or fanatic, and he was quick to see the needs of the new situation. Nor was he unfruitful in expedients. Under his hand a much-needed police was organized, a commissariat established, shops opened, and employment found for the idle. The domain was laid off into building lots, with regular streets and alleys, and the relations of the new community put on a more decent footing with their curious neighbors.

The sudden assembling of some hundreds of idle, low, and often vicious or depraved spirits, freed from the restraints and habits of usual life, with the stimulating effect of association, all firmly believing that they were the elect of the earth, and that after a rapidly approaching day all the rest of the race were to be cut off, and that they were the direct heirs of the universe; that the earth and its fulness were the Lord's — that the earth was given to the saints — and that they were the saints; it was not much to be wondered at that they should, by indirect ways, exceptionally anticipate the day of full delivery to them, to the great inconvenience and loss of temper of their ungodly neighbors.

Unquestionably, these lawless tendencies among his followers coincided very nearly with the Prophet's primitive ideas of acquisition, if not with his earlier habits of appropriation; but the shrewder Rigdon, and the entirely practical Brigham, could easily see that if they would remain in peace with their neighbors, the usages and forms of civilization must be observed, and that buying and not paying, however artificial and unregenerate, were preferable to the simpler and possibly more attractive mode of taking without leave, and attended with less danger.

Brigham soon developed a talent for speaking — somewhat rare among the followers of the Prophet — was called, and ordained an elder, and coming rapidly forward, was finally set apart for missionary service. He early strengthened himself by a judicious marriage with a young woman of a good family, a resident of Kirtland, and outside of the church of the saints.

In nothing is the sublime egotism of the race of men more conspicuous, than in the great powers it claims for all those to whose government or leadership it has submitted itself; and it never will tolerate the idea that it has been deluded and imposed upon, save by men of wonderful powers, although it is often difficult, as in this instance, to show wherein consisted this vaunted capacity and genius.

Joseph Smith undoubtedly had a fair share of the lower elements of wisdom and sagacity which we call cunning; was fertile in expedients, and possessed much intuitive knowledge of the lower springs and motions of human conduct. He was naturally courageous, always cool, and his impudence reached the sublime; while the gambler's faith in luck, with him, was a chronic fanaticism. " I will become the Mohamet of America," was his oft-repeated declaration to his confidants.

The ideas of veneration and reverence were unknown to him; and the levity and familiarity with which he joked about the most sacred things, shocked even the practical atheists who shared his confidence. The nameless One with Mary and Martha, the reasons why his brothers the apostles were sober on the day of Pentecost, and Paul's excuse for not marrying, were staple topics of irreverent comment.

His estimate of men was the simplest and most comprehensive. They were knaves or fools, or both. Not without skill in dealing with those about him, he often affected to place them in a nominal rank with himself, and played them off against each other. He was without culture, and never acquired the capacity for any sustained extemporaneous 'speech. He had some readiness in the use of Scripture phrases, and often employed its figures with effect. Sensual, and fond of the society of ladies, like many such men, he was not without address to commend himself to their favor. He had a lively sense of the ludicrous, and appreciated wit ; and while there was in his speech a prevailing tone of coarse levity, that broke out at times most unseemly, and was always feared, there was also a vein of sentiment almost poetic, which at other times toned him up, and rendered him impressive. He was in no way an original, even in his eccentricities. His self-assurance was unsurpassed ; and after full preparation and careful rehearsal, he was always equal to his public occasions.

The secret of the wonderful success which attended him, must be looked for in the common blindness and weakness of the race brought from the caves and woods of its far-off pilgrimage, by a very common human nature, plastic and impressible, and in the tone and temper of the religious atmosphere of that day.

After all, I have a little story to tell; and I deal with this movement, its sources and course, only as they bear upon the fortunes of one already brought prominently to the notice of my reader.

CHAPTER XV.

DURING all this time, John Green was a zealous and devoted saint, unremitting in his religious exercises, and faithful in the duties assigned to him. His peculiarities of manner and language did not much commend him to the favor of his new and strange associates; but his whining, caressing, and confidential ways had acquired a warmth and earnestness that seemed to be real, while his efforts to deprecate and prevent intrusion, and give assurances that it was all right — that in fact there never was any cause of apprehension — were at times ludicrous. Naturally his confession and new faith had brought a momentary rest, almost peace and confidence. He, however, soon began to show signs of physical change. He became slightly stooped, and wrinkles and furrows were planted and ploughed over his large face with a depth that showed that the transforming hand was in earnest; as if the shadows, whose presence were fictions, assumed to flatter a favored visitor, had become palpable and real, — were the mocking attendants of the host.

Sally had really awoke to a fresh interest in life. The fossil remains of heart and sensibilities, withered or exhausted in early life, had suddenly sprung into

(88)

new vigor, called up by a wailing cry of deserted and helpless childhood, and in their renewal embraced a brother with a tenderness never before felt; even him who, in his callous and criminal selfishness, had not hesitated to inflict the gravest injuries upon her. From a life of the narrow torpor of mere existence, she found herself lifted to the warmth of human love, and the anxiety of a needed tenderness. Fred, thoughtless, heedless, warm-hearted, impulsive, wayward, but frank and passionate, needed her care, and had the unselfish love of a mother; and John, old, perhaps criminal, stricken and wretched, misguided, as she thought, in surrendering up everything to Smith, Prophet though he was, was, as she could see, becoming helpless, — how helpless she knew not, for she did not know the full grasp with which he was holden. Partly from her native vigor, and partly from the knowledge that she held a considerable property free from the clutch of the church, Sally received much respect at the house, where she was a sort of housekeeper, and where Jake occasionally came when he was in Kirtland.

Sam Warden tramped from Kirtland to Mantua and back, an unconverted Lamanite; his real purpose in visiting Kirtland was to see Fred, whom he really loved, and of whom he was becoming very proud.

Fred was a favorite with the Prophet, who distinguished him with many marks of favor, and had been placed under the care of a competent teacher, not only in the ordinary English branches, but also in Hebrew and Greek — the Prophet having an absurd fancy for the former language — and not only required that his higher priesthood should acquire it, but even undertook it himself, and learned the alphabet. Indeed, his whole polity was a servile copy of the Hebrew original, never fully carried out till the migration West.

Fred developed no remarkable quickness in study, but was docile, and had a great steadiness of application for a boy of his age. He was permitted to retain and use his pony, and often went on hunting and fishing excursions; yet, in some way, while life was bright and joyous to him, he began to feel the presence of a hidden restraint, the existence of which manifested itself in various ways, and which was the more irksome, as he had no wish to escape, and evaded no requirements. The terms on which he lived there he was never curious to understand, and perhaps no one could explain them. He was neatly dressed, well cared for, yet who or what managed and controlled him was not apparent. It was the will of the Prophet, which no one questioned. He attended the public worship of the saints, and was attentive to his studies; he was not instructed in religious matters at first. Nobody asked him questions about himself; nobody asked anybody about him; he was admired and envied; yet who or what he was, if any one knew, no one told. In some way it came to be understood that nothing was to be known of him, and he was thus surrounded with a nameless mystery. Faces were turned to him, with mute questions, and when he approached they turned away, or suddenly became blank; whispers ran about him, mentioning his name, and when he turned to ask, they suddenly ceased, and the persons were not talking, — were not there. He seemed to be haunted and isolated, and the poor boy turned inward upon himself; precocious in this, as deep, thoughtful, and isolated children become. If he went out, and met men and spoke to them, they returned his greeting, but made no conversation : the boys rather avoided him, and little girls looked curiously at him, and were silent. He read books, — not many, for not many were to be had : the intellectual life of the saints was as poor and starved as could well be. He looked in the glass, and saw a tall, well-formed boy, with dark, speaking, grave face. with great, and, to him, sad, dark eyes, and brows that bent almost over them, curling hair, which Aunt Sally — he called her so now — liked to have grow long.

What was it in him that people saw and did not like? It never occurred to him that he looked well or ill, but he sought to find out what it was, and could not discover it. Not as at Mantua was he avoided, but more as one set apart ; while something like an intimacy sprang up between him and the gentle Hyram, to whom Nature had denied the marked qualities of his brother, compensating him with a more pleasing person and many attractive characteristics. Nor was he long to remain without other companionship.

CHAPTER XVI.

THE PROPHET'S HAREM.

THE social life of the new community brought out the features always produced under similar conditions. Called, by the command of revelation, from the outer world, to a new, tenderer, and warmer brother and sisterhood, from which the forms of ordinary life were banished, with their minds liberated from the restraints of old faith, and in a measure from the habits of its old morals, with their moral natures and imaginations shaken by supposed supernatural manifestations, while their minds were perverted and blinded with a delusion that took the form of an infectious mental disease, in the new freedom of manners and license of association which formed the basis of this singular community, the Mormons speedily gave occasion for the comment of the idle and the strictures of the uncharitable outside observers.

In the summer and autumn of 1831, many important accessions were made to the new Zion. Some of the new converts were men of wealth and culture, who, with their families, united with the zealous, fervid throng. The wives and daughters of these men, many of them beautiful and gifted, with the accomplishments and graces of culture, were warmly welcomed by the Prophet and

(92)

his chiefs, and became the centre of their society. if
not the enlighteners of their counsels, and the possible
inspirers of some of the Prophet's revelations. The
graces of these fair devotees were not lost on him; and
it was his habit to unbend, in their presence. from the
awful strain to which his mission called him, and to
find relaxation and pleasure in their society. There
was no banishment of the light and sweet graces that
spring from the presence of women, and the austere
and self-denying virtues and mortifications of the an-
chorite found small space in the discipline of the Prophet.
The violin, and gay joyance of the dance, and little
pleasant attentions of gallantry, were rather acceptable
to the preacher of the new dispensation, and found
ample toleration, if not encouragement, in the militant
church of the saints of the last days, and fulness of
time. With ladies he affected playfulness, and in-
dulged in the half abandon of gay banter and *persiflage*,
not unbecoming his years, but which, in the eyes of ladies
less favored of nature, or by the grace of the Prophet,
seemed not a fitting garland for the awful brow of the
specially called of God. Among his conceits he
affected a fancy for old Scripture names, which he
applied sometimes, happily, to his favorites of the sex,
and which their friends usually reverently adopted.
Judith was a young widow, splendidly formed, with
regal brow, and straight, thin nose. flashing eye, and
a perceptible shadow on her short upper lip. Two
beautiful sisters, a blonde and a brunette, were Mary
and Martha, with an aptitude for the *rôles* of those
of the old days. One budding brunette of thirteen or
fourteen was the Rose of Sharon, and another sylph-

like blonde the Lily of the Valley, and so on. He had
applied several different names to Fred, but none that
seemed to please himself, or that adhered to him.

Late in the fall, a spacious residence for the Prophet
was hurried to completion, in which was a ball-room,
with many unapostolic conveniences; and here, when
the Prophet took possession, he was wont to assemble
his favorites in the winter evenings, who came and
formed about him a sort of court, where, in the absence
of ceremony and reverence, joyousness and pleasure
ruled.

It was his wish that Fred, at first shy and bashful,
should be present, and take part in these informal
reunions; and he took pleasure in promoting an acquaintance between him and the romping, saucy
Rose, and the gentle and shy Lily; and it was amusing to observe the unhesitating advances of the former,
half warranted by her superior age, and inspired by
her frank and open nature, and the half petulant, half
disgusted way in which they were received by the
bashful boy, as yet unpolished by society, and unin-
formed by the gentle inspirations of nature. Is there
in the world a funnier spectacle than a boy thus tor-
mented by the torturing attentions of an elder fro-
ward miss, or in mortal man's experience a position
more intensely and painfully awkward? Patience,
playful, teasing, and all unconscious Rose; his voice
will change from its treble to baritone, and subside
to a sigh; he will soon be watching for a mustache,
and grow anxious about a necktie, and your time, or
somebody's time, will come, and you shall take sweet ven-
geance yourself, or some one of your sex shall for you.

Naturally enough, Fred preferred the gentler, younger, and less pronounced Lily, between whom and himself rapidly sprang up a sweet boy and girl kindness, half friendship, and half the love of brother and sister. Fred was tall and handsome, and it was natural to look up to and cling to him, as she had no brother, and was gentle and sweet and beautiful, almost beyond earth; and it was natural that the heart of the boy, the depths and strength of which had never been called out, should go to her, as something to love, cherish and protect. At his obvious preference for Lily, the mock indignation of the avoided Rose, and her pert and sharp speeches at poor Fred's expense, were a source of amusement to the Prophet and his circle.

The two girls—who became fast friends, as young and old girls do—with two or three others, were also placed under the instruction of Fred's teacher, and he was thus surrounded by and became a sort of centre of a bright group of young people of about his own age. Pleasant, almost happy, were these days to Fred, and helpful and almost wholly healthful in their influence in forming his mind and helping to mould the elements of his character. His teacher, though a disappointed, gnarled, and soured man, was not a proselyte of the Prophet, and had much capacity as a tutor. Fred was now in an atmosphere of cultivated and refined people, and at an age which, while it left him plastic and susceptible, was still too juvenile to permit him to be penetrated and stained by the hot and unwholesome influences which surrounded him.

Externally, the affairs of the saints seemed prosperous. They numbered nearly two thousand residents; a large store, a fine mill, and, at last, a bank of limitless issue were established, and friendly relations existed between them and the outside world. So the summer of 1832 found them.

The foundation of the temple had been laid with imposing ceremonies, and funds, and material, and artisans were in abundance to carry up its walls.

Internally, the poison-seeds were germinating, dissensions were in the presidency, and feuds between the orders of the hierarchies had already arisen.

A pale, sad-faced woman went silently about the home of the Prophet, and hung, with tearful eyes, over the cradle of the infant Joseph.

The haughty Judith bent her regal brow suspiciously upon the sisters Mary and Martha, and even looked curiously at Rose; while Mary and Martha were conscious of an estrangement, though perhaps unconscious of the cause. So the summer ripened into autumn, and faded out into winter.

CHAPTER XVII.

THE VISION AND CALL.

CONNECTED with the Prophet's residence was the prophetic tower, in which were the Pavilion of Vision, and the Tabernacle of Inspiration, sacred from all but the Prophet, and such as he chose to admit. It was in the first of these that he received visions, and in the latter, spiritual ministrations.

Stained glass softened the light, rich carpets received the feet, and elegant sofas and stuffed chairs, and various nameless and some indescribable appliances relieved the tedium of waiting. and offered attractive resting-places to the celestial visitants. Many closets and small rooms opened from the two principal apartments, always closed to profane feet, and unrevealed to unsanctified eyes.

On the couch of reception, in the Pavilion of Vision, arrayed in a loose silken robe, which left the throat exposed, reclined the Prophet, in the trance of expectation, and so disposed that a circle of softened and rose-colored light rested like a halo about his head. A subtle perfume pervaded the room, in a niche of which, and near the feet of the Prophet, loosely robed in white, and zoned slightly at the waist, with bare feet and bare arms, with her floods of blond tresses dropping in golden

7 (97)

waves and ripples about her, with her lips slightly apart, and her splendid blue orbs fixed adoringly on the Prophet, a rich flush on cheek and lip, and a tumultuous heaving of the bosom, that her pressed hand could not still, stood the Mary of this advent, breathless and rapt.

There was a slight motion of the entranced form, the hanging canopy opened, and a golden ray fell upon and illuminated the lips of the Prophet. A smile played over his hitherto moveless features, the lips parted, and in a low, soft voice he spoke :

" And the spirit said, Lo ! and as I looked, the thick clouds parted, and before me ran the beautiful river of life under the sunlight and margined with flowers, and on the thither bank stood the innumerable hosts of the redeemed, star-crowned, and striking their jewelled harps with gladness ; and at their head, towering above the sons of men, and with the form and beauty of an angel, stood he who had led them there. And the voice said, ' Lo ! he who hath delivered them was born of a virgin, and the Prophet of the Lord.' " The light flashed out for a moment with dazzling birilliancy, when the voice of the Prophet again, in the tones of earth, was heard, " Come ! the Spirit and the Bride say come," stretching forth his arms. A rustle of the white robe, the gleam of a white foot, the glance of white arms, and she sank on her knees by his side, murmuring, " My Prophet and my Lord." And the thick folds of the drapery, like enfolding noiseless night, fell with mute darkness about them.

CHAPTER XVIII.

THE LILY.

IN a little cottage low down on the banks of the beautiful creek, and under a bluff that juts down to its margin, now hoarse and murmuring with the autumn rains; under the golden and crimson maples, radiant with a flood of autumn sunshine that poured through a red-lipped rift in the dark October clouds; in the little sitting-room, warm with the West, reclining in a low rocking-chair, with her wondrous eyes grown large, but with the color still on lip and cheek, sat the Lily of the Valley; and on a low ottoman at her feet, with his great liquid dark eyes lifted with mute sorrow to her translucently spiritual face, holding her miracles of hands, sat Fred. Too frail for earth, too pure for its atmosphere, the golden-fringed wing of the angel had shaken its shadow of light and blight on the gemmed margin of life only to exalt and purify and beautify heart and spirit and form, as they stepped along the star-lit way that leads down to death and up to God; a sweeter pensiveness, a dreamy languor, came over her, like the far-off approach of sleep, bringing tender shadows into her eyes, like coming dreams in the drowsy orbs of childhood; a lower note in her laughter, a more caressing tone in her voice, just a lin-

gering in her step, and a clinging in her hand, and she
went brightly along the shining way.

The approach, made in the loveliest form, was per-
ceived by her widowed mother in the spring. At midsummer the physicians came and looked, and went
almost silently away. With the coming of autumn
the indications were marked, and in October it was
decided that her life could only be prolonged by a
flight with the birds, southward; so it was arranged to
carry her to beautiful Cuba. In the morning, a carriage would start with her and her mother across to
Cincinnati.

She was telling Fred of the wonders of Cuba. "They
say that in mid-winter it is warmer than our August;
that, day after day, the whole heavens are radiant with
white, brilliant light, that dazzles, and that every day
brings new and wonderful flowers, and that there grow
the wonderful palms — "

" I've seen them," said Fred, in a low voice.

" You? When and where?"

" In my dreams, I suppose, — when I had the fever,
perhaps," said Fred, looking puzzled.

" And then there are marvellous fruits, whose names
we've never heard, — and — oh, when I've seen them,
I'll come back, and tell you, — perhaps," thoughtfully.

Fred arose, saying he would come and see her start
in the morning.

" Fred," said the mother, "say your good-by to-
night. It will be better for both."

The poor boy looked with pain in his mute, appealing eyes, and, turning back, threw himself on his knees
by the now agitated child, and, clasping her in his arms,

sobbed out, "Oh, Lily! oh, Lily!" and buried his face in her robes in a paroxysm of sorrow. The poor girl bent over him, hardly less excited. "Don't, don't, Fred, don't!"

He remembered that he was almost a man, and raised his tear-stained face, now under control.

"Fred, there's one thing I want to say to you" — with a low, deep voice — "which I must say; don't stay here. It — it — is not good here. I can't tell, — I don't know why; but it ain't good. Go away; oh, go away from here!"

"Go!" exclaimed Fred, "I cannot go; I'm watched. Where could I go? I have no home, no father, no mother. I don't know who or what I am. A dog was the only thing that ever loved me, and he was slain for it. I would gladly die!" bitterly.

"Hush, hush, Fred! that is wicked. God is with you, and His angels will care for you, if you will be good. I love you; mamma loves you. You are almost a man, and strong and brave, and can go anywhere, and do anything; and if I live," said the beautiful girl, "I shall come back, and you can come to us."

"If you live!" exclaimed Fred; "if you live! You cannot die!" passionately.

"Fred, I may never see you again;" and, putting her lips to his, she murmured "farewell."

Fred could remember the touch of no lips to his, and none were ever to touch them again till —

Not lovers, as the world counts lovers, were this young girl and boy; perhaps would never have become such. Possibly, had the young girl ripened into womanhood, she would have carried the image of the youth in her heart, and have known no other. Possibly, the youth — Who will speculate upon the possibilities of the passions?

Fred, whose feelings lay deep, and who had been already taught the bitter lesson of repression and control, without a word passed out of the cottage, and took his way, amid the shadows of the young night, down the banks of the creek, toward the near forest.

CHAPTER XIX.

THE ROSE.

"THERE never was such a boy," said the piqued, petulant, and pouting Rose, one evening towards spring, after one of her teasing raids on poor annoyed, and half disgusted, Fred. How she had ripened within a few months, with her bright face flushing with audacity, and her eyes liquid and swimming with sensibility! She had stolen upon him, and snatched his book from his hands, and ran away with it, and he did not follow her, the booby, only looked annoyed, with his eyes turned from her.

"Will it have its book back again? Well, don't cry; it shall have it. then!" With a mocking gesture, as if to restore it, and snatching it from his extended hand, again.

"Oh-h-h, why didn't 'e take it? Didn't want it, did 'e?"

"'Jack the Giant Killer,'" she said, affecting to read the title. "What do you s'pose Jack would have done if a young lady had snatched his book away? You don't know? I guess you don't, stupid!" looking piqued.

"There, take your old book!" dashing it down upon the table at his side. "I beg your lordship's pardon,"

(103)

with mock humility, taking up the book again, and approaching him with exquisite grace ; " permit me to ask your pardon for my rudeness, and restore your book to you. You won't forgive me? Do now, my poor heart will break all in one small piece, and I shall burst into a tear," pressing her little jewelled hand, with mock agony, upon her exquisite bust.

" There now, let us kiss and make up. You won't?" Stepping around in front of him, and placing her hand under· his chin, and lifting his face up, with her own dangerously near. " Look up here — right into my two eyes — do you know what I've a good mind to do? I've a good mind to kiss you, right on your two stupid red lips." Fred placed his hand over his mouth.

" What a fool ! " turning away, and a moment later returning and taking the tip of his ear between her thumb and finger. " Who do you love? Nobody? Who do you like best? I know, — Aunt Sally, since Lily went. Don't mention Lily? Well, I won't, poor little doll-baby ; she'll make just the wife for you. You don't want any wife? of course you don't ; and you never will, — stupid. You sha'n't dance with me to night. You don't want to? Yes you will, when you see Mr. Hyde, and Mr. Young, and Ed Baldwin, and all that set around me, — when you can't get me you'll want me." And running back, and stooping down before him, and looking vexed and spitefully into his face, — " Your a fool ! " ran out of the room with, " there never was such a boy," to herself.

Fred knew he was a fool, and without at all knowing or even suspecting why, poor sweet innocence. He knew, to be sure, that he ought to jump up and run, and romp with her, and kiss her, and play at lover; but nothing in the world seemed to him so stupid, and he was disgusted, as he had been a dozen times before, that she should tease and annoy him so. He had found that girls were hateful as a class — "made to bother a fellow" — except sweet Lily, whom he had kissed, and as he had kissed her he would not kiss another, least of all this saucy tomboy of a Rose. Oh, silly Adonis! Oh, slowest and greenest of springs!

The games of romps played off by the audacious Rose were well known to many of the household, who had rather enjoyed the annoyance which they occasioned that young gentleman. The Prophet had piqued her, laughing at her want of success in winning some response from him; while the poor boy's want of sensibility and proper appreciation of opportunity which so constantly flouted him, in the shape of red lips and a supple waist, exposed him to not a little prophetic ridicule and sarcasm. The open manner in which the piquant Rose made her playful attacks, relieved them and her from the imputation of wantonness, or even levity, in the minds of all except Aunt Sally. She did not like it at all. She did not want Fred exposed to the annoyance, and whatever danger might some time come of it as he grew older. She did not feel so certain of this young and premature woman; she thought that it was her duty to put a stop to the present state of things, and she did change it somewhat. Something she intimated to the thoughtless Rose, who received her words not as might have been expected. Toward Aunt Sally she maintained a composed demeanor and dignified silence, which rather discov

fited that primitive lady ; but entering the room of poor
Fred, and pointing her finger at him : " And so 'e 'itt'e
baby-boy tole 'e aunty, didn't it ? well 'e should tell 'e
aunty 'boutey naughty Rosy, 'es 'e shouldey." A circle
of saucy laughter ran about him ; and had it been a
circle of fire, it would not have made him more uncomfortable.

Fred had not the slightest notion what had occurred,
nor of course to what she alluded. But her ridicule was so keen and incisive, that its sting pierced
him through. He continued to act upon his old and
only line of defence,— passive and silent endurance ; but
he knew that his poor boy-face was in a flame, and
tears of helpless rage came into his unchanging, unwink-
ing eyes.

The girl witnessed the change with surprise ; and
regarding him a moment, she approached, and in a
tone of sweet contrition, — " Fred," she said, " forgive
me ! " and left him to his reflections. Afterwards
when she met him, it was always with sweet deference
and respect, and a delicate consideration, not alone for his
feelings, but as if she cared for his good opinion. Fred
was surprised to find how pleasant and charming her
presence had become, somehow, and he now observed,
for the first time, what a developed and beautiful woman she had grown ; and as, like a true boy, he had
always vaguely, and afar off in the clouds of boy dreamland, admired the largest and oldest girl, resting his
affections upon substance and weight, so now he began
to gather the haze of his fancy about Rose as a dim
sort of a halo around a star ; and this transformation
was brought about by a girl not sixteen.

CHAPTER XX.

THE CRISIS.

SPRING was approaching, with an ominous intimation that it would bring some change to Fred. "Wait till spring," was the reply to any unusual request. He wanted to go to Painesville. "You shall go next spring, perhaps." He had never been in Cleveland. "Well, if he was all right in the spring he might." Fred thought this referred to his studies. He was a very good grammarian, and made good progress in arithmetic; was said to have an aptitude for language; was a fine declaimer, for a boy; a very fine reader and a good penman, — all for his age.

Little had ever been said to him about religion or the church. Of course he lived in the atmosphere of zeal, fanaticism and credulity, of deception, cant and hypocrisy. Not much impression, however, had been made on his mind, or the nebulous matter that was to harden into mind. When he first went to Kirtland, a circle was formed to read the Book of Mormon, and to him was assigned the place of reader. He found it dull; even its marvels could not relieve its opaque dulness.

It is said that even the gods, when they try a fall with mortal stupidity, are worsted.

(107)

He was nearly fourteen, and it was said that he must take a position ; in short, he was given to understand that, by the marked act of baptism, he must enroll himself unconditionally with the saints. It was explained to him, that when the temple was completed, a new service would be inaugurated ; that there would be a new class of young priests, with special privileges, and for whose duties special training was required ; that he was destined as the first of this new order, and that he and his associates, seven in number, were to enter upon their novitiate on a day in March not yet named. The repressive life of the student had formed in him the habit of taking things coolly, and this announcement was met with more than his usual frigidity. He said he would think about it.

"Think about it!" repeated the secretary, with amazement.

"I said I would," coolly.

"There ain't but one who thinks here," was the answer.

"Yes there is ; I think, some," quietly.

"You! who the devil are you, anyway, I'd like to know?"

"So would I," a little sadly.

With a stare of increased amazement, the messenger of the will of the presidency left, for it was of sufficient importance for the action of that nominal body.

The next day the Prophet took Fred from the dinner table to a sort of study, and in a kindly manner made known to him his destination : in a few days he would be baptized, and enter upon a different course ; he was specially called to it, his career would be distinguished, and finally, he would be one of the leaders of the saints. It was the only time he had ever seriously conferred with Fred. At the close of his communication Fred was silent, and the Prophet for the first time noticed something peculiar in his look, that a little irritated him. He did not stop to consider what it was; he was not given to much consideration in personal matters of this sort; nobody questioned or opposed his will.

Fred had a sort of liking for the gay, good-natured, easy-going Prophet. and had ever seen him in the inside life of his household; yet by that sort of instinct which governs the likings of children, he was kept from any close intimacy by a repulsion that he did not understand. and never thought of examining.

"I've left you too much to your own old Adam ways," said the Prophet, bending his brows upon him with unwonted severity. "You know, boy, that we can cast out devils, if need be." He now unmistakably saw something in the youth's eyes.—the same that Sam Warden saw, and that haunted John Green, and that flashed out into the face of Jake. Whatever it was. it looked to the Prophet like the spirit of courage, that had already reached the stage of defiance. He had encountered it in two or three women. and had found that the way to deal with it was not to assail it.

"My dear boy," he said. blandly, and laying his hand on Fred's head, "we cannot spare you. nor must you leave your studies; what a handsome young man you are becoming! The ladies would cry if we had to send you to the store; Rose would break her little heart." And picking up Fred's soft, but large and finely-formed hand, and admiring its texture, — "This was not made for a stone hammer or a yardstick; we shall have no trouble," lightly and gayly he withdrew.

The next day, Rigdon, whose sins had been purged away by special act, so that he could be the equal of the Prophet in everything but the prophetic spirit, the monopoly of which was to be perpetually enjoyed by Joseph, sent for Fred, and in a frank, bland, seductive way went over with the whole ground, and then he reminded him that they had taken him literally from a stable, housed and fed, clothed and pampered him, and educated him like a prince, because he had been called, so that he felt they might now urge that they had a claim upon him. Fred winced at this. But then, in his darkened mind, he thought it was funny that if he was called, he should not be given the mind to go.

Rigdon went on to say that it was his duty to obey the gospel, after which the way would open to him; that he was old enough to choose and have a mind about it; adding, "To-morrow, perhaps, you will be asked the direct question, — 'Will you obey the gospel by the outward sign of baptism?'" and bade him good-morning.

Fred was quite prepared to answer then, but returning the bow of the president, he withdrew.

As he went out he was joined in the corridor by Rose, who came up with a little of her old assurance, but none of the old banter, and passed her arm through his, clasping her little dimpled hands on his arm. Her touch had a strange, sweet charm for him. Looking up a little timidly in his face, she said, "Fred, you

will be baptized; I know you will; we've all been,—
even sweet Lily was baptized,—say you will! you
don't know how much we all wish it. And you are
quite a man now," dropping her voice and head with a
blush. The little curled head came very naturally
upon his tall shoulder; and it was all so like the things
in the stories; and it seemed to him that he ought to
pass his arm about the marvellous little waist, made to
be cinctured with a lover's arm.

Then she raised the little warm face, and turned and
looked up into his eyes. "What is it men see in your
eyes? I only see coldness," with a fainting tone. The
sauciness had gone out of hers; there was only a sweet
pleading in them, and her breath, like a faint incense,
came warmly upon his lips.

"And you will say Yes, and we shall all so love you,
—and, Fred—" the little head went down decidedly
on the shoulder. Voices came from a near, open door;
and the unconscious maiden passed it with a natural,
gay nonchalance, utterly bewildering to poor Fred.

There was another intensely interested observer.
Aunt Sally still filled the important post of housekeeper, attentive to her duties, prudent, discreet,
trusted, and in some vague, far-off way, feared. Apparently absorbed and preoccupied, and unobserving,
nothing escaped her about the household, and she was
the first to note the change in the manner of Rose
toward Fred. Nor was she for a moment deceived.
Poor blind, unseeing, unknowing, unthinking boy, only
beginning vaguely to feel the approaching revolution
that was so mysteriously taking place in him, as the
new forces of Nature were beginning faintly to pulsate

through his system! Already he was beginning to lose the control of his voice, the richer volume of which, failing to find utterance through the unchanged, childish organs, would shatter itself into piping quavers, or fall to a grum bass, much to his surprise, and often to his annoyance. Poor boy! he was becoming a man; and only thought he had taken a funny cold, all unaware of the fever that would follow it.

This, too, had Aunt Sally noted; she knew also, and better than he, what the Prophet wanted of him, and guessed somewhat the reasons why. She knew, too, the means that would be employed to secure that purpose, and looked darkly at Rose, and anxiously, apprehensively, at Fred. She had not anticipated that the final ordeal would be reached until further lapse of time. But how could she explain, how warn, how inform and put on his guard the unconscious boy who had been walking about this prison-house, for all these months, eating and sleeping, caring for and being caressed by these deadly foes, who might poison his food, and who had poisoned the air he breathed? Not in this order, but brokenly and fragmentarily, all these thoughts had come to her; and on this day, had she been the object of suspicion or of observation, care and anxiety would have been seen on her strong brow.

Deep in the following night, Fred was awakened by Sally, who brought a lamp into his room, and began with some needless words to allay any apprehension he might feel at her intrusion. Apprehension was the last emotion likely to arise in him.

" Fred, I want to ask ye one thing. Do ye trust me, Fred?"

"All the time, aunty."

"Bless ye! Well, then, — 'ave ye been called? — asked to be babtized, — ye know?"

"I was told I would be asked to-morrow."

"To-morrer? Massy! So soon? Do ye want ter be?"

"No."

"Will ye?"

"No."

"They may compel ye."

"Compel me?" with immense and contemptuous incredulity.

"Yer a boy, Fred, an' don't know; they may force ye."

"Force me? Let 'em try. They may drown me!" with a frown of angry defiance.

"Ye may see a vizyin."

"I saw plenty on 'em when I was sick," quietly.

"Do ye like bein' yere?"

"Not much. Why do you ask, aunty?"

"If ye's to go, whar 'd ye go to?"

"Somewhere, anywhere, — to Uncle Bill Skinner's, perhaps."

"They'd git ye thar."

"H'm, — let 'em try."

Aunt Sally stood silent a moment in thought: "Fred!"

"Yes, aunty."

"D'ye like ennybody yere? anybody in petic'ler, mor'n ye do other folks, — Rose?"

"I like her better than I used to," was the straightforward, unhesitating answer.

" Fred " — much relieved — " d'ye think this yer's a good place?"

" Not very."

" Fred?"

" Aunty."

" D'ye ever pray?"

" My mother learned me to pray."

" Yer mother?   Oh, Betsey Warden!"

" Was she my mother?" earnestly.

"Bless yer soul, what a question!   'Ow should I know?"

" There, good-night;" and she went away much comforted.

CHAPTER XXI.

THE CALL OF FRED.

THE next morning the Prophet was in a semi-prophetic state, very unusual in the household. Fred was called to the large common room adjoining the breakfast-room, and before that meal, where the Prophet addressed him in a solemn voice.

"It is a goodly youth. Let the spirit call in its chosen way;" and laying his hand upon the unmoved boy's head. — "Receive grace to hear and heed," he said; and spreading abroad his hands, in an impressive manner, he pronounced an invocation and breathed a benediction. At the action of his hands, all the assembled household reverently bowed, and then took their places at the table, when the Prophet, with his own hands, broke and blessed the bread, saying: "This, with water, be the food of the household of the Lord this day; and may it become the bread of life."

To say that Fred was much impressed by this simple and imposing ritual, is merely true: and, impassive as he had become, he looked upon the Prophet quite in amazement. He almost divided with him the attention of the awed spectators.

The Prophet remained about the house all day in rapt, austere silence. No work, not the lightest chore,

(115)

no word, not even a whisper, was done or said; but in silence or stealth the inmates sat or moved through the house, till nightfall, as if under a frozen spell.

The day was dark and rainy, and the night came on with snow and wind. The blinds of the whole house had remained closed during the day, and after nightfall the darkness within was pitchy.

It came upon Fred, in his own room, on the upper floor, and alone. He was a little faint for want of food, and not without a vague sense of something impending; but his pulse was at its usual beat, and his veins, like his will, unmoved. All the day long his memory had wandered back over his shadowed, straitened, stinted life, and found little to linger upon with pleasure. That little boat came again and again into his mind, and he wondered at the impulse that induced him to cast it to the fortune of the river. Whither had it been carried? Had some happy boy picked it up and kept it? Had it stranded and rotted by the river's side? Had it been fortunate, and swam out to the far-off great lake, which he had never seen save from the hills at the north? Its little fortune was like him, and the impulse came to leap into the outside current, and let it carry him along. Then the story came into his mind of the youth who, one bright summer morning, was loitering by a river side, when he came upon a little boat, into which he stepped, and pushing it into the current, committed himself to it; and it bore him down, past flowery banks and dark forests, past craggy steeps, that threw sombre shadows over him, and finally it landed him near a dark, battlemented old castle, which the river protected on the water-side. The youth stepped ashore and entered the old castle, in and around which was neither voice, nor sound, nor sign of living thing; mould, dust, neglect and desertion, held joint sway over all. He passed an open portal, and picked a rusty dagger from the stone floor, and while he was curiously observing it — a drop of red blood distilled from its point, and — a form in white entered Fred's room with an unheard step, which so coincided with the rapt current of thought, revery and mental vision of the youth, that when a voice said, — "The spirit leads, follow," he arose without hesitation, and laying down the dagger, as he seemed to do, he followed in silence. Out down the corridor, down a stairway, through other passageways, up other stairs, through doors all open, and in the darkness all strange, slowly they proceeded, groping and hesitating, on Fred's part, from the uncertainty of the way. At last a curtain parted, and Fred found himself he knew not where. A dim light, like that of the ghosts of many lamps, filled the room, if such it was, utterly unlike anything he had ever seen. A pleasant warmth and a faint odor, as the fragrance of fresh violets pervaded the place. Fred's conductor, pointing to a low, spacious couch, motioned him to sit; and indicated a low table near the sofa, on which was a goblet of water, and some bits of broken bread. The sight of the food recalled the healthful sensation of hunger, and taking up a piece he eagerly ate a few mouthfuls, moistening his mouth with the limpid contents of the goblet. He fancied that there was a peculiar, but not unpleasant, taste in the food or water, and laying himself back on the luxurious couch, mused

dreamily on his strange surroundings.   As he lay, there
came the sound as of heavy drapery moving and rustling in a slight breeze, pleasant to the whilom, over-
wrought, but now quieted senses of the youth.   Finally
the light died out, and darkness in heavy folds seemed
to fall about him, and wrap his benumbed perceptions
in almost oblivion.   Strange forms hovered for a moment across the fading margin of consciousness, and
the Lily, more beautiful than earth, but shadowy, with
her lips to his, and then, — utter nothing.   *   *   *   *
Was he sleeping or waking? was he still on earth, for
earth never saw, even its shadow, nor painter in dream,
nor devotee in ecstasy.   There in a rosy light it was,
not wavering nor shadowy, but firm and real, and
within his reach.   Was there ever such a face, transparent, yet suffused, such eyes and lips?   And all about
the glorious head — the wondrous head — such a cloud
of marvellous golden hair, flooding down full of spangles,
and confined with a golden circle.   He dared not drop
his eyes from the wondrous face, yet, in the bright
radiance which surrounded him, what was not given to
his gaze!   The left shoulder was veiled ; from it a bal-
drick passed over the left bosom, and below the right,
sustaining a shining robe of white.   The right shoulder, with the loveliness that only haunts dreams, would
assert itself on the entranced vision of the cold, pure
boy, and thus framed in the rose-tinted folds, held
back by one hand, this marvellous wonder stood.   As
the eyes looked steadily into those of the boy, a deeper
tint seemed to light up the celestial face.   " You are
called ! you are called ! you are called ! "   At first low,
and ravishingly sweet, then louder and firmer, and then

in a tone that seemed to command as well as announce. The right hand extended toward the youth a slender white wand, with a wavering motion, — the light faded, the vision melted, and the heavy folds of darkness again enveloped him.

Was he asleep or awake? Dead or alive, in trance or dream? He could neither think nor remember. Had the fever returned? Was it an angel? Did time move or stand still? He had neither the will nor power to move. Then unconsciousness; and then the vision of his fever, strange foliage and flowers, and palm-trees, and the radiant, happy face, and the name, heard only in dreams; then suddenly came the face and voice of Aunt Sally, speaking the name of Fred, and the day changed to a lamp.

This was real. She laid her hand strongly upon him. "Fred, Fred, 'wake!" low and earnest, — "come — this minnit!" With the touch of her hand, the charm was broken; he arose with an effort, and fell back weak and heavy, as if in a lethargy. There was a ringing in his ears, and a dry burning in his throat. He would have drank from the goblet, but found that it, too, had disappeared.

Partly dragged, and partly walking, Fred went hurriedly down a narrow, spiral stairway, down and down, till he met a current of sweet, fresh, cold air, and soon stood on the ground. A few steps more, and he found himself in the kitchen, where Sally gave him a bowl of milk, which he drank at a breath, and felt refreshed, though still dazed and uncertain.

"Fred, for the massys sake! What 'appened? What did ye see and 'ear?" What a wave of shadow

and darkness now lay between the waking, real present,
and the vision and dreams of the hour ago!

"I must have dreamed strange old fever dreams. I
wonder if my head is all right?" shaking it.

"You look scared, an' sort o' wild!"

"Do I?"

"Fred, this yer's a wicked, bad place,—don't ye
want to leave it?"

"Yes, I'll go now. I won't stay here another hour."

"War'll ye go."

"Where will I? Anywhere, everywhere, Aunt Sally,
—tell me who and what I am? You know,—don't
you?"

"Lord! how excited ye ar'! 'ow do I know? Jarvis won't tell."

"Jarvis! Who's—!"

"John,—John Green! Oh, we've all changed!"
confused and distressed.

"Aunt Sally—!"

"'Ush! 'ush! they'll miss ye."

"I don't care. Let 'em come," defiantly.

"Fred, see! 'ere's a bundle o' yer things. 'Ere's
yer cloak, an' boots, and cap, an' 'ere in this basket's
nice things for ye. Mebbe they'll follow ye,—ye can
eat as ye go. Pore, pore, 'omeless boy!" now breaking down.

"I don't care if they do follow me," coarsely; "I
wish they would."

"I've thought it over 'n over. It's near day. 'Ere's
a little money for ye. Ye'd better go to Mantua, and,
Fred, ye'll 'ear from me when I know. Stay thar,

ware I can find ye; as sure as the Lord ye'll 'ear from me, when I know."

The boy had taken another copious draft of milk, and swallowed some choice bits of cold ham. He now put on his boots,—there was his rich cloth cloak, with its fur collar, his fur muffler, and seal cap, his warm gauntleted gloves, and light-packed valise. He lifted and poised its weight.

"It 'as as many shirts an' things as I could git in it, an' 'ere's all the money I can raise," putting a small purse in his hands. "Get across to t'other stage route, from Chardon; an'—oh, Fred—yer the thing I love best on airth, ye lonely, 'ouseless wanderer; God will some time bless ye!"

A great, dry gasp arose, and was choked down by the poor boy. For a moment, the strong, true arms of Sally were about him; then he found himself alone in the wet slush of snow and mud, traversing a lane that led out from the rear of the house, to the Chillicothe road.

With the directness of his nature, Fred walked boldly, though rapidly, along the street. The storm had subsided, and the approach of day was lighting up the eastern sky. He felt a little sick at the stomach, and heavy about the head, and at first his step was a little unsteady; and the cold air struck him with a sort of nervous chill. The exercise of walking quickened the circulation to a pleasant glow. The respiration of the pure cold air seemed to restore the wonted tone of his strong, healthy system; and above all, the first joyous and exultant sensation of freedom, of liberty, of escape, flashed electrically over his nerves, and he seemed to tread the air. With what a wonderful glory the eastern sky was glowing, as if the sun was hastening up to greet and cheer him! How limitless was the expanse that bent so far off, and so free over him, while the very earth spread and stretched and ran out, in endless perspective, asking him to traverse it!

For a mile or two the road gradually rises to the south, and from its elevated summit Fred turned and cast his eye over the little huddle of houses and huts, of shops and cots, and sheds and hovels, that lay but a step below him, in the midst of which, dark and solitary, arose the house of the Prophet, and the home of the presidency, with the Tower of Prophecy at one angle. There was Aunt Sally, and Rose, and the Prophet, and there was the scene of vision, dream and trance, fresh in his still distempered fancy, and bright and distinct in the grasp of young memory. Above all, and not far off, seemed the ridge of the lake, vast and boundless as the ocean, from which his eye fell again upon the still sleeping town, from which, with its shows and shams, its pulleys, springs and curtains, he now turned forever. Mantua was twenty-eight or thirty miles away, and all around him was the bright, free, happy world.

CHAPTER XXII.

TWICE BOUND.

IN the north-east corner of Mantua was the farm of Deacon Carman. At the beginning of the century he had followed his elder brother into the woods, and chopped and logged, and burned and cleared, and fenced and built; hunted with the Indians, and fought against them; married and reared children; and now still hale and vigorous, moral and abstemious, honest and religious, he had the year before taken the premiums for the best farm, and for the largest yield of corn. His farm lay on beautiful slopes, rolling swells, and wide vales of wonderfully fertile land. An east and west road bounded it southerly, extending into the wooded hills of Hiram east, which it traversed as a trail, crossing the Cuyahoga River at the Rapids, while a north and south highway divided it, and led into the extensive woods of Auburn and Welchfield, north.

A fine two-story farm-house, barns and out-buildings, occupied the north-west angle, made by these intersecting roads, in front of which was a wonderful pear-tree, flanked by a thrifty growth of cherry-trees of many varieties. The yard was neatly fenced and clean, the house one of the best in the township; in the rear of it were extensive orchards, enclosed fields, and

(123)

broad pasture lands. Below the highway, to the east, spread out wide and beautiful meadows, through which flowed a stream, formed by numerous springs that arose on the farm.

In that far-off time, no more valuable, or a better-cared for, domain acknowledged the ownership of any single proprietor in all that region, now rapidly filling up, and growing in wealth and beauty.

Mrs. Carman, a stoutish, comely dame, of a little better origin than the average, had a still bright face, flashing black eyes, and a temper that also flashed at times. The eldest daughter, Sarah, was a tall, well-grown, honest, handsome country lass, of fifteen. The only son, Elias, was a square, broad-browed, promising boy of twelve; and Martha, the youngest, was a dark, demure little maid of eight. These, with hired help — men on the farm, and spinning-girls — constituted the family.

In those days of practical democracy, the hired young men and women were from families of the same level with the master, and had the usual privileges and consideration of the regular members of the family; and it excited no comment when the eldest daughter of the Chief Justice of the State, a resident of this region, with the entire approbation of her family, married the hired man on her father's farm.

In this family, to work on this farm as a bound apprentice, Fred willingly found himself, a few days after his escape from the saints.

He had gone at once to his old friend William Skinner, who had consulted Fenton, Sim Shelden, and especially Judge Carman, the elder brother of Seth; and it was thought that under the purview of the stat-

utes, the trustees of the township had power to bind
him out, as a destitute, homeless waif, who had as
much business to be in Mantua as anywhere, though it
was more than doubted that he had any business to be
at all. Deacon Carman had been applied to, and was
willing to try him. Aunt Mary, as Mrs. Carman was
called in her neighborhood, came into the arrangement
with pronounced reluctance and great misgiving.

She did not know about this boy, who came out of
the dirt, and nobody knew where, or how, he crawled
out, and who had lived two years with the Mormons,
and nobody knew what he had learned there, or why
he left. She finally gave in; and with the same for-
malities and provisions with which Sam Warden had
bound him to John Green, the authorities made him
the thrall of the good, pious, and honest Carman.
Being now of nominal discretion, Fred had signed the
indentures, and out of abundant caution, the mark of
Sam was also secured to the instrument. It was
thought that possibly John Green might attempt to
reclaim him, and hence the action in the premises.

On his first arrival, madam regarded him with a
wholesome and uncomfortable distrust, and for a long
time looked at him askance. She carefully kept count
of the spoons, and intimated to her trusting and simple-
hearted spouse the necessity of keeping the saddles,
bridles, and halters under lock and key. The fact that
the poor lad was tall and well-formed, and had a frank,
honest, open boy-face, and was so quiet, and gentle,
and respectful, so seemingly well-bred and modest,
was at first all against him. Then his hands were
white, and he brought with him broadcloth clothes,

and seemed so anxious to do, that she was quite decided that he never would. He would grow up there with her girls and Elias; and there was always something in persons of his sort that was sure to come out, and often in the line of their parents' offending. It was not here as in New London, in her father's family, where a bound boy had a place which was not in the family circle. Well, she could only trust in Providence, — and what was practically much more effective, she would watch and manage, and whatever might happen, she would at least have this enduring and accustomed comfort, — " I always told you just how 'twould turn out."

To the kind, true, honest-hearted Sarah, he was at first a pleasant surprise, and then an object of steady, friendly regard. She had not then been away at school, and her Windham cousins did not gain much by her mental comparison. He was not noisy and rough, nor sulky and shy and awkward. He was quiet and gentle, and so anxious to oblige and please. It did not occur to her that he was handsome, or looked well; she could look right into eyes as honest as her own, and she trusted him. Besides, he helped her about her flower-beds. Elias was not, at first, inclined to consort much with him; but he could manage horses, knew all about guns, and the woods, and seemed brave and fearless; so that he soon grew to the proportions of a hero.

Uncle Seth took him with confidence and trust. The poor youth had much to learn, and was not very quick, or very ingenious or inventive; but he was true and docile. Whatever he was told to do he did, and as he was told; no obstacle hindered, and no difficulty dis-

couraged him. If a hindrance arose, his courage and
determination arose with it, when his mind became
quick and active. Before he had been there a month,
the old man was satisfied that there was not a hair or
fibre in his whole make-up that was not true and manly.

They found him disinclined to speak of himself or his
past life. He never mentioned the Greens, and avoided
all reference to the Mormons. They were surprised at
his intelligence, and the extent of his reading, and were
glad to note his avidity for books. One thing alone
brought a shade of unquiet to the Deacon. Although
Fred went cheerfully to the South School-house, and
resolutely and heroically kept awake through the sermons of Darwin Atwater, he evinced little interest in
religion, and a disrelish for the Millennial Harbinger,
and did not take very kindly to Niles's Register. In-
wardly, Uncle Seth always had misgivings whether Fred
ever did read clear through Mr. Campbell's masterly
dissertation upon the Holy Spirit, although he was
never heard to give utterance to such doubts; still he
had them, and they troubled him.

To Fred, how inexpressibly kind and sweet was the
change which had now come to him! How gently and
lovingly the sky bent over him! How green and glad
the earth was to him! With what wonderful kindness
the woods waved their boughs to him! The springing
corn seemed to peep up on purpose to see him; and the
birds sang, and the returned swallows chirruped to him
from the sparkling air. How pleasant to care for the
sheep, and pick up the weakling lambs; to nurse the
young calves; to be all the day in the glad, open
air, rich with the perfume of apple-blossoms! He did

not find it hard to plant and hoe corn, or to drive the
oxen. He got very tired, at first; but then how hungry he would be! and never was there sweeter food
than the profuse plenty which Aunt Mary furnished,
and which she never stinted or grudged. She was a
famous cook and housewife. The nights came full
soon, and full of rest and unbroken sleep.

Did he remember Lily? Did he think of Rose? It
is not in healthy nature for a boy of fourteen to remember much; to retrospect or introspect, or think at all,
save passingly, as the healthful, sweet breeze of summer passes on, and always on, never lingering much,
never turning back, and only at times breaking into a
gentle sigh. Yet, after all, here, as elsewhere, the old
nameless shadow from the never-seen cloud was on
him. Had Aunt Mary told Sarah? What was it in
the look with which she soon regarded him? Why
could he not have one kind, dear, true, unknowing
friend? She was not less kind, perhaps, but more distant; not less considerate, but less talkative. Fred
could only lift his eyes, and turn with a mute sadness
away. He could ask no question, say no word. His
path might cross the paths of others; his orbit, for a
moment, touch that of another; but, without knowing,
he could feel that, in this beautiful, crowded, many-
voiced world, he was to journey in solitude, — ever and
ever alone.

CHAPTER XXIII.

THE GREAT PREACHER.

AN event of the season was the visit of Alexander Campbell to Northern Ohio, to counsel, comfort, consolidate, and confirm the churches upon the Reserve. Not wholly had they recovered from the secession of Rigdon; and, although the strong-headed Ryder soon recovered from his momentary tripping, the churches had languished, and minor differences in dogma had sprung up, — notably in reference to the many-sided and eminently practical doctrines of the true nature and office of the Holy Spirit. Mr. Campbell had never been upon the Reserve, although his venerable father had ministered much in that field. He had formed the purpose of this mission two years before, and his coming had long been anxiously looked and longed for among the disciples. Not only among them did the announcement of his coming produce a sensation. He was the most distinguished and formidable controversialist of his time.

He had already won the gratitude of Christians by the battle royal which he had fought for the general cause of inspired Christianity, with the powers of the common adversary, led by that amiable and wrong-headed philanthropist Robert Owen; he was the cham-

9   (129)

pion of Protestantism against the scarlet-robed woman
of doubtful reputation ; and, later still, he had laid
lance in rest for the comforting dogma of endless
perdition. So that, Cœur de Lion as he was, of schism,
in the Baptist Church, and general heresy against
creed and man-usage, the granite basis of his theology
retained the genuine imprint of the most essential Cal-
vinistic dogma.

Late in June, after the second corn hoeing, when the
meadow grass was maturing over the ripened straw-
berries, and ere the turning of the grain, long after
the calves had been weaned, and the sheep sheared,
whose fleeces in soft, white rolls were running into
threads through the rosy-tipped fingers of spinning-
girls, and a lull had fallen upon the severer work of
the farmer, the great preacher came.

It had rained the night before ; and that Sunday
morning was one of marvellous fragrance and freshness, when Deacon Carman, mounted on his favorite
Bay mare, Kate, and accompanied by Fred, on the
snip-nosed chestnut colt, rode out to the great meeting
in the woods, near the centre of Aurora. It was to be
a primitive gathering, in a grand old beech and maple
forest, of all the faithful, of the inquiring and curious,
of the adjacent parts of Portage, Geauga, and Cuyahoga Counties, then as populous as now. To and
across the State road, west, and then south-westerly, the
ride was nearly ten miles to the point of meeting.
They started alone, passed footmen and heavy wagons,
and joined other horsemen, till, as they neared the
place, they were lost in a general procession, that
broke up and gathered about the stand. The woods

were full of horses and carriages, and the hundreds already there were rapidly swelled to many thousands; all of one race, — the Yankee; all of one calling, or nearly, — the farmer; hardy, shrewd, sunburned, cool, thoughtful, and intelligent. The disciples were, from the first, emancipated from the Puritan slavery of the Sabbath; and, although grave, thoughtful, and serious, as they were on this Sunday morning, it was from the gravity and seriousness of the occasion, and little from the day itself, — an assemblage that Paul would have been glad to preach to.

At the hour of eleven, Mr. Campbell and his party took their places on the stand; and after a short, simple, preliminary service, conducted by another, he came forward to the front. He was then about forty years old, above the average height, of singular dignity of form, and simple grace of manner. His was a splendid head, borne well back, with a bold, strong forehead, from which his fine hair was turned back; a strong, full, expressive eye, aquiline nose, fine mouth, and prominent chin. He was a perfect master of himself, a perfect master of his theme, and, from the moment he stood in its presence, a perfect master of his immense audience.

At a glance he took the measure and level of the average mind before him — a Scotchman's estimate of the Yankee — and began at that level; and as he rose from it, he took the assembled host with him. In nothing was he like Rigdon; calm, clear, strong, logical, yet perfectly simple. Men felt themselves lifted and carried, and wondered at the ease and apparent want of effort with which it was done.

Nothing could be more transparent than his statement of his subject ; nothing franker than his admis-
sions of its difficulties ; nothing more direct than his
enumeration of the means he must employ, and the
conclusions he must reach. With great intellectual
resources, and great acquisitions, athlete and gladiator
as he was, he was a logician by instinct and habit of
mind, and took a pleasure in magnifying, to their
utmost, the difficulties of his positions, so that when
the latter were finally maintained, the mind was satisfied with the result. His language was copious, his
style nervous, and the characteristic of his mind was
direct, manly, sustained vigor ; and under its play he
evolved a warmth which kindled to the fervor of sustained eloquence, and which, in the judgment of many,
is the only true eloquence. After nearly two hours,
his natural and logical conclusion was the old pente-
costal mandate of Simon Peter, and a strong, earnest, manly and tender call of men to obedience. There
was no appeal to passion, no effort at pathos, no figures
or rhetoric, but a warm, kindling, heated, glowing,
manly argument, silencing the will, captivating the
judgment, and satisfying the reason ; and the cold,
shrewd, thinking, calculating Yankee liked it.

As the preacher closed, and stood for a response, no
answering movement came from any part of the crowd.
Men were running it over, and thinking. Unhesitatingly the orator stepped down from the platform, upon
the ground, and moving forward in the little open
space, began in a more fervid and impassioned strain.
He caught the mind at the highest point of its attain-
ment, and grasping it, shook it with a half indignation

at its calculating hesitation, and carrying it with a mighty sweep to a still higher level, seemed to pour around it a diviner and more radiant light; then, with a little tremor in his voice, he implored it to hesitate no longer. When he closed, low murmurs broke and ran through the awed crowd; men and women from all parts of the vast assemblage, with streaming eyes, came forward; young men, who had climbed into the small trees from curiosity, came down from conviction, and went forward to baptism; and the brothers and sisters set up a glad hymn, sang with tremulous voices, clasping hands, amid happy tears.

Thus, in that far-off time, in the maple woods, under the June sun, the gospel was preached and received.

Fred, who had tied the horses in the woods, and placed the saddles between the spreading roots of an old elm, near the stand, in such a way as to form a convenient and elevated seat, sat or stood upon them, and never took his eyes from the face of the speaker during the delivery of his masterly oration. Much of it was within the easy grasp of his comprehension; as a whole, it was beyond it, and the labor was too sustained for his boyish mind to follow. Nevertheless, the impression upon his imagination was very great, and the wish of standing in the midst of an immense concourse, as on the present occasion, its centre and dominant soul and mind, and of pouring out upon it an oversweeping tide of irresistible speech, argument, logic and metaphor, and of seeing men move and bow before it, as now he saw men about him, took, for the time, complete mastery of him, and gave rise to dreams that ever after haunted him. After the service, he went with Mr. Carman to the house of one of the disciples, where they had dinner, and rode home in the cool of the sweet June night.

CHAPTER XXIV.

AUNT MARY DOES HER CHRISTIAN DUTY.

AFTER the wheat had been harvested, and hay made and stacked; after the deep noon of summer, when the white apples were ripening in the north orchard, and the thick dark corn loaded the breeze with its odor; when the wild turkey-hen ventured to glean with her brood in the remote harvest fields, and the shrill voices of the grasshopper and cricket came from everywhere, and idle little urchins, with a many-branched goad. chased the brown-coated, gay-winged "flyers," amid the grass and ragweed. along the margins of the lonely highways; before the wheat sowing, and corn and potato harvesting, and apple gathering and cider making of fall, and the nutting over the chestnut hills; in the richer, longer, sweeter pause in farm life, from late August to mid September, the Carmans — Uncle Seth. and Aunt Mary, and little demure Martha — went to visit the Morrises, in their home near Newton Falls, twenty-five miles away, — quite a journey at that day.

The elders had met two or three years before at one of the great gatherings of their common faith; and although there was little else in common between them, they became good friends. and the Morrises had the

(135)

autumn before made the first visit to the Carmans — a courtesy which the latter were now to return.

The visit was a matter of much anxiety and agitation. The Morrises were wealthy, cultivated, and in a certain sense grand people, in their region. They lived in what was great style for the West; ate with silver forks; had been to Europe; were a branch of the revolutionary Morrises, — in short. Uncle Seth had been induced to buy a new carriage — a sort of a wagon on springs — the harnesses were cleaned up, and a pair of fine work-horses had been kept up for many days for the occasion; and Fred, with his good clothes, was to go as driver, partly because he could handle the horses well, partly because his appearance was creditable, and a good deal because Aunt Mary still maintained her jealous mistrust of him. The little journey was made in mid September, when the weather was splendid, and the roads at their best.

Mr. Morris, a cultivated gentleman of travel and leisure, had a few years before moved to Ohio, to take charge of a large inherited property, had built a spacious residence, surrounded it with beautiful grounds, and filled it with elegant furniture, and a few genuine works of art.

Mrs. Morris was an accomplished woman of refined culture. The eldest daughter, fast maturing into womanhood, a lovely girl, was with them under an instructress; and the youngest, Belle, a child of ten, with wonderful eyes and hair, rich in possible beauty, with a far away cousin, young Williams, a boy of ten or twelve — the last of an attenuated race, that had declined under the artificial life of luxury and intermarriage, so fatal to families in large cities — constituted the family.

The Carmans were received not only with the warmth that then characterized the intercourse of the disciples, who were preëminently governed by the democratic notions which are the basis of Christian social life, but with the simple naturalness of thorough refinement, that will not endure the clogs and hindrances of ceremony, and artificial phrases. They were at once at their ease; and Uncle Seth always maintained that brother and sister Morris were the most genuine Christians he had ever met. So much so that they dropped that endearing title of brotherhood from their conversation.

When Aunt Mary decided to take Fred, it was in the exclusive character of driver, and this fact was duly impressed upon him, and stated to others; and in her often-repeated programme and rehearsal of deportment to her husband, Martha and Fred, he was reminded of the *rôle* he was to fill; Fred was used to the stable and drivers. He had not forgotten the first rude months at Green's, nor the promotion that followed it, nor his gilded and pampered life among the saints; and on his arrival at the Morrises, he expected to remain in charge of the horses, lounge about the barn, stray about in the open air, eat in the kitchen, and sleep anywhere. Indeed, he had not thought much about it. He was very glad to go; liked to drive horses, found almost an ecstacy in riding through the country with little prattling Martha by his side, who was too young to know any reason why she should not love him, who had come to be her watchful, thoughtful, big brother, whom she would as certainly admire and love all her childhood and girlhood through. This at least would be his.

When the carriage drove through the maple and elm avenue that led up to the mansion, Fred was at once relieved of the horses; and hardly knowing what to do, stood apart while the host and hostess, with their young daughters, received their guests. Mrs. Morris was about conducting them into the house, when, for the first time, her eye fell upon the solitary boy. "And who is this?" with inquiring surprise.

"Oh! that's our driver, our bound boy;" with indifference from Aunt Mary.

"Indeed! What is his name?"

"Fred."

To the immense surprise of Aunt Mary, Mrs. Morris at once went to him, and giving him her hand in the sweetest way, led him forward to her husband, and named her daughters, and young Williams, as if he was of the party.

Was it possible that these Morrises, with the inherited instincts of generations of culture and refinement, recognized this sun-browned, modest boy as one who, without question, belonged to them? They acted as if they did; and Uncle Seth always cited the conduct of "Sister Morris" on this occasion, as proof of the elevation to which the spirit of Christian meekness and charity at once raised its happy possessor.

Not wholly in vain, so far as his manners and deportment were concerned, had been Fred's residence with the saints; and not without advantages in this respect, had he associated with sweet and tender Lily, and teasing, coquetting Rose. More than once did

Mrs. Morris, during supper, cast her eye to where Fred sat by Maud, and study the dark, large eyes, and finely-turned and cut nostril, already thin and beautifully defined, for a boy of fourteen or fifteen, listening to his quiet, gentlemanly answers, and the many questions of the vivacious Maud.

The false position in which Fred seemed to stand in this innocent circle, disturbed Aunt Mary, and she thought that "Mrs. Morris ought to know." True, they should be there but a day or two; still she felt it her duty to tell her, and put her on her guard, as she did everybody; and Aunt Mary had easily attained that Christian excellence that rendered every duty of this kind a pleasure as well.

As for Fred, a sort of pleasant glamour came over him the moment he entered the house. The lofty, spacious rooms, with their hangings and pictures, their carpets and furniture. — something in the air, somehow, vaguely made impressions, like the haunting memory of a dream; and he could not help looking about as if from something he would catch a clue to it; and more than once Mrs. Morris found his eyes upon her, as if he would ask a question, and as the impression deepened on him, perhaps he would have done so.

During the next day, and while the young people were amusing themselves in the grounds, Mrs. Carman, seated in an arbor a little remote, and exposed to the sun for the benefit of a rare grape that covered the south side of it, discharged her Christian duty to Mrs. Morris, telling in a very straightforward, intelligent, and pointed way, everything which she did not know about the origin and life of her driver. Mrs. Morris

was surprised and pained beyond measure; and not the
least cause of her surprise was, that her visitor should
have told her at all. Perhaps Aunt Mary would have
been no less surprised had she known how widely her
sense of Christian duty differed from that of the noble
and exalted woman who sat looking at her in amazement. When she recovered, she inquired, "Does he
know anything of this?"

" Of course. It is talked about all over Mantua."

"No doubt of that;" quietly, with a little strain in
her voice. " Does he ever say anything about himself?"

" Not a word."

"God in mercy pity him! Oh, poor boy!"

Fred, who had been strolling about, talking and
laughing with the girls, and brighter and happier than
he had ever been, was attracted by the ripening clusters
of grapes on the arbor, unaware that it was occupied.
He reached it just at the pause that followed the performance of Aunt Mary's Christian duty, and was an
involuntary listener to the conversation that followed
as above. He heard the whole of it without taking
its application; but the last words gave it point, and
smote him like a blow. After a moment of stunned
amazement, he turned away with hot tears in his eyes,
and his face burning with shame.

" Oh, poor, poor boy!" The atmosphere of Mantua
was full of this; but to his ears the words had never
before been spoken; and now they were uttered by the
woman whom he wanted to kneel down to and worship.
He rushed away, clambered over the enclosures,
traversed the fields, and found shelter in the woods.
More than once he looked up at the sky and sun,

and around, to see if his shadow still followed him. He dashed into a thicket of brush on the margin of the field, and gathering the young stems in his arms, he threw himself on the ground with their branches and leaves over him, and groaned, and longed to die. The shadow that was over him had darkened into a palpable cloud. The invisible chain with which he was so darkly bound was now revealed.

Death would not come, and he thought of flight; he would run away, and never stop running. He thought of the little hovel by the river, of the dying woman, not his mother, and of little John, and then of his boat; why did he not commit himself to it, and float down the river or drown?

But he was born to it; he might not escape. He thought of Aunt Sally, — perhaps she was his mother. He knew that he loved her, and she had enjoined him to remain in Mantua, and then came the image of sweet Lily. Mr. Carman, of course, knew it, yet he liked him; and little Martha, — but she would know, — and he arose and wandered about the woods till he grew cooler and more thoughtful. Then his pride came up, and his inborn manhood, and he grew indignant. What had he done? Was he not as perfect in form, strong, and as full of courage as other boys? He would face this world and fight it, and would not be despised or scorned. Beside, had he not always lived alone?

They should go back to Mantua in the morning, and it was now mid-afternoon. He would linger about till evening, and then go in. They need not see much of him; nobody would want him. He had talked of riding that evening with Maud, and Belle, and Martha, and Ed Williams; but what would they care for him?

Fred was missed, and nobody knew where he was; nobody had seen him, and the girls took their ride without him. As they were assembling for supper he came in a little pale, and looking weary. He explained that he was tempted into the woods, had wandered about, and took the wrong way out; apologized to Miss Maud, and sat down to the table. He had not looked at Mrs. Morris, and when he ventured to raise his eyes to her, he met her glance full of sweet tenderness and compassion. He didn't want pity and compassion; he had found his pride; nobody need pity him, and he avoided her as far as he could while they remained.

The next morning, after breakfast, the horses were driven around; kind words were being spoken on the piazza; messages to Sarah and Elias, and all the little nothings and somethings of leave-taking were being said and done. Fred, who had kept himself reticent and aloof as much as his good breeding would permit, was standing a little apart, and posed naturally against a pillar that sustained the roof of the piazza; while Ed Williams, who had become his great admirer, stood near him, observing him with silent admiration, with Belle resting her two hands on one of his shoulders, and admiring Fred because Ed did. As Fred returned his kindly look, he could not help contrasting their conditions. True, Ed was an orphan, but he was the heart and centre of this enchanted castle of luxury and love, petted and cherished; while he —

Patience and endurance, my poor boy! This page

has received something beside the ink that tells your story. Can't you see, by the preternaturally large bright eyes, shrunken temple, and light thin hair, by the compressed chest and sloping girl-shoulders, that life, and its riches of achievement, of strength and power, are not for him? He may not endure, and at the best may only dream. Endure, work, and grow strong; be docile, and learn to obey. Grow, spread out your shoulders, let your spine become a column, let your lungs expand and deepen, your blood-vessels enlarge, and the base of your brain increase. No matter about the rest; unfold and develop slowly. The germs of great events are being deposited here and there, and a wonderful field is to be reaped; men must spring and grow up for the day of harvest. They don't always come from cities or the old crowded ways. They as often spring up in solitude, and come from obscure places. Of the boys now fourteen years old, no mortal can select one of the ten or fifteen who shall rule forty or fifty years hence; and probably no man could designate one of the one hundred distinguished, or even of the one thousand prominent men of that coming time.

It is bitter and sad for you, as you lean against a post this bright morning, so young and friendless and un-knowing. But a field shall be listed, the trumpet shall call the champions, with no common men among them, the array shall be set, the charge sounded, strong arms shall wield trenchant blades, and plumes and crests shall be shorn away, and helmets sundered, and skulls cloven; men shall go down, and standards swerve and be lost ; some shall win, and there shall be a crowning for some.

While Fred and Ed and Belle were thus admiring each other, the adieus had been said, and the horses came forward. Mrs. Morris, coming up to Fred, asked him to accept a beautiful new volume of Shakespeare, which he had admired, saying that he must receive it as a token of the interest she felt in him ; and that if Maud visited Sarah the next spring, he must furnish her with a good riding-horse, and attend her, to see that no harm came to her. This may have been intended for another as well. Fred, though greatly surprised, managed to thank her decently and simply. Then they all shook hands with him, when his party entered the carriage, and he drove away.

CHAPTER XXV.

TWELVE YEARS. — TIME'S CHANGES.

WHEN we lose the grasp of details, we lose the
grasp of interest as well.

What a long period of time is twelve years to look
forward to! What a little gasp of breath, choked
with dead dust and ashes, to look back upon; on the
thither side of that period I linger a moment, to mark
the vicissitudes of these years upon the persons of my
story, ere resuming the threads of it with such as
have survived.

Jones, with whom was little John, had moved West,
taking that young specimen with him, and Sam Warden, somewhat improved since the change in the pro-
prietorship of the Green Tavern, had migrated with
him.

Lily — the sweet and tender lily of the valley — never
reached Cuba. Her disease developed so rapidly, that
from New Orleans her mother carried her home to die,
and herself never again struck harps with the saints
of the latter days.

Rose, in time, married a prominent young saint, and
leads and lives the life of a woman in Utah.

Mary — Mary found all too soon the inspiration of
the revelations made to her — that instead of being

10   (145)

called by a miracle to a holy maternity, she was to become the —. This was indeed a true revelation; its shame and agony drove her mad, and in her frenzy she washed life and memory out, in the waters of the creek. — Act of Providence!

And Judith, — and the Prophet: on the twenty-seventh of June, 1844, the log jail in the dreary little town of Carthage was surrounded by a murderous mob. Inveigled to give himself up on the solemn assurance of safety from the Governor of Illinois, the Prophet, with his brother Hyram, was now to suffer martyrdom. Hyram, blameless, save as the brother of Joseph, calmly confronted the murderers, and fell praying for them. Not so the lion-hearted Prophet. He confronted them with a revolver, which he emptied among them, and then with marvellous strength and agility sprang to a window, supposed to be out of his reach, and, strongly guarded, dashed it out, to fall dead on the outside. As his assassins gathered about him, a woman, with a cry of agony, leaped into their midst, and throwing herself upon the fallen man, eagerly explored the face, the eyes and mouth; and when she found no sign of life, she rose to the full majesty of her splendid form, and in her dark and terrible beauty confronted the cowardly slayers, and was left alone with her dead.

In the struggle for the supremacy which ensued among the followers of the late Prophet, the deeper, shrewder, and more politic Brigham Young prevailed against Rigdon. The latter was contumacious, tried, cut off, and consigned by an elaborate curse to expiate his sins by a thousand years of exile from the communion of the saints, and departed. An adherent of his lingered until, by artifice and simulation, he secured certain papers, supposed to be of advantage to the fallen chief, with which he too departed, some time in the winter following.

In a small, close, wretched vault of a room in the basement of the Presidency, in the centre of the city of Nauvoo, a strong building, part residence, part castle, half tavern, half brothel, half gambling saloon, and all hell; in a lower sink, strong in wall, strong in stench, and strongest in polyglot filth, grovelled John Green. Long ago, but slowly and very surely, had John awaked from a delusion which an infirmity in his moral conduct had helped him into, — stripped utterly of his money and lands, while under its first influence, to which fear and remorse lent their help. As he escaped from the thrall of superstition, something of his courage returned, and all of his old greed. At first he hinted at full restitution, then at partial, and finally asked to be placed in some position, or helped to some business, out of which money might be made. He grew desperate, and with desperation came more courage and less prudence, and from begging he changed to threats. These were fatal. The Prophet had become really powerful, and brutal as well, and in a way felt that he was but meting out deserved punishment. He pronounced John possessed of the devil, and sentenced him to be delivered over for buffeting.

This was upon the first emigration West, when a cell was constructed on purpose for Green, and where, in the late autumn, after the Prophet's death, emaciated, bent, grisly, tattered, and foul, he lay grovelling, as he had done for years, in his vile den, with his sunken eyes peering fearfully about in the gray light, with his matted, unkempt hair, in filthy dangles, hanging about his wrinkled, hideous face, and his shrunken arms, and skeleton, long-nailed fingers reeking with the filth in which they raked. For a marvel, he was not mad. One human being alone hovered near to watch over, aid, alleviate, and possibly love him, and he must have sorely tried the capacity of even woman to love. The sister whose early life he had embittered, whose mature life, for his own safety, he had slandered, and whose whole life he had darkened, had followed, waited, watched, helped, and when she could she had cheered and consoled him. She had always held a certain consideration in the household of the Prophet, who had a shrewd suspicion that she had aided in the escape of Fred, whom he had summarily cut off, and she found occasions to ameliorate the wretched condition of John. One steady incentive urged her to this: the fact that a secret dearer to her than life, she had never been able to penetrate.

Upon the change of the head of the Mormon polity, Sally had besieged Brigham to release her brother from durance. He knew nothing of the case, and was too busy. When again urged, he found nobody who knew anything of the case, nor did any record or memorandum show anything of it. Sally had a reputation for honesty and fidelity, and was personally well-known to the new President. Finally, toward the spring of 1845, he gave an order for John's enlargement. It did not come a moment too early. The door was finally opened unwontedly, — a party came

and, nauseated by the liberated effluvia, fished him
out.   He was clarified, and carried to Sally's room,
but he never rallied. Beckoning her to him, and pulling
her close down to his blue, shrivelled lips, with one hand,
while with the other he feebly deprecated the approach
of intrusive spirits, with a mental declaration to them
that he would make it all right now, he brokenly and
still hesitatingly whispered into her eager ear a few
disconnected words, which would have conveyed nothing to another, and which, after all, he intended
should convey nothing to her.   Something more she
would have known and waited for — was about to
ask — but the voice and the breath that formed it
never came again.   And the only conscious gleam
of satisfaction that solaced that final moment to the
dying man arose from the thought that he had conveyed but a doubtful meaning, and was bearing one
item away with him, while the onlooking shadows
must suppose that it was all right at last.

A few kind hands laid the remains of John Green in
the Potters Field of the saints ; and in the early spring,
without money, and a little bundle of worn clothes,
on foot, and alone, the faithful and now aged woman
turned her face eastward, to fulfil the only wish of her
heart.

Twelve years had brought many changes to Mantua ;
the settlers had increased, new houses had been built,
fields and clearings had spread out, improvements been
made, roads were much better, and the whole was rapidly assuming the appearance of an old, long-settled,
prosperous, and wealthy community.   Uncle Bill, and
David Fenton, and Chapman, were little changed ;

Delano had left the store, and Lewis Turner, who drove stage when we were last in Mantua, and was a friend of Fred's, was now the prosperous owner of the old and greatly improved Green Tavern.

At the Carmans, to the eye, thrift and prosperity seemed to have dropped from the passing twelve years. The old pear-tree had risen many feet ; the house was newly painted ; the fences were upright and neat ; ornamental trees larger ; the yards clean ; the farm had stretched east, and ascended nearly to the summit of the Hiram hill, where it presented a rough and stumpy aspect under the afternoon sun.

Uncle Seth was as composed, sturdy, and cheerful as when we left him faced towards home, on the return from the Morrises. His face was still to the New Jerusalem of his faith, cheerful and hopeful. He still arose, did the chores, had his breakfast, read whatever chapter was reached in the course, and said the same old, sweet, simple, hopeful prayer ; after which he arose, and supplying his mouth from the same old steel tobacco-box, assembled his workmen on the little north porch, where hung the saddles and harnesses, and announced the day's programme, which, like the syllogism, was an argument of three propositions : the invariable " Fustly, Nextly, and Finally." He still sold his young horses, and took promissory notes, which he always failed to collect. Indeed, so chronic had this practice become, that when one was paid he looked grave over it, as a strange event, betokening the end of all things. He still sold his young cattle to Heard, who never failed to pay ; and his pork and cider and apples to a hungry, promising set of settlers in the Welchfield and

Hiram woods, to be paid for in days' works, at fifty cents a day, at chopping wood or in haying and harvesting; and he always spent a week on old Kate's back, drumming these unperforming forces together, and then went and hired two or three good hands, and did up the work in two weeks. He still, on every first day, drove to the South School-house, and heard Darwin's sermons with unabated interest and profit, and in his quiet, serene way, got about as much out of human life as it will yield.

Aunt Mary was still comely and fresh-complexioned. She still distributed flax and wool among her hand-maidens, and furnished her harvest tables with the most marvellous dinners. Her face had softened, and the old flash came more seldom to her still black eyes, and her voice was an octave lower. Possibly her views of Christian duty may have practically changed, and much had happened to modify them.

Sarah had matured to a tall, handsome young woman; had been away to school, was married, and lived with her husband and three beautiful children in Rootstown.

Elias came home from school at the age of twenty, laid his great square-browed head upon his pillow, and died. He was smitten with a fever; and when his case became desperate, and the family, worn and exhausted, knew not where to turn, Fred came in upon them, after years of absence and estrangement. In his gentle way, with his cool strong hands and great calm eyes, tender and considerate, and nerves that never knew a tremor, he took him and them in his arms and carried them to the end; then, without awaiting thanks, went his way.

Little demure Martha was twenty, a shapely, sweet girl,

with black piquant eyes, and full of womanly ways. She had been very thoroughly educated, and her hands and presence had shed an air of grace and refinement over and through the farm-house, which such a young woman can only glamour a home with.

In her maiden reveries, had the thought approached her that it would be sweet to have Fred return in a different role from that of big brother? If it ever had, it disappeared in the presence of an actual lover; and now the conscious young maiden was the happy promised of a deserving youth, to whom May-day, or some early day of the coming season, was to see her united.

And Fred, — what of Fred? Do you really care for him? Patience, for a little, we shall soon see and hear much of him.

CHAPTER XXVI.

BELLE MORRIS.

IN mid December, in Aunt Mary's sitting-room, sits Belle Morris, as she was still called, notwithstanding her marriage, alone and musing, as was her habit ; she rises and walks to a window, against the wainscoting of which she poses with a marvellous unstudied grace. Indeed, her form could never fall outside the folds and lines of grace. It seems at first above the ordinary American height, owing to the perfection and harmony of all that makes up its completed whole.

Her hair — of a rich brown, from which, in her day of half asceticism, she never could expel the wave — was disposed of purposely, a little low over the broad brow, to shade its height. Her eyes, also brown, with a violet shade, wide apart, were almost too large for her face, though that was by no means diminutive, and were full of dreamy power. What perfect cheeks and chin, with a mobile mouth, made specially to win and to defy description ! How short its upper lip, and how straight the almost Grecian nose, with its thin, delicate nostril ! The face wore an almost religious calmness, but was warm, and sweet, and alive ; a possible St. Catherine, or St. Theresa, but not a bit of a Madonna ; she had been married, was a widow, and

now, at twenty-three, had never dreamed of the later
energy and strength that lay under her softness an
sweetness; and she would have been startled, an
possibly shocked, at the depth and fervor of the passion
that were so deeply hidden, that they had never whis
pered of their existence. If they had, it was like th
leaves of a tree moved by the breath of night; the tre
feels the stir, all unconscious of the cause, or of th
power of a tempest. In all the wide world within ker
what can the eye fall upon that so interests as a gifte
woman, perfect in her parts and forces, and all ur
conscious of her possessions and capabilities, save
indeed, the same woman, fully developed, swayed an
controlled, and swaying and controlling by her laten
powers? Does she dream to-day, — of what? Doe
she think? What occupies her mind? Does sh
remember, — what images of the past come to her
Does she look forward, — for what does she hope
She has suffered, as all do; she had lost the rarest o
mothers; she had her young husband severed fror
her — oh, years ago! — and the image of each cam
with the tender halo with which time invests all our dead

In the spring following the visit of the Carmans, i
that now old time, Mrs. Morris had mysteriously diec
Death is always a mystery, no matter how natural th
cause, or how clearly foreseen and expected. Why wi
people die? The blow shattered the family, and sen
the survivors abroad. The Ohio property was sold, a
but the homestead, so sweetly sacred to the mother'
memory, and so haunted with her presence. At lengt
Maud was married to a Philadelphia gentleman, bu
lived a good deal of the time with her father, when a

his Ohio home, — and he really had no other. Wherever the father went, he was accompanied by Belle, and young Williams, a ward of Mr. Morris, and a shadowy relation. From an early day, it was the wish of Mrs. Morris, and Edward's mother, that their young children should ultimately become husband and wife. After the death of Mrs. Williams, her son resided with the Morrises; and this favorite idea, accepted and acted upon, became the controlling one in the association and education of the young people, who grew up with and into it. There was a vein of religious enthusiasm in the nature of Mr. Morris, which, in a less cultivated man, would have developed into fanaticism. Belle shared it somewhat, and the idea of a restoration to the church of the primitive faith and practices, and, possibly, of the gifts and graces of the first disciples, always a favorite idea with him, after the loss of his wife, came to exercise great control over him. Into this current the slight, dreamy, imaginative Edward early fell; and the three, living much alone, and always together, and with few others about them, save the teachers of the children, floated dreamily and pleasantly into unpractical ways and habits of life and thought.

When Belle was fifteen, they had spent many years in Europe, and partly by reason of the failing health of Edward, whose physical frame and stock of vitality were incapable of carrying far, or of enduring long. It soon became apparent that a few years would, at the farthest, bring his life to a close. The children were greatly attached; but their love was purely of a spiritual, unimpassioned type, and such as might well subsist between two enthusiastic young girls. On the

part of Edward, it was the love of a rarefied devotee
for a canonized saint, which no touch of earth, had colored ; on that of Belle, the tenderness of a sister for a
helpless brother, elevated by her spiritual sympathies,
and an ardent and exalted wish to associate with such
celestial essences as a purified soul may become in
beatitude after death. As it became apparent that
Edward must inevitably soon undergo this change,
the desire to be united in the bands of marriage
became strong in their hearts, and Belle's father was
in a morbid frame of mind, which made him readily
acquiesce. Maud and her husband were in America,
and no voice was there to suggest delay, or a doubt of
the expediency of the proposed marriage. When Belle,
who matured slowly, was sixteen, and Edward, who
was twenty, and incapable of maturity, at the American Legation, in Naples, they were married. No difference in their relations occurred, and none in their
mode of life, save that they occupied a suite of rooms
in common ; and when, at the end of six months, the
feeble flame of Edward's life grew fainter, and at last
went out, the bride, who had become a widow, with the
deep, earnest sorrow of a tender and devoted sister for
a lost brother, mourned for a husband who was only a
bridegroom. Nothing on earth was purer, tenderer,
and holier than this union, and none so free from
the passion and ecstasy of the lower world. The
mourners returned to the United States with the remains of the lost one. He had lived the full and
ripened life allotted him, and performed the only mission
possible to him. He had been the love, stay, and hope
of a bereaved, unknowing, hoping mother ; had touched

the life. without mingling with its deeper current, of a gifted young girl, and yet with a force sufficient to shape and prepare it for a high mission; and in the fulness of his time he departed.

On his return to his own country, Mr. Morris felt a revival of his old interest in human affairs. and he devoted himself to the education of Belle, travelled much with her, and finally, resuming the occupancy of his Ohio residence, felt a return of some of the old health of spirit.

Within the last year Belle and Martha had met, and formed very suddenly one of those miraculous young-women friendships; and, while her father had permitted himself to be called off for a month or two. she had accepted Martha's invitation to spend the time with her. As she was also informed of Martha's engagement, though removed from the possibility of such a position by her spiritual wifehood. which she regarded as untouched by her husband's death. and which would render any earthly love a spiritual bigamy, she yet had, in an intense degree, a young. fresh. woman's — it may be said, a girl's — interests and sympathies in the loves, engagements, and marriages of others; for, with her, marriage was eternal. The wish to be with Martha, to talk over with her all the thousand sweet and interesting little nothings that spring out of the rich and romantic soil of an engagement and approaching wedding, for which many preparations were going forward, was much stronger than the wish of joining Maud in Philadelphia; and so she came to Mantua. as we see.

Her association with her boy husband. her life with her father, her sisterly intercourse with Maud's husband, a man of the most refined manners, had given her an exalted ideal of the purity and tenderness of man's nature, while her life, her readings, and study, had not led her to explore the annals of his lusts, cruelty, and brutality ; and when instances of his grosser nature fell under her observation, they were the exceptional outbreaks of exceptional monsters that still sprang from the great original perversion of the race. Not without noble uses was her life ; and in her surroundings, especially in Ohio, the objects and opportunities for charity were rare : such as came to her — and she was diligent in searching them out — she accepted thankfully, and improved to the utmost. No languishing, shrinking, frail, helpless girl was she, but full of robust health and spirit, and womanliness, that delighted in horses, and out-door, exciting exercise, while the serene and pervasive inner life, in which she impassively floated and dreamed, was due wholly to the free consecration of herself to the dim shadow of the past, and the absence of any strong and inspiring cause of change or emotion.

CHAPTER XXVII.

THE PORTRAIT.

BELLE brought her riding-dress, saddle and whip with her, and a plenty of robust disposition to use them, maugre the December weather. She had a room adjoining Martha's, and communicating with it, and in the atmosphere of these cultivated young women a little world of glamour and romance sprang up, joyous with mirth, and bright with ripples of laughs, and glad with gay streamlets of womanish talk. Both had deep veins of feeling and sympathy; both had suffered losses, both had recovered the old buoyancy, and both were healthy in soul, mind and body. They had no beaux, no male callers, were remote from a town, two miles from a post-office, with no near neighbors. But they had a lover, — one who for all social purposes was held in common. Martha had an engagement-ring, and one large room was even then in the hands of a dressmaker from Ravenna, and many bright odd things of brides' wear were in mysterious process of fabrication, or growth, or conjuration, by the hocus pocus unknown to prosaic man.

Martha's lover lived in Louisville, was a merchant, and a darling. Next to the luxury of a lover, was the luxury of a friend to confide him to, and talk him over

(159)

with. These, both in perfection, were now Martha's. There never was such a dear, sympathizing, ingenuous love of a confidant as Belle. It all came out very soon and very naturally. Martha at first was coy about details; but nothing could resist the pertinacious, coaxing, teasing Belle, until she knew it all, and they talked it up and over, and in reverse, and by enfilading. How inexhaustible it was! It was the old story, and contradicted the poetic maxim. Their true love ran smoothly, from its inception, and as true should and would, if let alone. The curious Belle was anxious that Martha should analyze her feelings and emotions, separate and explain them, so that she might know how she felt towards her lover.

"I love him!" with a sweet frankness.

"Yes, I know; but how do you feel toward him?"

"Why, Belle! and you, who married the youth of your choice, to ask such a question! Didn't you love him?"

"Of course; but different girls may feel differently, you know."

"Well, how did you feel? Perhaps we are alike."

This seemed fair, and Belle answered: "Well, you know, Edward and I always lived and grew up together; and our child liking simply grew with us, and in no way changed with our marriage."

"Was he dearer to you than all the world, — your life and soul?"

"Of course he was very dear to me."

"Did you prefer his presence to that of all others under the sun?"

"All my friends — my father, my mother, Maud, and Edward — all give me exquisite happiness."

"Oh, fudge!" exclaimed the mocking Martha; "you were never in love."

"So Maud says, and sometimes she is out of patience with me, and asks me why I cling to that ghost of a shadow. She says our marriage was the union of a doll with a rag baby, and wonders I will regard it as binding."

"Do you?"

"It was a marriage, — sacred and solemn, and for eternity; 'the twain became one.'"

"'One flesh.'" said Martha, a little contemptuously, "not one spirit."

"Why, Martha; you sweet, pious girl, — you shock me! Don't you look forward to an eternal union with your Henry?"

"Of course I do. He is a man to me, the one of his sex, my ideal, — and I love as a fond, weak, passionate girl loves such a man. I believe in him; I want to be his wife. To serve him, cheer him, make him happy, die for him or with him, and go and be with him!" said the warm-hearted and somewhat excited girl.

"And this is woman's love for man," musingly; "and man's for woman, the real noble and true, is worship, made up of reverence and tenderness; cherishing, sustaining, protecting, carrying!" And dropping her face for a moment, she arose and went to a window.

"Oh, Belle! Belle!" said Martha, "with all your

11

wonderful gifts, which the noblest man alive hardly deserves, I wish you'd fall in love."

" Why, Martha! I have a husband. You wicked thing."

" Well, I do, and I hope to live to see it."

" Thank you, Martha. Do you believe persons ever fall in love, as you call it? You did not. Do you put so much faith in the poets?"

" Yes, I believe it. I believe that it sometimes happens that two who are specially fitted for each other, and neither has any existing fancy, may see and feel this fitness at once, and so fall in love. Don't you?"

" I don't know. The nearest I ever came to such a thing, was with a portrait which I saw in Florence. It was of a man who had died, and the husband of another, and as old as my father. It was the portrait of the last of one of the old Huguenot families of South Carolina. There were generations of that old Norman blood, once ennobled, in him, and you could see it in every lineament of his face. Something lofty, and noble, that would easily become haughty, but was soft, sweet, and somehow compelling. When that portrait — it was full length — steps down from its sort of rustic frame, like the entrance into an arbor, and comes to me, I shall fear for myself."

" Why, Belle, you are enthusiastic. I hope you'll meet him."

" I used to go every day and stand before it; and the original was one that a noble, true woman did fall in love with, and her life has been tragically wretched. I will tell you the story some time. We were then at her house, every day for weeks, and Edward began to dislike my looking at the portrait so much."

"Jealous of a portrait! He was a queer man."

"No, not jealous; but he thought my interest in the story was, perhaps, almost unhealthy."

"Tell it to me, — do."

"Not now; we were talking of love, and bright things. Wait till some day when we are in the mood."

"I've been wondering whether Fred might come while you are here. Mr. Skinner said that he saw him last summer, and he said he meant to come to Mantua this winter. I wish he would. He is of the high and noble look of your portrait. Oh! I'd give the world to have you two fall in love."

"Tell me about him. I remember him as a very handsome boy, and my mother was much taken by him, and I want much to know what became of him."

"Not to-night," said Martha, pensively. "His story, too, has something of sadness, even the little I know of him, and his last visit here was in that awful time, — not to-night; to-morrow, or some time."

CHAPTER XXVIII.

FRED.

"YOU promised," said Belle, one day, when the girls were in a grave mood, "to tell me something about Fred Warden; do you feel like it now?"

"You will not think ill of poor, dear mother. She, like others, has her peculiarities, and one of them was to dislike and distrust poor Fred. She was honest in the feeling, and could not help it. Poor, dear mother, what would she not give, and all of us, to recall some things of the past!" very softly and sadly.

"Fred lived with us for about two years, as a bound boy. How strange that seems to me! He was faithful, quiet, and unassuming. You've heard — ?"

"Yes," a little impatiently.

"Well, of course he knew of that, and seemed very sad for a long time after we came back from your house; I think he must have heard something while we were gone. He never went anywhere, unless specially asked, and seldom then; when not at work he was reading, unless he was in the woods with a gun, or training a horse. He went to school the two winters, and I remember him as very quiet, very pleasant, and thoughtful. Father was very much attached to him, and he and 'Lias became very warm friends, or would have been. Well, mother

did not like him, could not bear him; he could do
nothing to suit her, and finally did not try much. She
seemed somehow to fear that Sarah would think too
much of him, and was finding ways to keep him at work
in the kitchen, or somewhere, and I fear he did not forget that he was a bound boy, whatever else he may
have had to remember; and the older he grew, the
more attentive mother became, and her watchfulness
increased. Father is easy, and perhaps was not very
observing, and I don't know what he could do, had he
known everything. Fred never complained to father,
and never answered mother back; but I could see, as I
grew older, that the poor fellow had a sad life of it.
Sarah was gone away a year to school, and then he
was less annoyed, but then mother seemed to be afraid
of his influence over Elias. When Sarah came home
from school, things were worse than ever. She was a
young lady, and Fred almost a young man, and could
do many things for her. Heaven knows no young
man could be more modest and respectful, and Sarah
was very much inclined to treat him as he deserved. I
never knew what mother's real intentions were, whether
to annoy him, until he would go, or what. It came
finally to a crisis. I can't remember — don't know
that I ever knew — what the last cause was. I fear
what preceded it was more than ample. Sarah and I
were both present, — it was in our garden, and he had
been doing something for her, when mother came, and
spoke sharply to him for it. Then he turned to her
very quietly, and said — he was very pale, and there
was something queer in his eyes which I will never
forget — 'Mrs. Carman' — he was always accustomed

to address her in this way — 'Mrs. Carman, I will
go.' 'Go — go where? you ——' Poor mother had
a temper and a tongue; and " — holding down her
head — " we had to hear her. Sarah walked away.
I remained. Fred soon went. He went up to the
room — which is now mine — where he slept, and packed
up his few things, and came down. Mother remained
under the influence of her temper, and told him to
leave them ; that if he went he would go as he came,
a ——. He laid down the bundle, his overcoat and
boots, and, without a word, walked out ; and " — with
a tremor in her voice — " we never saw him for six
years."

"Martha ! Oh, Martha ! " cried Belle, in anguish.

After a moment : " Father was away from home, and
when he came nothing was done, and little said, —
father gathered up all Fred's things, had them put in
good order, and placed in a small trunk, and took them
to Mr. Skinner's, one of Fred's friends ; but he never
took them, and I don't know what became of them."

" If he should ever marry," said Belle, " his wife will
reclaim that little trunk, if it is in existence. What
became of him.? "

"Oh, I can't tell ! I think he was away for a year
or two ; he never did stay in Mantua after that. His
aunt or mother — she may have been neither — gave
him eight or ten eagles when he left the Mormons ; he
showed them to us once when he first came. He
bought a few books with some of the money, and must
have had the rest when he left. We used to hear about
him, and all manner of stories, — that he had gone
back to the Mormons ; that he had gone off with a

circus; that he was driving stage; I don't know what all. There was no truth in any of them, as we came to know. When Jo Smith was tried at Chardon, for attempting to murder a man by the name of Newell, he was there as a witness, and seemed to have taken the idea of studying law; and it seems that he did, with a lawyer by the name of Cartter, at Canton or Massillon, or somewhere there; and then, for a time, we did not hear of him, and he had partly gone out of our minds.

"Four years ago"—after a pause—"early in July, Elias came home from school, ill. We did not feel alarmed about him; he was up and about a week, and then grew worse. Father, in those days, was a full believer in the Thompsonian practice, and had a book. Well, he and mother undertook to carry him through a course of medicine, as it is called, but he grew much worse, and we sent for Dr. Joel Thompson, a son of the Dr. Thompson who lives, or did live, in Shalersville.

"Oh, dear! I can't think of those days of horror, and quackery, of No. 6, and lobelia, without anguish and indignation. Everything was as bad as bad could be; Elias was raving, delirious. We had never had any sickness, and were ignorant and helpless. Mother was distracted, and father, poor, dear, good, precious father, was helpless. Our uncles, aunts and cousins could do nothing; father would keep Thompson; the haying had come on, the wheat was falling, and everything, everywhere, was as ruinous and wretched as could possibly be.

"In this distressed and awful condition of everybody and everything, we found Fred suddenly in the house. Oh, Belle, what a wonderful and glorious thing a man

is; what an angel he can be! Fred seemed like an
angel; he was beautiful, like an angel,— then. What a
miracle he worked! tall and strong, and cool and brave,
and low-voiced, with the step and touch of a woman.

"From the moment he stepped in he was king, as
such men are. Dr. Thompson vanished, and his old
steam-tub and pepper went with him. A man went off
with his horse on the run, for Dr. Moore and Dr. Earl,
who came, and held a consultation, and the battle for
Elias's life began in earnest; father and mother abdi-
cated. and Fred and cousin Martin took the whole care
of Elias. Fred would take him up and handle him as
easily as if he had been a baby, and as tenderly. For
ten days — for ten days — I believe he never left him;
and when the fever broke, and he came to, and it was
less labor to take care of him. Fred went out among
the farm-hands, where everything was at loose ends,
and in two or three days he put things to rights. He
was born not only to command, but to do also. Elias
continued to mend. I remember Fred spent an afternoon with us, and how cheerful, and hopeful, and happy
we all were; mother could not do and say enough; and
Fred waved her off, and would not let her talk; he told
her when Elias was well it would be time. He was
then about twenty-two, and still boyish, but had that
lofty look and way which you described as belonging
to that portrait. He told us something of himself. It
seems that ever since he heard Mr. Campbell, he had
dreamed of becoming a public speaker. He described
the trial of Jo Smith, and the advocates, whose
speeches made a great impression on him, especially
those of Mr. Andrews, of Cleveland, and Mr. Cartter

and it seems that Mr. Cartter had taken a fancy to him, and helped him, and he had then just completed his studies and been admitted. He told us, too, how he heard of Elias's sickness, and came to us at once."

Here she paused for a moment, while Belle sat silent, with eyes fixed intently upon her face.

"Oh, dear! Elias had a fatal relapse; nothing could help or save him, and in two days he — died —

"We lived through it; — folks will. I only know that in it all, and through it all, Fred stood in our centre to do and cheer and comfort. Well, when we came back from the cemetery he had gone, and from that day to this we have never one of us seen him." And she covered her face, and for a moment gave way.

"Martha! Martha!" throwing herself on her knees at the sobbing girl's feet, and clasping her waist, "don't say that! Surely, surely he would stay to be thanked. You have seen him since?"

"Never; and we never quite understood it. He did not go to the grave with us. I don't know why. Perhaps he who thought of everything and everybody, was himself forgotten; nobody asked him to go; and you know he could not help being sensitive, when you remember —"

"I would have gone after him," said Belle, impetuously.

"So would I, now. Father and mother were old, and utterly prostrated. We had no brother; we wrote him, and all joined in the letter, — such a letter as you may imagine. He answered it, — a very kind, gentle, but to me, a very sad letter. I won't try to repeat it, — I will show it to you some time. Its sadness was more in what it did not say, perhaps." A long silence.

"Well, what became of him? Is he alive still? Surely there must be a future for him."

"He lives at Massillon, I believe, about forty miles from here, and occasionally attends court at Ravenna, and we hear him very well spoken of. Father don't like lawyers. Indeed, the disciples in this region generally do not."

"Martha"— from her place on the carpet —" that young man should have been brought back here, and you should have been his reward. I don't know about this Henry," seriously. "Would that — you know what — have prevented your loving him?"

"No; a true woman would only love him the more and better," decidedly.

"You are a true woman, Mattie, dear, ain't you?" After a pause: "What a sad story this is; after all, he could not be quite perfect, or he would have remained, at least, for thanks."

"Don't blame him; I won't hear that, if I do condemn my own mother."

"And what does she say about him now?"

"Not much; but I believe she nearly adores him. There would be nothing too good for him now."

"Oh, Mattie, what a mistake! He should have come back, and you and he should have loved and married."

"I think," said Martha, "he will never marry a common woman; he would not love such an one. Oh, if he would only come while you are here!"

CHAPTER XXIX.

THE PORTRAIT STEPS FROM ITS FRAME.

SO Belle stood musing at the window, as we see. All the matters sketched in the two last chapters had occurred, and were narrated to her before. Her eyes were fixed musingly on the outer wintry world, her thoughts with her real self were on the story of Fred, which had somehow very much impressed her; so much so, that, cool and unimpressionable as she was, she was surprised at it. As her unseeing gaze wandered along the line of the front fence, from the large gate at the left of the house, where the old pear-tree stood, to the small gate leading directly across the little front lawn to the front door, and over which was a rustic arbor covered with climbing, leafless vines, she started with amazement. Was it a dream? Had her revery, in its strength, grouped all the fragments and elements that had occupied her thought, and framed the wonderful optical illusion that for a moment flashed on her vision? For there, framed in the rude arbor's entrance, living and breathing, was the portrait of Florence. The same lofty, noble countenance and speaking eyes, the half wilful mouth, that would break into a smile, or set with will and pride. There was the brow in its strength and volume, with its

(171)

possible haughtiness; but now bending with softness over the eyes, youthful and full of more excellence than mere beauty. It was but a moment; but it was all there, and real. The figure moved forward, — the hat was replaced; and taking the path that led around the back way, instead of coming to the front door, passed before her eyes a real, veritable man, in the flesh, walking and breathing, and leaving his impress. — Did she remember what she told Martha?

Belle placed her hands over her eyes, and tried to think. She could only see. A mystery was somehow solved, or rather an awful mystery was made palpable to her. She knew, as by revelation, that there must be the nearest possible relation between that portrait and this vision, if it was real. And while she stood still transfixed with this certainty, Martha flashed in, watery and radiant, from the dining-room:

"Oh, Belle, he has come! Fred, Fred has come, and more glorious than ever;" and taking the half-entranced girl by the hand, she drew her into the dining-room. The vision was very real. There was the veritable young man, bending over the clinging, sob-bing, broken, repentant Aunt Mary, and trying to assure and reassure her, — "That he was not one to be loved or regarded. He was only to love and serve others, and go; he was born to that."

How the words went into the heart of the still wondering Belle!

"Fred," said Martha, as her mother recovered herself, "do you remember Belle Morris?" The young man turned, and never, not even in the Pavilion of Vision, had his eyes rested on such, to him, unimagined

loveliness. A moment, and recovering his seldom-dis-
turbed self-possession :

"Belle Morris? Can this be Miss Morris? I remember her, and her kind, very kind mother, perfectly
well." Yet wondering if this could be her.

Belle, still dazed, for the illusion was now real, gave
him her little marvel of a hand, and only murmured
some indistinct words, like the warble of a bird.

"Not Belle Morris, — I must correct. — Mrs. Williams ; Mr. Warden." And marking the effect of this
announcement, — "The case is not desperate ; Mr. Williams was always a little shadowy — you deserve that,
Belle — and vanished while Belle was a little girl, —
and for you, she is Belle Morris."

"Martha, Martha, you are awful ! " from Aunt Mary.

"Mother, I'm kind and merciful," said the wilful
girl, a little archly.

"She who wears this," said the recovering Belle,
taking Martha's hand, and exhibiting the betraying
solitaire, "might, in her happiness, be forbearing."

"Oh, Martha ! " exclaimed Fred, " let me congratulate you," taking the now blushing girl's hand
warmly ; "in the world there is at least one very
happy man, I know."

"I hope so," in a little, sweet voice ; "and now I
here appoint you two bridesmaid and groomsman."

"You forget ! — I am a widow," said Belle.

"You a widow ! Why, it was only the other day
that you said you were a married woman. We won't
be defrauded this way. Maid, wife, or widow, or all
of them, if you are not my bridesmaid, I will not — "

"Be married ? " asked Belle.

" Not have any — I hope to be married," with the little voice again.

And now, Aunt Mary, having fully recovered all her motherly, housewifely instincts, came back in force.

" You must have some dinner."

" I had my dinner at my friend Turner's."

" Have you a horse, — or carriage?"

" I walked up from there;" and after a pause: "Mrs. Carman, may I stay here a day or two? I won't much annoy the young ladies. I came back to Mantua, and the wish to come back here was so strong, that I haven't even called on Uncle Bill Skinner; for, after all, this is the only home I've ever known." He was not sentimental; but, spite of him, there was a tremor in his voice and a moisture in his eye.

" Stay here! stay here!" cried the again sobbing Aunt Mary; " you shall always stay here! Let this always be your home! Oh. I'm so glad you came! I thought I was never to see and thank you, and it —"

" No matter! not a word of that! I am a thousand times repaid!" very brightly and gayly; and, turning off, he dashed at a dozen things, — asked all about Mr. Carman, and Sarah, and her husband and children, and the farm, and old-time things, going back to his residence, and then about the neighbors, — Hiram Spencer, Judge Carman's folks, Uncle Zach, and so on. Then he turned to Belle, and grew grave and thoughtful; and all the time she watched and observed him, and asked herself a thousand insoluble questions. There could be no mistake; this was the veritable son; there was crime, or an awful mistake somewhere. Could there have been two sons? And she thought of what was said of the shadow on Fred, and sighed.

Soon Uncle Seth came in, and broke completely down, and *would* talk about Elias. That preciously sad subject and dark day had to be gone over with.

They were almost made happy by the many pleasant things that Fred remembered of him, — things many of which they then heard for the first time. So they passed out of gloom again into warmth and sunshine, mellowed and softened by the renewed memory of a great and common loss.

Aunt Mary was to have company that night — two or three distinguished preachers of the disciple persuasion — and was under preparation for a supper. Uncle Seth had been benignantly looking forward to their arrival as a season of refreshing, and even Martha and Belle were not without some exhilaration consequent upon the expected advent of the ministers, and not without a little anxiety on Fred's account, who was rated an unbeliever ; one of the expected was noted for the honest fervor with which he admonished that class, with little reference to time, place, or circumstances, having regard to eternity alone.

When the guests arrived, they came in the usual way in farm-houses, and entered by the rear, where they were received by the expectant elders, removed their outer coats and wraps, and lingered for the warmth of the generous hickory fire, always burning in the huge, jammed old fireplace. Then they were shown into the front sitting-room, to interrupt a very pleasant flow of talk between Belle and Fred, who, sitting in the glow of the red fire at the twilight, felt wonderfully acquainted within the two hours since their meeting. In their rambling talk, Belle, in the most innocent way in the world, had told him of a singular name, and how it came. A gentleman, a descendant of the Huguenots, blessed with a beautiful infant son, had a Saxon friend by the name of Ethwold Alfred, and he bestowed both names upon his heir, and insisted upon using both as if they were a single name. The child's mother had, for convenience, formed a new one from the two, by putting the first and last syllables together, and called him Ethfred.

"Ethfred, — Ethfred," repeated Fred, thoughtfully, "I've heard that name!"

"That is very strange," answered Belle. "I presume there never could have been but one child named Ethfred."

"I've heard it; it has haunted my dreams; and I never, while waking, could recall it. Ethfred, — that is it. I could remember that it had some sound of my own name."

"The last syllable is Fred; and by dropping the first, which is not pleasant, you would be Fred, as you are," playfully. "What else have you dreamed of, pray?" lightly and brightly.

"Oh," laughing, "I had a brain fever when I was twelve, and I know not what when I was with the Mormons, — that was the land of dreams."

"You must have had some funny experiences. Did you dream of this name there?"

"Yes; I dreamed I was lying on the ground on flowers, with wonderful flowers about me; the air was full of fragrance, and a beautiful face was over me, —

the face of a woman, who called me 'Ethfred'—I'm now sure that was the name—and before me arose a wonderful tree,—a palm, such as we see in pictures of the East. I seem to have dreamed this two or three times."

"It is very funny. Did it ever—"

The door opened, and in strode John Henry—not the Rev. John, they never had that title appended—a large, gaunt, gray, coarsely-arrayed figure, with a New England type of head and face, now much out of date. The deep gray eyes, overhung by shaggy gray brows, were shrewd, keen, but kindly; the voice strong and loud by nature; his manners were plain to rudeness; but he was, nevertheless, a man of power and mark in his day and way. He was accompanied by a younger man—Morse—a gentlemanly person of fair culture and much ability, and rather reticent.

"Father Henry!" cried Belle, springing to him, and extending her hands, which he took very cordially, and bending down to her, with a warm smile lighting up his rugged face, framed in a fell of iron-gray hair; it never could be white,—the iron would never leave it. "Daughter, daughter Belle, bless you! I fear for thee, precious one, lest the snare of thy comeliness entrap thee in vanities." And holding up her soft little hands, and changing his style of address: "They toil not, neither do they spin, O daughter Belle, but they do meet works of charity and kindness!" He inquired for Brother Morris and Maud, and bent his brows several times on Fred, who stood near, an amused and interested spectator. "And who is this? He looks like a goodly son of the unbeliever."

12

" Mr. Warden, let me introduce you to Father Henry," said Belle, a little anxious to know how they would receive each other.

" Mr. Henry," said the youth frankly, stepping forward, and giving his hand with a warm, natural grace, that few could resist, " I've often heard your name, and always with respect ; I am very glad to meet you."

" I never heard your name before, and am not very much rejoiced to see you ; I may be next time," was the response.

" He's not only an unbeliever," said Martha, mischievously, " but he's a lawyer, — one of those awful sons of Belial."

" A lawyer, and he finds shelter under this roof! Young man, don't you know that lawyers were specially cursed? Woe to ye lawyers !" with a sepulchral voice.

" I've heard of that somewhere, I believe," smiling, almost laughing ; " but then I remember that the same high authority denounces the priests with greater severity and justice."

" Indeed, young man, you should distinguish between the Jewish priesthood and the preachers of the Word."

" I think a slight distinction might also be drawn between the Jewish lawyer and those of our time. But really, my kind, dear sir, I'm not lawyer enough to fall within the curse," laughing, with infectious good nature. The old man hesitated in his opening of half banter, as if a little in doubt what turn to take.

" Brother Henry," said Aunt Mary, rushing in with real apprehension, " this is the young man of whom

I've told you, who was with us in our days of tribulation, when our son died."

"And it is good to remember that.   Young man, I think I shall like you, but touching thy profession, it smacks wholly of darkness."

Then Fred was introduced to Mr. Morse, who evidently was pleased with him, and very soon the girl called to supper.

CHAPTER XXX.

PUT ON THE DEFENSIVE.

THE old-time farm-house dining-room was one capacious room originally, which was kitchen, dining, and family room, generally ; but under Martha's direction new space had been found in the L part, and a new wall had separated the dining and family room from the kitchen. In the former, Aunt Mary now received her guests, and seated them at one of her profuse and well-cooked suppers. The little, funny, quaint old teaspoons, the bowl of one of which would hardly admit the tip of a lady's finger, were in regular service, in honor of Belle ; and these were now supplemented with real old China cups of a great-grandmother, imported by a sea-faring progenitor.

A large and beautifully-browned turkey was the object of principal interest on Aunt Mary's table, which Uncle Seth regarded with foreboding. surrounded as he was by guests. He thought of the old time when he was assailed by a raging she-bear, as comfortable and pleasant, comparatively.

"Mr. Warden," asked Aunt Mary, suggestively, "have you lost your knack of carving?"

"It's part of a lawyer's trade to pull people and

(180)

things to pieces." remarked Father Henry; "let us see
how cutting he can be."

"Lawyers, as you call on them, have been known to
cut up witnesses and other innocents," said the young
man, advancing upon the common enemy, and taking
up the formidable knife; "and as they always carve
the whole to themselves, as Mr. Henry will testify,
they ought not to object to such a service."

A rap from that gentleman called the company to
order for a short, sonorous grace, when, with a twinkle
of his eye that could be kindly, he asked, "What can
be done with the sinner who good-humoredly confesses
his sins, but refuses to repent?" Fred, who had no
disposition to discuss his profession, and was quite
content to accept this as concluding the subject, addressed himself seriously to his task. He was that
rarity among American gentlemen, especially at the
West,—an artistic carver. Had he known the approving admiration with which his labors were regarded,
and that it was fully shared in by Belle, he would
have felt rewarded for the, to him, slight labor. As
the noble fowl lay in neatly sundered parts, while Fred
was learning the wishes of the guests,—"I'll warrant,
now," resumed Father Henry, "that if he was before a
jury, he'd put that gobbler together again, and contend
that it was untouched,—perhaps that 'twas alive, and
ready to strut off." No answer, but a good-natured
smile from Fred, who dexterously served the whole
party, and gladly took a seat reserved for him between the young ladies. "It is a little remarkable,"
observed the usually taciturn Morse, "the vehemence
and seeming sincerity with which lawyers contend, on

directly opposite sides; and that, you must admit, Mr. Warden, leads candid men to doubt the sincerity and candor of all lawyers. One certainly must be wrong."

"Both may be," quietly remarked Fred, disposed to conclude any argument. "I think I have been informed that you were formerly a Presbyterian?" he observed, by way of inquiry.

"I was, at one time."

"And that Mr. Henry was a Methodist?"

"So I am informed."

"It is a little remarkable," he went on, "the vehemence and seeming sincerity with which a Presbyterian and a Methodist clergyman contend on directly opposite sides of the same question, and that too a matter of direct revelation, about which there should be no doubt; baptism, for instance, in which you now admit that you were both wrong. You must admit, Mr. Morse, that this leads candid men to doubt the sincerity of all preachers." This grave turning of tables was done with a mock serious voice, that made it irresistible, and was greeted with a loud laugh from Father Henry.

· "Don't argue with the devil, brother Morse,— don't argue with the devil, even on Bible questions."

"I know one honest lawyer," observed Uncle Seth, quite decidedly. "Mr. Day, of Ravenna, is an honest man, if there ever was one."

"And everything in the world but a fool, also," said Fred. "I suspect that he must have been counsel for you, in some case."

"Yes, he was."

"I thought so. Our lawyer is always honest. It's the chap on the other side who outruns total depravity."

"I believe," remarked Aunt Mary, quietly, "that Mr. Carman thinks that Mr. Tildin is a very bad man."

"He was on the other side. Oh, that's too bad!" laughing. "Tildin's heart would compel him to nurse a dying fly ; and that mortal man should suspect him of possible wrong, is too bad."

"Well, I am not so sure of that," replied Aunt Mary, with judicious doubt and gravity.

"Oh, they are a bad lot," still laughing ; "and so bad, that we go into open court, in the face of the court and jury, and in the face of immediate and certain exposure, and lie, and re-lie, right along, and the fun of it is, everybody, though knowing that we lie, nevertheless feels obliged to believe us,— it's too bad. While your only reliable men are your preacher and doctor."

"You are a necessary evil, no doubt," observed Father Henry, who rather enjoyed the play of the young man's spirit in the defence of his profession.

"Did you ever think what a real compliment that is to the bar? The world is so hopelessly bad, so much worse than we, that it cannot get on without us. Then if it was virtuous, and holy, what use would it find for preachers and priests? Poor, wicked old world, let us each serve it in our way, and not quarrel with each other."

"I fear the young man was born for a lawyer," said Father Henry, turning to Belle ; "and perhaps we should not be too hard upon him for what he can't help."

" Especially," added that young lady, " when he says that he is not lawyer enough to fall within the curse."

The supper was finished, the guests arose, two or three neighbors dropped in, new groups were formed, and new interests were discussed, with cider, apples, and nuts, by the hickory fires, and the winter night wore on to the hour of retiring.

CHAPTER XXXI.

BELLE'S REVERY.

THE thoughtful Bell sat, — not musing. but thinking, actually and not illogically. as women can think, and often do. How passing beautiful she was. as she sat with her peerless head upon her hand, whose little slender fingers were bent back by the weight, with the ruddy glow from the embers rich on her cheek ; and what funny thoughts for a girl! He had heard that barbarous name — Ethfred — in his dreams, he said ; but why in his dreams? of what are dreams made? Then there came into her mind the discussion of dreams between her father and Marbury. Is there a new faculty born of sleep. or do we get new power? or do some organs sleep and leave others awake, which, thus unbalanced, play such phantasies? Dreams must be made of something seen or heard. of course they must ; so if he dreamed of this name. he must have heard it. and there never was but one child who bore it. No wonder it brought bad luck. He has seen pictures of palms, and their surroundings, and could dream of them. though he undoubtedly dreamed of what he saw, and the woman bending over him was his mother, and called him by name under a palm in Cuba.

(185)

He was not a cousin, for the father had no brothers or sisters, nor could he be a brother, for his name was "Ethfred," and she clasped her hands. It might not be, and not a word would she utter to him until it was made certain. The germs of these thoughts were intuitions. They formed their final crystallization naturally, and by no conscious process. And then the man himself stood before her, warm and gentle, with the mute beseeching light in his eyes, so noble and tender, and so abused by fortune through all the cruel years.

Oh, to serve him, to have his gratitude, to have — Well, what was the danger? Hadn't she a husband, — in heaven, to be sure, but it did not occur to her that he thus left his widow defenceless. But where was Martha? Could she have stolen off to bed? Did she mean to throw her and Fred upon each other for society? It was like Mattie. Her watch showed that it was half-past eleven, when nine or half-past was orthodox bed-time, — broken over this evening by the elders for company. So she tripped lightly up to her warm room, cheery with the red light of the wood embers, with grave thoughts in her head, and a little glow — just a little flutter — in her veins. She arrayed herself for the night, and pushing open the door into Martha's darkened room, stepped lightly to the side of the sleeper. She stood for a moment, and lifting the clothes, "You bad, bad, Mattie," in a sweet little voice, laid herself in her night robes, close by a warm side, and was about to pass one arm over the sleeping form, when — . Shocked, but without sense of injury; confused, but with clear perception; alarmed, yet feeling no fear; repelled, yet singularly attracted, she stepped noisely upon the floor, and in an instant the door softly closed between the two.

Poor Fred! "Poor Fred?" Yes, poor Fred! It might mark my page were I to portray the low ideal which the average young man has of the purity of woman. It may possibly not be given to the masculine perception to fully appreciate the innate, healthy, inner stainlessness of a true woman. Possibly the language which would express it might convey no meaning to him; and were I to see it, by some miracle in my text, I might find it cloudy, transcendental, and needing change. I suspect that nothing so alarms the sensibilities of a woman as when she comes, by a slow succession of shocks, to apprehend as well as she may the gross nature of man. Fred may have shared in his sex's want of discernment in this respect, but like a great, a very great many young men, he had set up in his soul's inner shrine an ideal of womanhood, the crowning grace of which was this uncomprehended purity. — a thing to be worshipped, if not understood; any profanation of which would be, in his eyes, that nameless crime for which no pardon could be possible; and in some sort he now felt guilty of this crime.

Miss Boothe had stepped in late, and he had, with Martha, accompanied her home. When learning that she was alone, Martha had consented to remain with her. On his return, he missed Belle from the room where he left her, and regretfully went for the night to his old room, as Aunt Mary had directed, full of the one idea — no, not one idea, that is a mental entity — and with this the mind, save by perception and consciousness, had nothing to do. He was full of the image of Belle, her grace and beauty, and for an hour his own atmosphere had been cleared of the old shadow.

He entered, without noticing, the old and once familiar room, which seemed larger, and in some way strange. Absently he removed his clothes and placed himself in bed; but when he passed the line of waking unconsciousness to the realm of dreaming reality, he did not know. At some time, however, he heard the low voice of Belle coming naturally into his dream, and, for an instant, she who filled his sleeping vision filled the place by his side, — and was gone. Had she actually been there, or was that a phase of his dream? He fully awoke, and she was gone, and there came to his awakened sense the idea of having committed a crime against her purity. True, he was in dreamland, and as innocent in thought as act; but he wondered why her approach had not awakened him, — he thought he would know if she approached his grave; and the shock, the offence to her would undoubtedly be as great as if he, knowing of her mistake, had permitted her to complete it. He was in no condition to reason or think at all. He had long realized that the love of woman was not for him; that a name tarnished by such a birth, and in a way infamous, he could never offer to any woman. Here now was this one woman of all the earth and heaven whom he should love, whom he felt and knew that he now loved; against her he had so sinned, and she would necessarily regard him with loathing and abhorrence. This would be his punishment. So in a weak, foolish, young man's way, it haunted him the long night through, and he arose languid. How could he meet her again? He would make an excuse to the

Carmans and go away — if indeed Belle had not already left the house — and take himself out of her sight!

He found Belle standing by the window from which she first saw him the day before, and as she turned, her look betrayed to him something that he translated into suffering, — possibly dislike or loathing. She was alone.

"Mrs. Williams," with humiliation and contrition, "I know not how I can approach you, or how frame a possible apology. I dare not hope for pardon. I was dreaming of you when you approached; I heard your voice; I should have spoken, and saved you; I could not; I wish you could know how impossible it is for me to harm woman;" a pause — she had turned away — no answer. "I will go away at once, and relieve you of my presence."

A little hand came out to him deprecatingly. "No, Mr. Warden, you will not go; you will stay, we — shall"— a little motion of the hand finished the sentence.

"Oh, that this should have happened! I, who have never hoped for the love of woman, and yet would gladly die for you."

No answer, save a little wave of the hand again. Fred stood a moment; he could say no more, and Belle would say nothing. He could make no apology, and none could be accepted. He could only relapse into the abashed awkwardness of the clownish feeling of a man who blunders into a position to which no human tact is equal. Had he possessed the finer nature of the woman, he would have felt instinctively that it was not a matter for words, unless, indeed, at some blissful future, when everything might find words for expression. He saw in a moment that he had help-lessly blundered, yet he felt that a woman should have sympathized with a manly effort to apologize; and as the only thing left he escaped from the room, out through the dining-room, and so past the kitchen, into the back yard, off across the orchard, and down by the cider mill, across the road into the meadow below, to where a young man was feeding a herd of young bullocks and heifers from a hay-stack. He thought it all over, and it did not look to him, on this bleak wintry morn-ing, as amid the dreams of last night. It was all like a dream now, and at no time while Belle was in his room, was he well awake. He knew he was uncon-scious of the thought of ill, and should she be so re-lentless? After all, the shock to her might be as great as if, with a full knowledge on his part, he had permitted her to commit the error. No matter, there came up a sensation of anger to mingle with the sore feeling that possessed him. What mattered it? She could never be anything to him, and he less than nothing to her; if she did scorn and despise him, it was but natural. She could not be above the rest of the world. What was he, but a ——. It was not a pleasant frame of mind in which he turned back to his kind hosts and their guests, but it would carry him through under the eyes of Belle, or in her presence; she would not look at him, anyway, and he would not care.

And Belle? She remained by the window, only turning when she heard the door close at his exit. Her face wore a thoughtful, but anything in the world but an angry or disgusted look. Under other circum-stances one would suppose that something deep, but

not at all unpleasant. was in her mind; and withal
there was a little look of distrust about her. She
turned again to the window, wondering, perhaps,
whether that portrait would come again through the
arbor, and started to see Martha flash in it a moment.
This sight sent her to the glass, to see what her face
might tell. but she was evidently satisfied with it. as
well she might be, and the next moment turned to
scold the truant. "Well, upon my word, if —"

"Don't scold me, Belle; I expected to return; I
sent back Master Fred; of course I knew I wouldn't
be missed."

"Indeed! Miss Martha, take a timely warning if
you wish us to cultivate each other. Don't you know
that if parties get the impression that friends wish
them to fancy each other, and make little conveniences
for them, that they take pleasure in asserting their
independence? and your friend Fred would be no ex-
ception."

"You wise Belle! I never thought of that. Where
is that young gentleman, pray?"

"How should I know? He idled through the room
but a moment ago, finding it more attractive elsewhere,
of course."

The quick Martha looked keenly at her. "What has
happened, you cool, indifferent thing?"

"You went and left me alone, and without notice;
is not that excuse for coolness?"

"Answer me one thing, — don't you think he is
handsome?"

"He is better looking than handsome." very seriously. "Don't call him handsome,— anybody might be that."

"Well, what?"

"Noble, and true, and good; any woman would trust him in a moment," seriously.

"Oh, Belle, Belle, and you a married woman! Look out!"

"I think that it is when a woman sees all these qualities, and keeps them for her own secret admiration, that she is in danger," answered the cool and wary Belle.

"And you're deep, after all, with your great wide eyes staring about in wondering innocence. Never mind"—as she passed forward to aid about the break-fast.

CHAPTER XXXII.

A WEIRD HUNT.

FRED came in rather late to breakfast, and was remitted to his place between the young ladies, receiving from Martha a quick, sharp glance, and reproof for his tardiness, and an answer to his excuse that "Pete would attend to the young cattle." Father Henry turned his shaggy brows not unkindly upon him, and pleasantly referred to the discussion of the night before, remarking that brother Morse thought that lawyers were, on the whole, a sort of worldly philosophers, not without their use, though not very well appreciated.

Fred answered : "That a man with danger on either hand, as you see me" — with a glance at either fair neighbor — "has need of philosophy; what can the church do in situations like these?"

"The church can furnish the exact remedy," sparkled up the piquant Martha, with a mischievous glance at Belle.

"You are to try your own prescriptions, I believe, which proves your sincerity, at least, Miss Carman," said that perfectly placid person, with a little emphasis on the first word.

13   (193)

Some general talk of the weather. and of the departure of the guests, between the elders, with silence among the younger ones, till the meal was finished; then a chapter in Mr. Campbell's translation of the later Scriptures, a hymn which Fred helped the young ladies to sing, a sonorous prayer by Elder Henry, who pointedly reminded the Lord of the existence and outside condition of Fred, and recommended prompt measures in his case. Then the preachers went their way, attended by Uncle Seth, with the understanding that they would return the second evening after.

Somehow, it was a dull day at the farm-house. Belle was silent and thoughtful, and went to her room to write letters, and was by herself most of the day. Martha, with her vivacious nature and sweet thoughts, relapsed into her little demure ways, and Aunt Mary was uneasy about the mysterious absence of Fred, who -had disappeared.

In the afternoon, Pete relieved this anxiety, by saying that Fred had passed by where he was chopping in the east woods, with Hiram Spencer's rifle, making over the chestnut ridges towards the mouth of Black Brook, he presumed for turkeys. It was quite late, however, when he returned; and the three women in the fire-lighted room were waiting in the weird loneliness that may come about women at this hour, in the absence of the masculine element, that at least sheds. about a lonely farm-house, at the oncoming of night, a sense of protection and safety. Three rather sombre faces broke into warmth and gladness when he came in.

" How now, you runaway!" exclaimed the vivacious Martha, springing to him; "don't you know you've behaved very badly, running off to the woods, and leaving us alone all day?"

"Excuse me, but really, when your good mother consented to harbor me for a day or two, it was on the express condition that I would not annoy the young ladies, you remember."

"I don't know any such thing; and besides, you should wait till we showed our annoyance."

"A gentleman would prevent the possibility of your being annoyed."

"Well, we are annoyed, you see."

"I can only implore your pardon," meekly.

"We won't forgive you now, — I hope you haven't killed anything, you unlucky wretch, running off to murder things!"

"Only a very dark day, and a very black turkey, notwithstanding the maxim that assigns luck to fools."

Supper was announced, at which Martha asked an account of the day's adventures, and how he came to act so.

"Well, Mr. Spencer had told him of a flock of turkeys, over by the Dean Place, and offered him his rifle, and he thought Mrs. Carman would like a bird for her table, on the return of her guests. So he went out, and had struck the fresh track of deer, and was enticed to follow it."

"Just like a man!" put in Martha.

"Well, he came upon the deer, and his gun snapped."

"Served you right; and the deer snapped her fingers at you, I s'pose."

"Exactly! Well, he saw it several times; it had a funny way of disappearing, and then suddenly being before him, like the white witch doe, that nothing was to kill, and finally away across Black Brook, he found himself lost."

"The Irishman found himself lost!" exclaimed Martha. "Well, sir, when did you lose yourself found again?"

"Not till now. Well, having got me hopelessly snarled up, the deer disappeared."

"Appeared to disappear, perhaps," suggested Martha, "and served you right for disappearing yourself. Let this be a warning."

"Well, I didn't look for her, him or it, but thought of Hiram's turkeys, and found myself so bewildered that I really thought of nothing. Finally, I found myself somehow in the midst of a flock, and shot a fine, large, and glossy black young tom, when — "

"You piously thanked your stars, and gratefully started for home."

"I started, but for no definite where, as I found. I finally grew weary of carrying the young tom, threw him down, consulted the moss on the trees, and made a very direct course for home."

"Of course, — well?"

"After a half-hour's walk I came upon a fine, black, young tom turkey, that somebody had just shot, which looked somehow familiar; and sure enough, close by, was a track which my boot just fitted."

Laughter from the ladies.

"I resumed the turkey, and my journey. That particular tom had the peculiarity of rapidly growing heavy, and I soon abandoned him, notwithstanding Mrs. Carman's possible wishes."

" Well? — "

" Well, I came upon another freshly shot young tom turkey, in a few minutes. and, as he was rather fresh and fine, and thinking Mrs. Carman might find him acceptable, and as he was thus providentially thrown in my way, I thought I would carry him to her. After a little tramp, I changed my mind, remembering that she had turkey last night ; so I dropped him also, but somehow he wouldn't stay dropped, for within ten minutes I came upon him again. You see, ladies, go where I would, do what I would, that particular and very unlucky young tom haunted me. This time I took a very deliberate survey of him, and of myself, mentally, and of my whole life."

" What an ugly view you must have had ! "

" I did, — I assure you."

" Well, what was your conclusion ? "

" To adhere to that tom, and change my course of travel, and possibly of life."

" That was profound, though late. Well ? "

" It was not well. I soon found myself in the trail leading up through to Troy — I believe Welch- field is now called — and of course thought that my resolution had met with an immediate blessing. I had gone perhaps a mile, when just at that moment the clouds lifted at the horizon, and the sun shone out exactly in the east ! It was apparent that the world or I was very much turned around : and as it was easier to reverse myself, I turned immediately the other way, and am here, ladies," with a bow to each. The man- ner was very vivacious, with a little flavor of irony.

" And the turkey ? " gravely asked Martha.

" Is on the porch, or was. I won't answer for that young tom, however."

" Susan ! " to the girl, " take a candle and go and see ; this tale needs confirmation." Sue soon returned, bringing in an immense and glossy black turkey, so black that it seemed to shed twilight through the room.

" Why, what an unearthly, weird monster it is ! Take it out," with affected fright.

" Fred," resumed the young lady, with immense solemnity, " let this day's wanderings and misadventures, with its warnings and sufferings, remain an awful lesson to you, so long as you live — and remain young, and unmarried — never again to desert two distressed damsels, one of whom is a widow, and the other has not a lover within five hundred miles ; and that the lesson may not be without improvement by us all, Susan shall dress the young thomas, and maybe he will inveigle two hungry preachers, and the rest of us, with other woes. It is our duty to submit to these trials of the flesh, — when it promises to be savory."

During the delivery of this unctuous exhortation, Fred had drawn down the corners of his mouth, and dropped his eyes, with ludicrous contrition, and expressed his acquiescence in a sepulchral " Amen " at its conclusion.

CHAPTER XXXIII.

THE EXCURSION AND RESCUE.

ERE they left the table, Martha informed him that the State-road young people, the Reeds, one or two of the Mays, and others, had sent over, and asked them to go the next morning, with a little party, to the Rapids. The ice above was splendid, and they would skate and drive on the river, have a dinner at old Furman's, and a good time, and would he go? Belle had consented.

Of course he would, and gladly. He had an immense relish for outdoor sports, in which he excelled. It would furnish him employment, and be an excuse for remaining near Belle, who had been almost bodily with him all day, notwithstanding her contemptuous rebuff that morning, and her silence this evening.

The rest of the evening was spent in the front sitting-room. Fred *distrait* and silent, notwithstanding his evident effort at careless gayety, in which he signally failed. The charitable Martha attributed his manner to over-fatigue, incident to the forest enchantment of the bewitched doe. Aunt Mary kindly insisted on his early retirement, while Belle seemed somewhat lost in a revery. Martha fell back upon her own exhaustless, happy thoughts. Fred was up early. He

(199)

found Elias's skates, and restrapped them. Uncle Seth had driven off the cutter, an old one was hunted out, a pole extemporized, a seat fixed up, and a harness and pair of horses adjusted to it. One of the horses was young, unaccustomed to work, and quite unmanageable; Belle, from her window, admiringly watched the skill and address with which Fred controlled and finally subdued the spirited animal. The morning was brilliant, with sun, snow and frost; about mid-forenoon the State-road party arrived, and Fred had his horses ready to start with them.

When they were about to go, Belle, under pretence that his sleigh was scant of room, having but a single seat, accepted a place in another. The excuse was sufficient, perhaps, but the sharp-eyed Martha saw that the act cut Fred like a knife. No remark was made about it between them, and the party proceeded south, towards Judge Carman's, and took the old diagonal road that led down past the old Elam Spencer place, and thence east into the road up the hill, and across the intervening table-land, past the Norton place, and so finally down the slope into the valley of the Cuyahoga, to Furman's, a quarter of a mile from the river. The whole way was still an almost unbroken forest, and one of the most wonderful growths of splendid chestnut-trees on the continent.

After a little pause at Furman's, the party pulled up on the still solitary banks of the river, just at the upper end of " the Rapids," where the waters, breaking through the sandstone ridge that here, cropping out, had imprisoned them, and caused them to stand and flood back, deep and still, for miles, and finally go

madly plunging and foaming through and over the
broken, worn, and torn fragments of rock below, — now
an impassable, dangerous, wintry torrent of considerable width and depth. Immediately above, the ice was
smooth and firm, and for any extent upward. Sam
Furman had a cooper's shop near the bank, which the
party took possession of, and which was warm with a
roaring fire.

The sleighs and cutters were driven at will on to the
firm surface ; skates were adjusted, and very soon the
young men were flying over the ice, and sometimes
pushing the young ladies in chairs, or some other extemporized means of conveyance, before them. At that
time young ladies seldom skated.

One of the young men, who drove a single horse,
and had two young girls in his sleigh, amused himself
and them by driving up and down on the river. At
one time he incautiously approached too near the
margin of the ice, where the boiling water broke from
it in its swelling plunge down the Rapids ; he
headed his horse about in time to save him, but the
momentum carried that sleigh over the smooth ice, so
near to its edge, that it broke with the weight ; and
although the spirited horse, at the call of its excited
driver, took the carriage away in safety, one of the
girls, a little Hebe of fourteen, in her fright, finding
herself sweeping in a giddy circle out over the water,
sprang from the sleigh into the current. Her clothes
buoyed her for a moment, and the rushing torrent carried her below. Her red hood floated at the surface
an instant, and disappeared.

The accident was witnessed by many of the party,

who, at the apparent danger, raised a cry of alarm,
when, under an apprehension that the ice had given
way generally, everybody in terror sprang toward the
shore.   Fred was a few roods away, pushing the
laughing Martha before him in a chair.   He had discovered the approach of the sleigh, raised his voice in
warning to the driver, abandoning Martha, and was
already in full career for the scene of peril.   With an
almost perfect form for strength and activity, strong
and agile, he sprang forward.   Dropping his gloves
and cap, and flinging his coat from him, he leaped into
the open water and disappeared.   A moment, and the
red hood reappeared, and then the upper part of Fred's
person, sustaining the insensible girl.   So far down
now were they, that the current, in its first leap, dashed
him downward — a rock projecting stayed him — when,
with a prodigious effort, he reached the flat surface of
another, over which the waters ran smooth, but with
almost irresistible force.   Unable to stand with skates,
he sprang forward, stemmed successfully a deeper current, and under his burden reached the margin, in
which, standing to her knees in swift waters, stood
Belle, with her arms mutely extended to him, and a
light in her great eyes such as he had never seen before.   From this point she aided him; a sleigh was
standing near; pushing the loose seats aside, they laid
the girl on the straw in the bottom.   "Take her on
your lap," said Fred, in a low voice; "so, — now roll
her to and fro."   Seizing the lines, he headed the
horses towards Furman's, and lashed them to their utmost speed.   "Tear open her dress, if possible," were
the only other words he said.

Ere they reached the house, the nearly drowned girl showed signs of returning consciousness; and when Fred took her in, she was struggling and breathing, though with difficulty. "Strip and wrap her in hot flannels at once," he said to Belle, to whom he resigned her; "and care for yourself, — you are drenched."

He removed his skates, one of which was broken at the toe, and ran back to the river, meeting on his way the whole terror-stricken party. His cap, coat and gloves were restored to him; and directing one of the young men to go for the nearest doctor, he entered the now deserted shop.

An hour later, limp and stained about the bosom, with his hair still damp, he entered the Furman house to learn that the rescued girl was doing very well. There the whole party were, and now gathered about him in eager and rapturous applause. Oh, it is much to be the hero of even a moment, and feel the strong rush and gush of human praise and admiration; and so did it overwhelm poor Fred, that he could make no reply; a choking sensation arose in his throat, tears came to his eyes, and a devout thankfulness went up from his burdened heart; and all the time he could feel a pair of great wondrous eyes upon him, that he would not turn to meet.

"Miss Carman," said he, finally addressing that now radiant young woman, "I owe you an apology. Permit me to beg your pardon for the very unceremonious manner in which I left you on the ice a few moments ago."

"I will not only forgive you for that, but for all past and all possible future transgressions. How glad you should be that you are a great, brave, heroic man!" admiringly.

"And Mrs. Williams"—he had now found his tongue, turning, but still avoiding her eyes—"I owe you a thousand thanks for coming to help me out of the river; and the poor girl is indebted to you for your care in the sleigh."

"Oh, I am so glad!" said the sincere girl, "gladder than I can say."

Then all resumed their interrupted versions of the matter, and each of the young men explained very clearly why it was that he did not also plunge into the mad and boiling waters, and carry out the drowning girl.

"Oh, boys!" exclaimed the appreciative Martha, "it is all perfectly clear,—you all cleared out. In a moment you rendered it the clearest case that ever was clarified,—no use to protest, Dave: I saw you climbing a tree,—you thought that there was a miraculous rise in the river. Well, we weren't all born to be heroes. You all wish that you had done it, and we are all too glad that it was done, and well done, because it was done quickly. Fred, ain't that a little Shakespearish, or something."

"That, or something, certainly," laughing. Then the young lady wanted to see her deliverer; and Mrs. Furman, with Belle and Martha, took him into a large warm room, where, in a bed, propped up with warm woollens about her, a sweet bright face, and mischievous black eyes, were anxiously awaiting him. Her face was warm with color; and poor Fred approached her blushing, the only embarrassed one in the room.

The attendants made way, and putting up towards him her honest brown hands, she said, "I want to thank you and can't ;" and pulling the poor youth down to her, she kissed his cheek. "God bless you, God bless you, and of course He will!"

When they had a little recovered from this natural exuberance of feeling, "There," said Martha, "that must do! You are a precious little puss, Millie, for jumping into the river. There ain't another girl in the world who would have done it, and we are ever and ever so much obliged to you for it, and so is Fred; for how could he save you if you hadn't? But, you see, you mustn't go to falling in love with him and being unhappy. Of course, it would be your duty to marry him, but you won't have to, for I've promised him in another direction ; so you'll have nothing to do but remember him in your prayers, you precious little goose you!" Then Fred was permitted to go out without a word. Indeed, the case was a little too trying for him, lawyer as he was.

After dinner the teams were brought around, and, of course, the party went home, the young girl remaining till a later hour, for more complete restoration.

Fred was desirous of going to Turner's, where his baggage was, and turned down a new road, which followed the river valley, accompanied by Martha. The strain of the last two or three days had been severe upon him mentally and physically ; and if Martha found him a less pleasant companion than he otherwise might have been, with a woman's tact she accommodated herself to his man's moods uncomplainingly. As they approached the neighborhood of Fred's young boy-

home, he became alive to the surroundings, and pointed
out to the sympathizing Martha various localities;
among others, to a little heap of stones and one or two
apple-trees in a deserted space, which marked the site of
Sam Warden's hut.   Further on, he pointed to a little
knoll in the now thin fringe of forest that bordered the
river where he stood when his little boat passed forever from his sight.   Never before had he said so much
of his old-time life, and he now suddenly relapsed into
his wonted reticence, saying little more upon any subject, and left his companion to wonder over the light
that his words let in, not so much upon his history, as
on his inside life and experience.

They remained long enough at Turner's to permit
Fred to make the needed change in his dress, called
at the post-office, and returned home by Uncle Bill
Skinner's, where they made a brief pause.   When they
got home it was already twilight; and when Fred
returned from the barn where he drove his team, he
thought, at first, that the sitting-room was deserted.   A
moment later, Belle stepped out from the shadow, and
came forward, holding out her hand.

Fred grasped it with both his own, pressed it for a
second to his face, and abandoning it, wet with his tears,
hurried from the room.

CHAPTER XXXIV.

FATHER HENRY QUOTES PAUL TO BELLE.

ON their way home, Mr. Carman and his guests heard very exaggerated rumors of the incident at the Rapids. They reached his house a moment after Fred, much excited, and entered the sitting-room just as he returned to it. As he came in, Mr. Henry stepped up to him: "You can tell us all about this wonderful deliverance," he said, in a way which was an assertion, a request, and command as well.

"There is not much about it," said the now fully-recovered youth. "We were all on the ice, when that little wayward Way girl jumped, or fell, or was spilled into the water; and as she did not get out immediately, a fellow skated along and skimmed her out," with a gesture of his hand, as if dipping a butterfly from a pool.

"Skimmed her out, did he?" asked Father Henry, very incredulously."

"Father Henry," said Belle, coming forward with a beautiful enthusiasm, "the young man who was driving the sleigh in which the young girl was, turned suddenly too near the edge of the ice, just where the water, deep and black, begins to move, and that sent the sleigh around in a circle, when this little Millie, in her fright, attempted to jump out on to the ice; but when she sprang, the sleigh had moved so far that she jumped into the water. She gave a shriek as she went in, and everybody was frightened, and hurried off the ice. She floated a moment, and went down; just at that instant Mr. Warden came flashing over the ice, throwing away his gloves and cap and coat as he came; at the edge of the ice he sprang into the air, and I thought he would leap to the shore. He struck the water just where the girl disappeared — the world whirled a moment — and then I saw the red bonnet, then Mr. Warden with Millie; then the current dashed him down to a large rock; from that he seemed to spring to a shallow place, where he plunged toward the shore with Millie in his arms. It was a brave, noble, heroic act, such as few men in the world could perform, and such as the world is better for having done in it. I saw the whole of it." Her voice trembled, and a sweet dewiness came into her eyes as she closed.

"And so, young man, your statement was not quite true?" with affected, but very kindly, severity.

"Would you have him become a braggart?" asked Belle, laying her hand on the old man's arm, and looking up into his face.

"And she has not told you," said Fred, in a soft voice, "that when I was almost overcome, and struggling on my skates against a sweeping current, she plunged in to her waist, and helped us out, and that she brought the drowned girl to herself."

"He told me what to do," said the generous girl.

The old man looked with a softened surprise from

one to the other of the noble pair standing so near him, each so anxious to praise the other.

"Let this noble act be a bond of union to you." And turning to Belle,—" It is a goodly youth, and 'the unbelieving husband is sanctified by the wife'; let us return thanks for this great deliverance;" which he did in a few sonorous words, to the great relief of the blushing Belle. As for poor Fred, broad as the allusion was, it conveyed no meaning to his dazed perception. Supper was announced, where all the details of the interesting incident were talked over in all their relations, and many similar incidents called to mind. Father Henry was interested to know what were the mental exercises of Fred accompaning his act.

"What did you first think?"

"That I would save her."

"Well, what next?"

"I was afraid I would be too late."

"Weren't you afraid of losing your own life?"

"I never thought of that, I thought only of her."

"When did you gain sight of her?"

"Just as I leaped, and I feared I might strike her; she was partly down on the bottom. The water was but a little over my head, but it had an awful suck."

"Weren't you afraid you would not get her out?"

"I knew I should; I pushed out, came near falling, caught my foot in some rocks, and broke the skate iron that turns over the toe; just as I thought I would fall, I saw Mrs. Williams within two yards of me, and,— of course I got out then easy enough," with a soft and

14

falling voice.—a silence with expressive looks that Fred did not see.

" Didn't you nearly freeze?"

" I never seemed to know I was wet until I found my clothes frozen. The water was genuine Cuyahoga. I turned two quarts out of each boot with the true Black Brook tint. from away above May's mill-dam; " 'and so he went gayly on in answer to questions.

A little later. Lewis Turner came in. as he said, to carry Fred off. He had not seen any of his friends at the Corners yet. and he would return him in a day or two. Before Fred left. he had some conversation with Martha about a visit to Sarah. whom Fred had not seen for years. It might be too much to ask her to leave Mrs. Williams to go with him. and he hardly had the courage to ask her to go. he said, with a deprecating look at that conscious young woman.

" I will be very glad to go," was the prompt response to the look.

So it was arranged. when, with kindest adieus from the other guests. and many admonitions from Father Henry, he took his leave of the rest, and went out.

CHAPTER XXXV.

AN INTROSPECTION.

UNTIL long after midnight had Fred, with a cease-less stride, tramped up and down his room at Turner's, in the vain effort to analyze himself, and the emotions and vicissitudes which he had experienced within three days. The prominent incidents he went over and over with,—his arrival at the Carmans, his meeting with Belle, the impression she made upon him, the strange incident of the night, his attempted explanation and apology, and the disgust and contempt with which she extinguished him,—his wandering in the wood the next day—her seeking a seat in another carriage, with strangers, that morning—the exciting events at the Rapids,—her bold plunge into the river to aid him, her look, her joy at his commendation.—above all, her meeting him that night, and her glowing recital of his conduct. Then he recalled his own emotion, when he took her hand; his intention to kiss it, which he dared not do, and his weak breaking down over it. What did that matter? She must have seen, before that, exactly what were his feelings toward her. Over and over with it all, and then he thought back of his fruitless quest,— a hunt at the South for the place whence he supposed the Greens came, if mayhap he might lift the veil from his origin, and of its fruitlessness. Then he remembered how the name Jarvis had escaped Aunt Sally, and other remote things, and then his thoughts came back to Belle.

Finally, he sat down, from physical weariness, to endeavor to think, to strip and lay himself bare to himself. Who and what was he? It all seemed accidental and purposeless, tending to nothing. He was, because he had to be, and not because anything was to come of it. It was all the result of an accident, that should not have happened, an oversight of Providence, and hence no provision was made for it, and none ever would be. He was to go on, or rather other things would push him on. He was mixed in with others, who were going on that way, and the current they made took him along; that was all. He was to have nothing on the route, no basket had been filled for him, and nothing awaited him when he got to the place; indeed there was no place for him. When the rest landed, he and the stream stood still, and became stagnant; he would float about decaying on the surface, until he acquired the power to sink, and would finally rot on the bottom with other drift. Why should he have this stain? What had he done? Why should children ever inherit disease, and depraved appetites, and abnormal tendencies from their parents? It wasn't the fault of the child, and yet he was born to it as certainly as if the transgression was his personal crime. But why were people made so? Why were they made at all, for that matter? He had inherited a disease in the form of an infamy; why had he escaped the condition of Jake and Sam? Why not remain low, and coarse,

and brutal, and so remain down, where the mark had
not struck and stung him? No man had ever got
above it. The proudest in history always carried it.
The great Bourbon, was a——, to the end, and is never
named now without this reminder. He used to rage at
this, and wander through thick dark nights, conjuring
up shadows to buffet, and had at times grown familiar
with the thought of death. Then would come some
shadow of a thought that it might not be, after all.
What comfort was there in that possibility? Nobody
doubted it, and never would. Now he had met this
Belle. He had seen ladies before whom he could have
learned to love, and would have gladly set himself the
easy task had he felt free. Now at once, without
thought, without warning or note, he loved her deeply,
intensely,—pshaw! he had only seen her two days
before.— Out of poems, was there ever such madness?
Yes, it was a madness, a mere rioting of the fancy.
Lord! what inspiration came to him, fainting and
staggering in the icy waters from her eyes, as she
stood braced against the current to help him! Oh,
if her love was for him.— of course she knew. Why
should he go back there? Why should he go away from
her? If he had never seen her, he would never have
known what a wonder of loveliness the world held. He
was glad he had seen her. Then he sat, and tried not
to think. He was done fretting at or with the world.
He was in it, could not mend it; indeed, the world was
seemingly well enough to others. Belle? of course he
should love her. Oh, was it not for this, he would
win her. He would compel her to love him. She
should be made to see and feel, not that he was worthy

of her — no man was — but that he was not wholly unworthy. But a —— bah!

He certainly had not appeared very well in her eyes, — saving his experiment in hydraulics. That certainly wasn't much of an exploit. Oh, if it had been Belle, and if she had been with him in the very grasp of death, and he had dragged her hence, with just enough strength to lay her on the shore, saved, and had then sunk down by her side and died, — what a joy had been his! But this little girl in the Rapids, which he had waded in the summer, and where he had speared suckers, — faugh! somebody would laugh at the idea of such an exploit!

And higher and nobler thoughts, such as he was wont to cherish, came back, — old aspirations and inspirations. He had been marked, — came such from birth. The ordinary lower channels of human action were in some way clogged and choked up, and his life would not flow in them. He must vault above, and solitary. Was not this blot upon him merely on the outer wall of life, a wretched placard, by which prejudice advertised the faults of his parents? Did it reach the essential self, — the soul? Was not that pure, and good, and elevated? Were not his sympathies quick and warm, his aspirations noble and great? Was there anything mean and sordid, low and base, in him? Had he not always jealously watched every thought, and the springs of thought, — every turn and bent of mind? Had he not familiarized himself with the thoughts and lives of the pure and essentially great, and proposed for himself a pure and elevated career of labor, and devotion, and self-sacrifice? What if men turned from

him? What, after all, were the few years to which, at
the most, life was limited? What did it really matter
how this first gasp of time was spent? What were
sixty years to eternity? Had he not a soul, capable
of strong and steady upward soarings? He opened
a window, and looked out and up into the studded
vault. "What an awful sight, and yet comprehending
somewhat — at least feeling its sublimity — I confront
it. I am not abashed and overwhelmed by it. Something of the Father God is within me, and I look into
these shadowy realms, which darkness makes palpable,
as something belonging to me, and I to it. I am an
atom of even infinity, that cannot be lost. What
matter these few days and pangs, and shames and
abasements?"

Looking again, long and anxiously : "Yet where is,
God, who so reveals His works to us and hides Himself? By what means does He work, and with what?
Where does He hide His awful powers, and store away
His incomprehensible energies? Is He still creating in
the measureless infinities of space away from us? Still
fashioning and finishing? And when these new universes
are complete, will He return, and bring to our darkened worlds the summer of His presence? Or does
He occupy Himself with merely ruling these worlds?
How idle that would be for Him! Does it cost Him
much outlay to govern us — and misgovern — if men
say truly? What braggarts, to suppose that much time
or thought is spent on us. How weak and base we are,
— born base, some of us, and, when we confront these
blazing worlds, we know that we cannot be God's
noblest work. What creatures He might have made

us, had it minded Him to. Yet we may aspire, and in this lies our marvellous excellence. We may hope, and grow, and lift ourselves up. purify, and be ennobled; contemn ourselves, and sordid lives and surroundings, and escape from the darkened atmosphere of earth and its night-projecting shadow. I feel something of this," and he closed the window and sat down.

"Oh, I will struggle to purify my very soul and heart, and thought and desires, and be familiar with none but the pure and good and holy; and yet I am so lonely! Surely God means companions for us, and this beautiful one, — she may some time know and feel that in spirit, in soul, I am not wholly unworthy of her. Is there such a thing as love and communion beyond the earth, outside of the flesh, and above the senses? Has it ever been felt or found in this world? Has it not been sighed for. prayed for, and felt, and found only to be rags and filth. in which seething sense and lust have generated maggots such as. — horror! Why do I come back to this? How low and earthy I am, — not good enough to preach. Oh, what a luxury to go up on hill-sides, or in wooded valleys, and call men about me, and tell them of God, and lead them from their sordid lives. I? Ha, ha! I can't bear to think of what I am, or where I begun. What a preacher I'd be! I should avoid churches and meeting-houses. Lord, how the old theological pot-shells should be pulverized! Oh dear, I would never be good enough to preach, when I begin by this self-glorying. Then it might not do to preach the love of God as I would be glad to do. After all, do men ever accept a higher faith until they are fit for it? When they

really believe it, it saves them. If they did not, they
would be under the old restraining fear and healthy
slavery of the devil; so no harm would come in any
event" — a pause. " To go forth as in the older time,
or now, in the pure spirit, and preach a pure gospel,
with a high-born and beautiful woman, sweet and
angelic, to love as such might, and encourage you. — to
let you come to her, after long absences, worn and
poor, and to be cheered and nursed back to new
strength and life by her ! " He thought of Belle conse-
crated to her husband in heaven, yet loving and sustaining one on earth, and ever in unapproachable
purity.

CHAPTER XXXVI.

BELLE'S LETTER.

FRED finished this somewhat memorable visit to the old home of his childhood, and went away as he came, quietly and without notice. He went about among his early acquaintances, visited Sarah, accompanied by Martha and Belle, and brought his satchel down the next morning after the return; and, when breakfast was over, he arose, and unexpectedly bade them good-by. He walked out through the little arbor, where he paused a moment, and turned to flash back, upon the still astonished eyes of Belle, the Florence portrait. There was always much of admiration for him in Mantua, and now they found him so mature and manly, so modest and gentle, and so intelligent and well-informed on all possible subjects, upon all of which he spoke well, that well-read men — and Mantua had many — were surprised at the extent and accuracy of his information. He was not what men call showy, but sensible, and waited to be drawn out; and, though plainly dressed, he had a careless way of wearing his clothes, at once elegant and free from puppyism. It was noticed that he did not wear a ring, or chain, or pin, or marked color. His manner was a little reserved, like that of one who thought better of himself than he supposed he was rated by others, and who waited to be asked before opening himself out.

To say that he was not observed, and closely, by Belle, would do the perceptions of that young lady injustice. Accustomed to the ease and refinements of the best forms of culture in the United States, and having passed many years in Europe, whatever else she may have found or fancied about him, she found his manners and address very attractive. She especially admired the unconscious elevation of his sentiments, as well as the delicacy and purity of his tastes and manner, and the ease and felicity with which he expressed himself.

On the evening before his departure, Uncle Seth, who was somewhat hoarse, asked him to read the evening lesson from the Bible. and pointed him to the fourth chapter of Matthew, which Fred rendered so simply, naturally, and beautifully, that his listeners asked him to go on, as he did, through the fifth, sixth, and seventh. His voice was rich and soft, his sensibilities very quick and deep, and he seemed to deliver the narrative, and the grand, simple utterances of the Great Teacher, in the purity and spirit which inspired them. As he went on, a deep fervor seemed to grow up and glow, until the far-off scenery, with the spirit of loneliness stamped upon the Orient — the primitive and curious multitudes, and the wonderfully serene presence, calm and sacred, of the young Christ — seemed to be brought before the vision of his wondering, rapt, and exalted listeners. When he reached the last sentence of the Sermon on the Mount, his voice trembled in a softened cadence, and ceased. His auditors listened for a moment, breathless, as if expecting he would proceed, and a shade of regret fell upon their faces when they saw he had ended, and the young women turned dewy eyes upon him, as if he were a young prophet. No one thought of asking him of his faith, and no one for a moment doubted it. The face of Belle, in particular, wore a very sweet and satisfied expression; and, when he took leave of her the next morning, they happened to be a little apart from the others, and, whether either spoke a word, the anxious and attentive Martha never knew. Something mysterious there was between the two, she knew, — something unusual. Was it repulsion? Was it attraction? She could not tell; and, somehow, this deep Belle wrapt herself so completely from her approach, that she scarcely made Fred the subject of a remark to her. She thought, on the whole, that Fred had not been appreciated; and for nothing will a woman suffer sooner in the estimation of another woman, than for a want of sympathy in her admiration for her favorites of the other sex. What and whom does she like? thought Martha, and who does she suppose will come for her? If she thinks as I think she thinks, I think she will live to think differently, — that's all; with which thoughtful reflection she only mentally attached herself the more closely to the side of her unfortunate favorite.

Within a day or two after Fred's departure, Belle announced that a carriage would come for her the last of the week.

"Belle!" She arose, and went frankly to Martha, and looked her fairly and honestly in her eyes for a

moment, then bent down and kissed her. "I've over-
stayed my time for some days. I am expecting that
a letter has by this time reached home, which will
require serious attention."

For a day or two she was a little — just a trifle —
restless and abstracted, and less talkative than usual,
— a little coy of words, and not so much given to looking up when Martha called to her, nor always when
she answered; and she seemed not to hear so quickly
as usual, and answered a little away from the matter
in hand at times.

The fourth day after Fred left, late in the snowy
afternoon, Belle saw a youth enter the gate, and look
towards the house, holding a letter in his hand. She
stepped to the door. "Mr. Turner told me to give
this to Mrs. Williams." he said, as if doubting that the
young-looking girl before him was the lady. "Thanks
to Mr. Turner, and this for you," said Belle, taking the
letter, and giving him a gold coin. Martha had gone
down to the Judge's, and she was alone. She nevertheless went to her room, without looking at the letter.
When she entered it, she stood and studied the firm
hand of the address, in the way of people who so phil-
osophically question the outside of a letter as to its
contents. Perhaps she did not care to know what it
contained. She finally opened it, spread the pages
out, and looked at the strong, firm, man's handsome
hand, not like that of a clerk, yet full of character,
and, in places, thrown on as if by unrestrained impulse.

The first part of the manuscript was regular, easy
and flowing; then the characters grew large and sharp,

running and rushing with gaps and blots, and sometimes illegible, as if the writer had, in frenzies and spasms, dashed himself in broken and abrupt sentences upon the paper, and at moments with both hands.

Belle read in fits and starts, looking frightened, and casting her eyes about as in momentary apprehension. Thus it finally rendered itself to her on her last reading :

"I hurried abruptly from you, ere I should alarm or overwhelm you with the rhapsodies of passion. I must speak, — and as you must have felt I would. You may be amazed at what I set down here, but not at all that I write you. Why do I? Why do the waters finally break and rush?

"Oh, loveliest one — most beautiful — that makest the earth glad with thy loveliness, and yet a solitude in thy unapproachableness. I love thee, I love thee, — I love thee! Dost thou hear and comprehend? It is for woman to hear her lover, but she cannot comprehend, nor does he, the strong outgoing onrushing tide that would sweep about and encompass her with an ocean of worship and reverence. I would not pipe to thee on the lover's thin reed, nor sigh and bring flowers, and twist garlands of meaningless praises, but create a solitude, in the midst of which I would enthrone thee. I would snatch from the day its glory, and pluck from the brow of night its stars to crown thee, and then men, with palms and garlands, should come to worship thee. I would ask nothing, seek nothing, but to worship in distance and in silence.

"I am not frenzied ; I am not one to go fancy-mad. This is not the fantastic, frantic cry of a weak soul and a shallow nature, but from depths and strength my voice goes, — will go out to you; nature, art, man, God, almost, have conspired to manacle, to imprison me, — wall me out from your presence, so that I may not go as a man would go, and tell you his love. I assert myself, wrench from around me these chains, and dash the walls of my prison-house into shatters. I rush into your presence, and kneel at your feet, and tell you that I love you. Only that. only that! and then I put my lips in the dust, and, without cry or moan, remain forever mute.

"A young barbarian, from the depths of savagery, comes out upon the margin of the hoar and shaggy forest, out of night and darkness, and beholds for the first time his star. He knows that it is his, and falls upon his knees in adoration, and longs, — oh, so passionately and yearningly! — that the star should know of his worship."

That was all, — no name or initial was appended to it. Twilight deepened into darkness about Belle, as, with great heaving, gasping sobs, she still lay with her head buried upon the table. Is she woman? or more? or less? An hour later she appeared below, having suffered from a sudden headache, as women sometimes do. She was very quiet, and Martha, who was given to observation, thought that she had never seen so deep a light in her wondrous eyes.

When she left for home, two days later, she told Martha that she meant to be at her bridal, but that she thought that a widow should never be a bridesmaid, and that Fred certainly ought to be differently matched, — on that occasion.

CHAPTER XXXVII.

A MESSAGE TO FRED.

IN mid March, the whole State of Ohio and the country generally were startled with the account of a murder. In the limits of the newly-formed county of Mahoning, made up of the old counties of Portage and Trumbull, just on the margin of a wood, in the newly-settled part of one of the townships, the body of a man was found, just by the wayside, murdered. He was a stranger, middle-aged and dark, and nothing was found on his person indicating his identity. He was well clothed, and had spurs on his boots; about a mile from him, tangled in its bridle, saddled, and well caparisoned, was found a horse, supposed to have been ridden by the murdered man. It was said that he had been seen, at several places west of the point where found, mounted on this or a similar horse; and finally it was rumored that he had been followed by one, and some said two, men from the West. Later still, it was reported that he was a seceding Mormon, and had been followed and murdered by some of the Thug band of Danites, doubtless under instructions from the new head of the church.

Intense excitement prevailed all through the country. Acts of violence were rare, and in many of the Reserve

counties a homicide had never occurred. The news-
papers were full of the tragic event, and the wildest
and absurdest rumors prevailed among the people.
The authorities, unfamiliar with such cases, were on
the most confused alert, investigating and blundering
in the most compendious way.

The coroner called a jury and held an inquest on the
body, where it lay in the woods, with the March flowers
crushed under it. Hundreds of people attended, and
many from twenty miles distance. It was in proof
before the jury, that a man similarly dressed, and
riding the horse afterwards found, was seen to enter
the woods just at twilight, a mile from the scene, and
that a young man, on his way to his sugar-bush, found
the body early the next morning. Three or four
doctors concluded that death was caused by a blow
from a bludgeon upon the head, and other evidence
was given that the body had been robbed. Finally a
man came forward, who identified the body as that of
Oliver Olney. The horse was produced and inspected.
The jury returned that the man known as Oliver
Olney came to his death by a blow from a bludgeon in
the hands of some person to the jurors unknown. Two
days later, the body was buried with great solemnity in
the presence of a concourse of more than a thousand
people. The officiating clergyman preached a most
acceptable sermon from the words, " Whoso sheddeth
man's blood," etc.

About ten days later, Fred received, at his office in
Massillon, the following note:

15

" CANFIELD, March 26, 1845.

" FRED WARDEN, ESQ. :

"*Sir*,—Your old enemy, Jake Green, is now in jail here, charged with murder. He is without counsel, money, or friends."

There was no name signed to it; nor was there on the envelope any mark or clew to the writer. The note was in a man's hand, unmistakably.

Jake had been arrested in Coshocton a few days after the murder, while making towards the lower part of the State. He had been followed from the vicinity of the tragedy, near the scene of which he was observed on the morning of the discovery of the body. It was said that many things — some mysterious papers — were found on him, going to show that the deceased was Oliver Olney, a former resident of Geauga county, an early convert to Mormonism, and a supposed adherent of Rigdon's, and who, it was said, had fled from Nauvoo recently. It was rumored that Jake and one other had followed Olney from Nauvoo, and, as was believed, had come up with, waylaid and murdered him. The case was said to be very clear against Jake; and popular feeling, even among the cool, law-loving citizens of Northern Ohio, was intense against him. The bad reputation of Jake about Mantua soon reached the venue of his alleged crime, and tended much to deepen the feeling to his prejudice.

Jake had been absent from Northern Ohio for some years, and was supposed to be with the Mormons, among whom, as was thought, his father and aunt still resided.

At his arrest he began by a denial, and then maintained a sullen, dogged silence; proof, of course, of his guilt. The popular rule bears hard on a suspected man. If he talks, it is to deny and mislead. If he is silent, it is of course because he cannot deny his guilt.

Jake, a sturdy, sullen villain, whom the officers could hardly protect from violence, was heavily ironed, and lodged in the strongest cell of the new prison. Hundreds had been to gaze through the grated windows, and wonder and jeer, mock and taunt him; none to speak kindly, or express the slightest sympathy in his fate, or pity for his condition. He was the obtuse, hardened, blood-stained murderer, whom it was useless to try, save as a compliance with the useless forms of law, and to pity whom was a crime against justice and a sin against humanity. Whenever the jailer attended upon him it was always under the protection of an armed guard, and the outside world was daily startled and horrified with some new tale of the poor wretch's guilt, — this being the thirteenth or fourteenth murder he had committed.

On the afternoon of the fifth day of his confinement, when the western sun lit up his cell from the one small barred window, his prison-door was opened, and a tall, commanding, open browed, kindly-eyed young man stepped lightly in, and the door was locked on him. So bright and gentle and kindly beamed his face, that Jake did not recognize him, till the voice, — "Jake, old fellow, how are you?" and Fred frankly held out his hand. Jake took it mechanically in his hard and manacled hand, and looked wonderingly and abashed into the face, the lines and features of which came slowly back. " Fred, Fred, is this yer? Do yer come ter dam me?"

" I come to help you; of course I do. We are old acquaintances, and relations for aught I know; at any rate we are both human, and one of us wants help."

" Fred," said the touched Jake, " I killed yer dog when — "

" Never mind that now. Poor Walter would have died long ago. I am a man now, Jake, I am a lawyer; have been a good deal in the courts, have earned a little money, and I came on purpose to defend you, and get you out of this."

" Do yer mean it, — raly, Fred?" breaking down.

" Indeed I do. I came for no other purpose under the heavens."

They sat down for a long and earnest conference; Jake was broken and incoherent, and Fred held him and questioned as the *nisi prius* lawyer of all mortals only knows how to do; Fred had seen four years of considerable practice, was accustomed to go to his books instead of begging broken morsels of law of his elders in the streets, and had early learned to depend on himself. It is a marvel, the rapidity and clearness with which a strong legally-trained mind grasps, arranges and analyzes facts, and leaps to conclusions, while an unaccustomed mind, however strong and intelligent, is struggling with an undigested mass of details complex in their nature, and confused from want of method. They have crystallized in his; he steps from one governing point to another, and is at home, while the other still struggles with the tangled skein.

Fred made a few notes of names and dates, and at the
end of an hour arose to go.

"Have you any money, Jake?"

"No — but I — "

"Take that, for the present," giving him a ten-
dollar note.

At his call, the jailer came.

"Why is this man in irons?" demanded Fred, with
grave indignation.

"Why, to keep him safe, I s'pose."

"Safe, eh! Has he attempted to escape? Did he
resist?"

"Not's I know on."

"Call the sheriff, if you please." The sheriff came.

"I am Fred Warden, a lawyer, and counsel for this
man. May I know by whose order he is fettered and
manacled here in this cell?" The tone was very quiet,
but Fred was very earnest, and men were very much
in the way of heeding him in that mood.

"Well, you see, Mr. Warden, that there is a great
deal of excitement against him, and — "

"You chained him to keep the ignorant devils from
hurting him, I suppose?"

"Well, not quite that."

"What then? Your prison is new and strong.
He is not condemned, — is presumed to be innocent,
whatever excitement there may be against him. Do
you know of any provision of the Ohio Statutes that
warrants this?"

"Not as I know of."

"Will you remove those chains?"

"Certainly, if you wish it."

"Most certainly I do;" and the jailer was called, and poor Jake's limbs were liberated.

As he went out, the sheriff was very much impressed with the idea that Jake would be defended; and there was something in Fred's way and manner, something of force and strength, of undeveloped power, that would make light work of ordinary difficulties.

From the jail Fred went to the office of a young lawyer of the name of Wilson, with whom he had a long conversation, and the next morning they both, on horseback, proceeded to the scene of the murder, where they were met by a surveyor with his chain and an assistant. The young man who made the discovery, and others who saw the place before it was disturbed and tramped over, were summoned, and the most careful examination of every possible thing, and all the surroundings for a considerable distance, was made; distances were accurately measured, and a plat of the whole ground was prepared with great care.

The various witnesses were of course very willing to talk, and under Fred's questioning, were surprised at the numberless wholly unimportant things he called out and noted, and committed them to, so that it would be hard to vary from their statements, made in the presence of so many. What under the sun he wanted of it all was a puzzle to them; "and all the time he looked so pleasant and quizzical, and as if he did not care a cuss," as one of them said, in his account of the matter.

The proceedings concluded with a disinterment of the remains, and a most careful and scientific examination of them, conducted by Dr. Ackly, of Cleveland, in the presence of a distinguished practitioner from Warren, and one from Ravenna. This act was thought to be little short of an outrage upon public decency and propriety ; and folks said that if there was no law to prevent such shameful carryings on, it was time there was. What earthly use was there in digging up a dead man, as if he could be made to tell anything on their side of the case? Of course, that was all the doings of the doctors ; they would make anything an excuse to dig up and cut into a body ; and it was popularly believed that Dr. Ackly actually carried off the head of the murdered man to Cleveland, and pickled it in spirits, and that each of the others took some choice bit. At last Fred finished his survey and preparation. Before he left, he had an interview with the prosecuting officer for the county, who said that he should push the case to a trial early in June. When Fred suggested the difficulty of getting everything ready, he replied that it was an atrocious murder, and public opinion demanded a speedy trial and execution. Fred ventured to say, that in the present condition of public opinion a fair trial was hardly possible, and was assured that there could be no possible doubt of Jake's guilt, and that it was his own fault that public opinion was against him. Fred left him, with an intimation that the rules governing the continuances of cases of this importance were inflexible, and that a man would exhibit little invention if he permitted such a case to be tried until he was entirely ready.

Whatever may have been Fred's purpose in seeking this interview, he left in the bosom of the prosecuting attorney of Mahoning County, a healthy determination to try the case at all hazards, at as early a day as possible. He rightly judged that the cool, quiet, and unassuming young man who acted for the prisoner might, with time and delay, get up an embarrassing defence, plain and undoubted as the case was.

The scene of the exciting labors of these few days was not many miles distant from Newton Falls, and many times there came a passionate longing into the young man's heart to invent some excuse for going, or to go without any, into the neighborhood, only to look upon the house, haunted and made paradise by the presence of Belle. Reluctantly, and with sadness, he turned him homeward without this seemingly poor luxury. He had not heard a word of or from her since he left Mantua, four months before. He knew he could receive nothing from her in reply to his letter. He knew he ought not to have sent her that, but he couldn't help it. It went tearing and crashing out of him, — *would* go. He could not recall what it was, and did not feel much contrition for it. He felt that she was true and noble, notwithstanding her quiet, dreamy, nun-like life. When men fled in mortal fright, did she not dash into a wintry torrent to aid him in saving the drowning maiden? Not on his account, of course, but no common woman would have done anything but stand and shriek, if she had not fainted. Surely, would she not be willing that he should love her? Would she not come to see, in time, that no harm, no hurt to her purity, could come to her from his distant and sacred worship? Would he not struggle to make his soul not unworthy of hers, and might she not some time come to know and admit

that? Would she be at Martha's wedding? He doubted
it. He should go, and would at the least hear something of her. If she was there, what could he say to
her? He now regretted that awful letter; it would
keep her away, for fear of meeting him. So he mused
over it all, and rode home, as he worked now, in the
daily light of his great love.

CHAPTER XXXVIII.

AN OLD TIME WEDDING.

IN the far-off old time of which I write, ere the beautiful slopes, and hills, and valleys were denuded of the wonderful forests that once furnished homes, haunts, and hunts for Indian and beast; when the openings and clearings, protected and fenced in from winds, and traversed by innumerous small streams, which, in the absence of great evaporation, found head in every swale or cat-swamp, and a course or channel in every little vale, the tone of the climate was softer, the winters more moderate, and there was still an actual spring, out of the almanac and pastoral poetry, all over beautiful Northern Ohio.

The Carman farm, behind its protecting mass of timbered land which fenced it on the north with its southern inclination, and its rich warm soil, was always the first to feel the kindling glow of spring; and now, on May-day, was radiant and fragrant with light and blossoms. In the woods the shad-bush and dog-wood made little gay clouds of white, under which blossomed the blood-root, squaw-blow, adders-tongue, ladies' slipper, and myriads of the gay and unnamed children of April; the grand old pear-tree arose in front

(234)

of the house, a marvellous fragrant white pyramid, — one mass of blossom ; the cherries, peaches, and plums were failing, but the great orchards were one wilderness of red and white, while the whole air, faint and weighted with perfume, was traversed everywhere with little streamlet-like hums of loaded brown bees.

It was a great day at the old red farm-house. All along in front of it, tied to fence or tree, were many horses and carriages ; and men and boys, matrons and maidens, thronged on the grass in the yards, under the piazzas, and in all the rooms that were open, all in gala dress, and with bright faces.

It was Martha's wedding-day. All the family relatives were there : all the Carmans of Mantua, of Warren and Aurora ; the Sheldons, the Higleys, from Windham, many prominent persons of Mantua, and all the neighbors.

Uncle Seth, in his best plum-colored home-made, with his calf-skin boots newly greased, with his serene, fine face — that always had a touch of sadness for a wedding, and a ray of light for a funeral — was about busy with his guests, while Aunt Mary, in her rich old satins, with the color bright on her cheek, and the life quick in her eye, whose housewifely instinct had became an outstinct as well, managed and controlled everything as was her wont.

A little buzz — a lull of voices — and then a crowding into doors and up to open windows. The word had been given ; the sitting-room so often referred to, in which were the nearest friends, was opened ; and from the inner *penetralia*, Aunt Mary's best room —

too sacred to be mentioned — came the bride, and her manly, handsome bridegroom, and took the places designated. Near them, with a face thinner and a gathering moisture in his eyes, stood Fred, and with him — her hand in his and her eyes on his face — stood the little Hebe whom he had plucked from the Cuyahoga. Belle was absent.

Father Henry was there, and, in a few simple and impressive words, performed the sanctifying ceremony that made them one, amid the sympathizing tears of the women, and the grave, grim silence of men.

If there is one thing in the world more incomprehensible than others to the average masculine mind, it is the feeling with which a woman always witnesses the marriage ceremony. Of all sublunary or celestial things, the farthest from the mind or heart of the bridegroom are the ineffable thoughts and emotions of the trembling one whose hand he holds, when she literally gives herself to him. The *abandon*, the devotion, the unreserve of that act, he does not understand, and the words that would express it would convey little meaning to him. To him, a little pause in a wayfaring career — a bending for her hand — a slight sidelong deviation that he may receive her,— only that, and nothing more. To her, a perfect moral, physical, and mental revolution, — a coming out from her maiden life of dream and hope, of color and fragrance, to the world which she does not know ; coming out from the beautiful mysteries of her inner self, of which she knows as little, and placed at once in contact with the strong, coarse, and often vulgar and base fibre of man's compelling nature, that cannot understand, and would not regard, if it did, the subtle and delicate fibre of hers. No wonder that matrons, always from experience, and maidens from presentiment, weep at her sacrifice. Man extends one hand, with one side of his heart to her, while she abandons her whole self to him.

The ceremony was short, simple, and impressive; and Martha, sweet and arch, and blushing, was given over to the congratulations of her friends, while Fred did what he could to sustain the bridegroom under the untowardness which is so trying to a man on finding himself in a position subordinate to a woman. I trust this will finally be found to be but "inherited experience," and not nature.

Great baskets of rich cake were passed about the crowd, to be devoured by the men and preserved and carried home by the women.

Wine, cider, and other liquids were not wanting, and an hour was given to the hearty, not rude or vulgar, festivity of an old time country wedding, from which the guests departed with the day; and the bride and her groom were remitted to the seclusion of her room, in the sanctuary of her father's house.

Fred had not expected that Belle would be there, but yet more bitterly was he disappointed at her absence than can be told. Martha had hardly heard from her since she left. She had never, till recently, been acquainted with her, and she had acted very strangely, as she thought. She had written to Martha, soon after her return home, that matters of the gravest importance had arisen that demanded her immediate personal attention, and that she should go South, and possibly went at once, as Martha supposed she was now absent. She did not tell Fred that, in her letter, Belle had not named or made the slightest reference to him, which she thought very strange. Indeed, she felt disappointed in this Belle.

Upon the dispersion of the guests, Fred, under the melancholy that oppressed him, rode over the lonely road, through the woods, to the Rapids. Night was in the forests with its shadow, but musical with the plaint of the whippoorwill. How wonderfully sweet and melancholy to the ear of the pensive young man came the many voices of the shrunken river, no longer plunging madly over the rocks, but murmuring and gurgling musically in the channels between and around them. He rode across the river, and stood under the shadow of the unbroken wood on the east side.

With what force it all came back to him, — the bright sun and sparkling ice — the cry, the race, the disappearing red — the plunge into the mad, boiling waters — the grasp, and desperate struggle — the almost failure at last — and then the marvellous rescue of Belle's eyes first, and then her hands. He rode back, and slowly home through the darkened woods, and as he went he thought it all over: her repulse of his attempted apology; her avoiding him on the morning ride to the river, with every detail, upon which his now morbid fancy threw a strong adverse color. The rude, violent, and unmanly letter of his may have been coarse and vulgar to her ear and sense. She may have burned it without reading. But, in any event, it was a crime against her delicacy and self-respect. It had kept her from Martha's wedding, and would forever bar him from her presence. Could he apologize for this? Would it not aggravate his offending? After all, was he not entitled to some consideration as a human being? Was it not a part of his life and fortune, the recoil of the invisible, always-felt chain that so darkly bound him, — always most tense and galling when its absence alone could produce peace or render life endurable? He would address her one more letter:

"AT THE CARMANS, May 1, 1845. — *Evening.*
"MRS. BELLE WILLIAMS:

"*Madam,* — You were not here to-day, and the fear of my presence compelled your absence. I am hateful to myself. Inadvertently I was the cause of a deep wound to your delicacy. I was foolish enough to attempt an apology. Invention could find no words in which to frame it, and you turned your face from me in horror, and rebuked me with your hand.

"In my madness and folly, I dashed the fury and passion of my love for you upon paper, and sent it to you.

"It is a love that does you no dishonor. Your husband in heaven would not reproach me for it. It would give me infinite peace to know that I had not offended beyond pardon, by some word or token — a bit of soiled paper, a withered leaf — the most worthless trifle the world holds, — anything from you. If I may not receive such, I shall know I am to remain a stranger. If I do, I shall count upon only a distant, casual acquaintanceship, which is never to pass the line of cold recognition, at accidental meetings. Is this too much for me to ask?

     " Ever, with profoundest respect,

       " Your obedient servant,

          " FRED."

CHAPTER XXXIX.

HOW singularly remote events sometimes influence the fortunes of ordinary persons!

In the autumn before, the "Creole" cleared at Norfolk for New Orleans, with a cargo of one hundred and thirty-six freshly-imported Africans, — slaves, as we called such folk then. When at sea, under the inspiration of winds and waves, they mutinied — these deluded Africans — without the least reverence for the Constitution, the greatest work of man, and with slight regard for the freest and best government God ever inspired man to make, — the heathen. They overcame the captain and crew, and then, under threat of death, ordered them to steer for the coast of Africa. They were taken to Nassau, and delivered to the British authorities. Mr. Webster — the god-like in this at least, — his action was inscrutable — then Secretary of State, demanded that they be returned into slavery, Onessimus-like. Great excitement followed; and early in the present March, Mr. Giddings introduced a series of resolutions into the House of Representatives, declaring that at open sea, outside of the reach of State laws, these wretches were free, and might assert their

16   (241)

right to freedom by rising upon their jailers, as they had done. For the utterance of this heretical formula, Mr. Giddings, on motion of Mr. Botts, of Virginia, was, by a vote of the House, condemned, and formally censured by a majority sufficient to have expelled him. He at once resigned, returned home, demanded from the Governor of Ohio an order for a new election, and went boldly to the people. The Whig leaders, at that time, even those of anti-slavery tendencies, condemned his course as impolitic. His sentiments were sound in the abstract, but it was inexpedient to put them forth at that time. Alas for abstract truth! the time for its utterance never comes. Most of those who voted to sustain him did so reluctantly, were glad of the censure, and thought his true course was penitently to submit. At home, the leaders stood away from him. The Democrats did not think it expedient to put a candidate in the field, and the leading Whigs, standing coldly aloof, permitted him to go over the course with such chilling cheer as they managed to give him.

The day of election was early, the time short, and Mr. Giddings was left to make such a canvass as he could. He came back quivering under the insult he had received, and indignant at the cowardly coolness of the party leaders, and went upon the stump, first set up on the Reserve in the campaign of 1840.

Fred, who was nominally, at least, a Democrat, had made some reputation as a young speaker in 1840, to which he had added in the Clay-Polk canvass of '44, and by many was thought to give much promise as an orator, was attending court at Chardon when Giddings spoke there, became much interested, and, at Mr. Giddings's earnest request, attended some of the called meetings with him.

Among the personal and political friends of Mr. Giddings was a prominent man of Turnbull County, not a politician, but of great wealth and personal influence. He was at much pains and expense to get up a gathering of the people for Mr. Giddings, which came off a few miles from Warren, about three weeks after Martha's wedding. A spacious out-door stand was erected, a band secured, immense posters placarded the adjacent portions of Geauga and Portage, flags and mottoes were extemporized, and with the day came the people also. They all came, — came with their wives and children, in their wagons and carts, carriages, buggies and carryalls. They formed processions on all the roads of approach, and, with old Harrison flags and banners, the log cabins and canoes of 1840, and the flags and banners of the last campaign floating and flying, with martial music, fifes, drums, and bugles, they came.

The meeting was in mid-day; for all these people were to return in time for many duties at evening.

Mr. Giddings arose amid breathless silence, and, under the tension of his feelings and convictions, he was never so thorough a master of his best powers as now; never in his long career was he so effective as during this short canvass. The hesitation of speech, and lack of language, which sometimes marked and marred his speeches were absent, and a steady flow of strong, nervous language carried out and delivered his meaning as he would. Simply, clearly, and grandly, he opened out the whole matter; and then giving himself up in his heightened warmth, he closed out a two-and-a-half hours' speech, almost sublimely.

Repeated cheers greeted and helped him on. He was one to be so helped; and when he sat down, three times three, as in the old Tippecanoe campaign, evidenced the fervor of this usually cool, calculating, and phlegmatic people; then the band played a stirring air when the young Democrat was announced, and Fred, from the rear of the stand, went forward to the front, standing upon its edge by the end of a table. He paused for a moment, silent, and the curious crowd bent eagerly forward to get sight of him. There he stood, in the simple beauty and grace of young and almost perfect manhood. The crowd expressed its satisfaction with rapturous cries of applause.

He began, falteringly and hesitatingly, the little simple formula which his experience had taught him to have ready until he was sure of himself. In a moment he did not hear his own voice, — for just then the crowd parted at his right, and a carriage was permitted to occupy the space; in it, on the front seat, and so near him that he could have tossed a bouquet into her lap, sat the peerless Belle. Not a lisp or whisper had she responded to his plaint. He was despised and scorned, and there she was, with her face at that moment colorless, but with her great wondrous eyes full of the light that came to him over the mad waters. In some way in his mind he at once identified himself, — contemned, walled around all his life, and now scorned, with the insulted representation, the contemned constituency, and the abused freedom of speech. He was indignant, excited and exalted, — and he was one who would bear any amount of inspiration. For a moment he did not hear his voice; and the next, it sounded to him like the voice of one near him, ringing out clear, silvery and sonorous, like a trumpet-call. How his few formulated sentences glowed and flashed! and how, almost joyously in the pride of his young, and never before so fully realized strength, did he leap from the last round, and open out his pinion for sustained flight! How real everything was to him, and how palpable! How he ignited everything he touched, and shed a glow on all he passed! Men crowded close to him, and gave him the full might of their lifting, inspiring power, and bore him onward.

He clutched the theme,— the outrage upon the freedom of speech, and debate, and thought, and held it up in bold and striking lights. "And it was done by slavery, which had dethroned God, razed out the Decalogue, and smeared the page with its own Gospel. It fashioned legislation, moulded judgment, poisoned the sources of thought, till at its command the minds of men warped and tortured the promise of salvation, to the threat of damnation. It laid its hand on our mouths and commanded us to be dumb. It placed its fingers on our pulses and commanded them to stand still. It turned the red-tide back upon the heart, which, in its grasp, it commanded to grow cold and cease to beat. But that heart shall store its accumulating energies, until, with one indignant throb, it hurls this silenced tribune of the people back upon the floor of Congress, where, throb by throb, it shall sustain him, and a shivering cry, a glad shout, shall hail this triumph of freedom. The capitol shall hear it. The waters of the yellow Potomac shall catch it up, and, in their downward sweep to the sea, they shall whisper to the Great Sleeper on their banks, that the city which bears his name is again worthy of it."

The rising of the slaves on the crew of the "Creole" at sea, furnished a splendid theme for his masterly powers of graphic description.

At first, repeated bursts of applause interrupted him, but it was soon discovered that these annoyed him, and he was permitted to go on; soon the interest became so intense, that nobody thought of applause. When his voice finally ceased, men bent forward to listen, as if it must go on, and then they looked into each other's faces, and again to the stand which they saw was empty; then they knew that the spell which held them was broken. They murmured, and then shouted, shout after shout, as if the pent and ravished feelings could find relief only in shoutings.

And Belle, through the whole flashing hour, with her eyes never wandering from the young orator, and her color coming back, and the light of her eyes deepening, and leaning forward in unconscious grace in her eagerness, helped to carry him on; and when he sank back from the front, at the close, her glorified face went down, and was veiled from sight.

As he stepped back, Mr. Giddings caught him in his arms in an eager, grateful congratulation. The band recovered, and struck up, and the enchanted people lingered to catch a glimpse of, and perhaps shake the hand of, the young orator, who had surpassed their conceptions of fervid and sustained eloquence.

Then it was remembered that he was to defend Jake,

and there was some vague sort of an idea that he
would acquit him, and it was hoped he would, — and the
poor devil might be innocent after all. What a funny
thing is the people !

CHAPTER XL.

THE GLORY FADES.

HOW gloriously possible even heaven seemed to Fred, for the last part of that hour. It is curious how the mind and faculties of a man aroused will act and play when at their best. While his main forces were concentrated intensely upon his speech, a score of little imps of fancy were in play, as they always are, all about and over the field, — flashing ahead, and glancing at the ground; backward, along the track, and anon away upon things having little to do with the immediate labor. And all about sweet and glorious Belle. There was some mistake. He should go to her, and take her in his arms as his, and with her sweet consent. Didn't she look all this? even that she would come to him, — almost! Dear, deluding imps! and as he sat down, and then got down on the ground, he knew he was on the earth again. He felt that his speech was a triumph; but what did he care? His cheating fancies, with their rainbow glories, faded and died in a moment, and he was the poor contemned wretch that arose an hour ago.

It is one of man's delusions that a woman always loves or hates, adheres to or opposes a cause, as it is represented by some man whom she loves or hates,

(248)

worships or despises. It is one of the oldest and most firmly fixed, as it is the most fallacious articles of the man creed, that a woman can never comprehend and accede to, or deny a proposition, or appreciate a cause in the abstract. But it was an error that Fred did not fall into in reference to Belle. It was, of course, her intense anxiety for the safety of the drowning girl that led her into the icy river; as it was her noble and instinctive womanly sympathies for the cause of freedom and justice, that made her lean from her carriage and cheer him so with the inspiration of her eyes and manner. What did she, what could she, care for him? He almost despised himself, that he could languish for other reward than the consciousness of doing his duty. Duty! what a word was that to a despairing lover; what were any words? All this ran through his mind, as, surrounded by a crowd of admiring young men, he was walking from the stand to the house of their entertainer near by, — catching their words and answering back mechanically.

As they entered the house, the host came forward, and taking him by the arm, led him into a parlor, and introduced him to several: among others, to Mr. Morris, Mrs. Marbury, and Miss Belle Morris, as she was called. This ceremony called up and aroused his pride to almost *hauteur*. Mr. Morris started to come forward as if to meet him, but evidently Fred's manner of dignified coldness repelled him. Fred made the profoundest of bows to the ladies, and, spite of his arctic manner, Maud, almost as beautiful in her way as her younger sister, managed to receive his hand. She even ventured to congratulate him on his speech, but his host brought others to his relief, and he made his way to other parts of the room.

Soon after, a dinner, more nearly a supper in the country, was announced, and upon reaching the spacious dining-room, Fred, to his dismay, was conducted to a seat near Mr. Giddings, and between Maud and Belle. No woman can comprehend or sympathize with all the feelings of Fred in this position. She cannot comprehend why every man is not a gentleman, and why he should not, under all circumstances, be at his ease with ladies. She knows that he will always receive proper consideration, and why her presence can ever embarrass him, she is unable to understand. But a man of quick and nice sensibilities will fully appreciate his position. Here was the one woman of all the world, who was the all to him, who shared the common prejudice against him, to whom he had declared his love, and of whom had abjectly begged as a boon the bare favor of a cold recognition of his existence, and it had been refused. Here now was he, the scorned lover, as a special mark of distinction, placed by her side. With a few commonplace words he took his seat, and under the pressure of a crowded table, as near as the seats would permit. So abject had he become in his own esteem, that, spite of himself, he was conscious of the charm of her presence, which he seemed to inhale as a subtle and entrancing aroma; all the time, too, he was conscious that he was closely observed by Maud, who with womanly tact was making such diversion as she might in his favor. Had he exercised the least perception, which, as we see, he never did where Belle was concerned, he would in a moment have discovered, by

Belle's look and manner, that the position was quite as embarrassing to her. Indeed, her face indicated not embarrassment, but anxiety, if not pain. The glow had gone out of it, and the wondrous light of her eyes had died in them; her air was not so much that of coldness, as of passive resignation. But Fred was in no mood to perceive or know anything. Humiliated and abased, he was thoroughly wretched, as must have been shown by his countenance and the tone of his voice. Men were staring at him, and calling to and at him, and he was, in a dim, confused, miserable way, trying to be interested in the complimentary remarks which he did not hear, and toying with food which he could not eat. Belle made no effort to talk. Once or twice her hand was raised to a bunch of beautiful half-blown moss rose-buds, fastened over the unimaginable loveliness of her bosom, and once she answered her father, who sat next her.

They had been a few moments at the table, when word was brought Fred that a gentleman outside much wanted to see him for a moment; and although many protested, yet, with a word to the host, Fred arose and went out; a few minutes, and a note was sent from him to Mr. Giddings, who looked at it in surprise, and then read it out:

"My dear Mr. Giddings:—I am suddenly called to Canfield, and go at once. I will try to join you at Warren to-morrow. Make my excuse to the host.
"Fred."

The call was a relief to Fred; he took his place with

alacrity in the carriage, glad to fly even from Belle, and drove away in as wretched a frame of mind as he had ever known.

Had he returned to the table, he would have found that bunch of beautiful rose-buds on his plate. It never resumed its place, and probably not more than one knew its final fate.

CHAPTER XLI.

BELLE.

IT is a sufficiently difficult task to sketch with graphic accuracy the character of a man whose traits are pronounced, whose characteristics are marked, and the springs and workings of whose mind are often obvious, — of a man who is permitted to speak and act directly as a primary and controlling force, and manifests himself more or less openly.

Who shall confidently attempt the character of woman, the lines of which are often so delicately traced as to be invisible to the eye of a man, and which may nevertheless control? Who shall estimate her emotional nature, and the balancing or controlling power of her affections? Who can tell where the springs of thought or sources of impulse lie, and how or why or when either may act, and how either will influence the other, or what shall determine or control their action? and what the result of both acting together. Accustomed to act through others, and effect by indirect means, becoming used to not having her way, until the way itself is not obvious; denied all play of ambition, until its possession is deemed unwomanly; permitted only to persuade, until it is a crime to argue, and treason to command; taught that her only strength is in absolute weakness, her greatest power in abject submission, that her true independence is helpless subjection, and her sole possession is to be the absolute property of another, her real empire servitude, and her crowning achievement constant self-sacrifice ; that she is aggregated negatives,— is not to do, is not to have, is not to be, is not to go, is not to see, is not to hear, to speak, or think, or know, and that her highest acquirement is to become nobody and accomplish nothing, and that in this she can alone occupy and fill her sphere. When the delicacy of her organization is remembered, it is apparent that her character may present difficulties that the ordinary artist, if he apprehend them, might hesitate to attempt. I might protest against these conditions which in all of the ages of man have changed the nature of woman to un-nature, but it would in no way help me to sketch the beautiful Belle.

It has been already mentioned, that Belle, reared in the atmosphere of the highest culture and refinement, from the singular currents of her existence, and the tendencies of the lighter elements of her nature, had floated dreamily in the sheltered and colorless streams of a half-nun life, touched and tinged alone with the ecstacies of a devotee, and only disturbed at times by the vague stir of the elements of a strong rich nature, lying so deep that their very existence was unsuspected. Her mystical, shadowy association with an imaginative youth, with whom real marriage was impossible, whose clearest perceptions took the form of misty visions, whose highest exaltations were feeble ecstacies, whose powers were too weak for fanaticism, and whose only hope and aspiration was languishing for the company of the angels. That the accepted and constantly acted .upon idea on her part that their union remained in full, binding, present force, and that their actual association was but temporarily suspended, had singularly isolated Belle even in the society of her equals, among whom she had freely mingled for the last four or five years. She could not fail of being very attractive to gentlemen, and frankly admitted the pleasure derived from their society. She was not now ascetic or prudish. She only and always conducted herself with the innate, unstudied, and exalted propriety of a devoted wife in the absence of her husband, and from this course she had in no instance departed. Gentlemen unexceptionable, with the profoundest admiration, would have approached her as possible lovers, but had never been able to do so. Her father had playfully chided her for her devotion to a shadow, and sometimes had seriously combated her notions ; while Maud, after pursuing her through every shade of badinage, had closed the light campaign with the declaration — half a wish and half a prophecy — that she would some day fall in love ; — it would not come through liking, or by any of the channels of growth, but she would fall into it, and under the in- spiring logic of a lover new light would be thrown on this phantasm. To which the laughing Belle answered that she always avoided precipices, and even in her romping days never had a tendency to climb. Maud ran and pinched her cheek, and then kissed her with, "We shall see." But with the hopeful watchfulness of three or four years, she had not seen.

Belle's vision of the portrait stepping from its frame, is perhaps remembered. The impression so singularly

produced was very deep.   It was not only deepened,
but became bewildering ; when, instead of its proving a
mere optical illusion, she found, when thrown into
Fred's immediate presence, that under the varying
lights, change of attitude and play of expression, his
resemblance in feature, from general effect to the
minutest lines, seemed to her memory, and excited imagination, perfect ; and then, like an electric shock,
came the thought that here was the mysterious solution
of an old mystery, a new link in the chain of events,
which made up a story of tragic love, that had fixed
itself in her memory as tenaciously as if the events of
it had occurred under her eyes.   As she looked, that
thought grew to belief, and passed at once into the
form of enduring conviction.

Then her mind, quickened by this assurance, recalled
the curious name which seemed familiar to Fred, as
well as the other coincidences of which he thought he
must have dreamed.   She felt and knew that she was
strongly drawn to him — almost irresistibly — and that
she thought him the handsomest, — no, not that — she
didn't like the word — but something brave, strong,
and noble — man she had ever seen.   Then there was
the mystery of his birth.   If not this child, who was
he?   It was this mystery, and her interest in the story
which must be his, that attracted her to him, of course.
But then he certainly had beautiful eyes, a deep, rich,
manly voice, and the same silky black side-whiskers as
the portrait, and the same wilful, finely-formed mouth ; —
he *must be* the son.

As to the mistake of that night — but so pure was
she in heart and soul that her purity was not alarmed —

she did not blame him; of course he was asleep, was dreaming of her. How funny that was! and she was careless; but then he knew how it happened. She knew the adventure was sacred in his mind. It was a rude shock to her delicacy; she could hardly think of it, and it must have shocked him as much.

Would he mention it in the morning? Was she afraid he would? Did she wish that he would — it was not necessary; she thought he would not, — but then men are queer sometimes; she wondered how he would look by daylight. Of course she was not quite certain of his looks. Then he came in, and she saw by his look that he attached much gravity to the occurrence, and it shocked her; she could not face him when he spoke. But his words, — that he dreamed of her, and that she was the only woman for whom he would gladly die! How these thrilled! That was not gallantry. The quickened blood came to her face, and when she turned around he had gone. He was somehow disturbed, and she could not quite say to him what she would. No matter; that was got along with now. A seat was offered her that morning, and though she would much prefer to ride with Martha and Fred, yet, as there was but one seat in their sleigh, she took the one offered. Then came the accident and rescue. Belle thought of and saw only Fred. She was not frightened; the world swam a little when he disappeared, but then she knew he would come out, and she could not help rushing in to help him. How glad she was that the poor little maiden was saved, and mainly because Fred saved her! How like a river-god he looked, coming out of the water! How glad she was when he praised her! She

17

did help bring the girl to, but Fred told her what to do. Then she recalled his conduct when Martha's brother was sick. He was gone a good while with Martha that afternoon, and she was very glad when he came, and was a little afraid to meet him; he took her hand in both his, and pressed his cheek and the side of his face to it, and left tears upon it; what did it mean? Did he love her? Was this love, a man's love? a real, splendid, heroic man's love. and for her, — Belle? What a heaven! How she choked, and how her heart throbbed; could it be love, and did she feel the same way to him? Of course, when he turned away from her the tears dropped from her eyes; but then she was a woman. She had never felt such a strange, sweet, exquisite thrill. How warm and clinging his hands were! Was it love? Surely, this was not all interest in him, because he must be the son of her friend Mrs. D'Arlon. But then, — it could not be; people could not fall in love so suddenly as this. Besides, she was a married woman, and a woman with a husband could never fall in love, or — was it something — that people sometimes called love? It was not that, she knew. Something of fear, shame, apprehension of guilt must come with that. Then she had watched Fred, been near him, heard his voice, seen the light in his eyes, and found somehow that she did not like to meet his gaze, and he was often turning to look at her, and that did not offend her.

She thought of his birth, — what if she was mistaken, what if the general impression of him was true? It could not matter to her, it should not to anybody. If anything, he was entitled to the more credit for the position he had gained alone, and in spite of it. Of course he would be a great man, and would marry somebody. Would he? Not if—not if—of course he did not love her. He had no business to love her; she was a married woman, and he knew it. But he did not know that seriously he must not love her as men sometimes loved women they wished to marry. Pshaw! what a silly girl she was! What had come over her? She never had such thoughts before; but then it was a whim—a fancy—and would pass. She found that she did not want to talk about him to Martha; Martha would suspect something. So it ran on more and deeper; and Fred left, and could not speak when he went. She wondered if he would write. Of course not to her; but when his letter came, she was not much surprised, and not at all frightened.

Somehow, the fierce and stormy way in which he told his love exhilarated, aroused, and almost intoxicated her, and for a moment seemed to carry her to the inner heavens—not the home of abstract, celestial, angelic, of cold, colorless bliss—but a heaven like the earth transfigured and glorified, with a thousand suns and endless flowers, and warmth, and glad and joyous singing, happy things. This was love—passionate, intense, strong—but oh, exquisitely sweet and beautiful! Then came the memory of Edward; she who, as his wife, was so loved, and was glad and happy for it,—she, oh, horror! felt no guilt and no shame, no trembling, no possible danger, but thrilling gladness. No, this could not be love,—it—it must be that alluring fascination which she had heard that some men could throw about some women, which disarmed fear, and changed the poor wretched woman's nature. What if this strong and fascinating man should insist on her loving him with what people would call a marriage? Then she turned and found exquisite consolation in the last two or three lines of his letter. He only wanted to worship as the young barbarian would worship his star; and only wanted that the star should know. Was there ever anything so beautiful, yet exquisitely touching? How unhappy he was, and why might he not love her? And why might she not joy in knowing that he did? But — but — could a married woman innocently be the object of such worship? — not of soul worship, soul love? Why not? She distrusted and doubted, as well she might. Did not this come wholly between her and the memory of Edward; between her and him in heaven; transforming heaven, in which he was, only to an unregretted memory, an uncherished dream? True, her form would remain pure, but her heart and soul — oh, blessed heaven, and all its hopes and joys, were never so shadowy and vague, so poor and filmy — were not heart and soul lost already? Had she erred in thought or dream? She could not feel that she had, and she felt that she ought to be sensible of guilt. Was there adultery of the spirit? Might they not commune with no thought of earth? She knelt and prayed with the deep, sweet, hopeful fervor and restful faith of the pure in heart, soul and thought.

CHAPTER XLII.

BELLE'S THEORY.

UNDER the inspiration of her love, whatever she may have called it, her mind, naturally strong and quick, and now doubly so in everything that had reference to Fred, and the conceded mystery of his birth, was, as we see, suggestive and inventive. The thought, of course, occurred to communicate her belief and its reasons to him, as the one most interested, and whose energy, knowledge and sagacity would be strong allies in an enterprise of his own. But after all it might prove that she was mistaken, and then, how cruel to him, who had suffered so much! She had only a portrait which she had not seen for years, a story, the names, places and dates of which she had only a vague idea of. Besides, deep in her woman's heart was the wish, strong as life, and which might lead her to confront death itself, to do this thing for him, — to restore him, crowned with his birthright, and let him owe her for it. Oh, what exquisite luxury! And these thoughts and voices   · inmost heart — this struggle with her soul — mu   be stilled; perhaps she might be mistaken even in her duty to the dead, and her estimate of her real relations. Oh, what a surprise to Fred it

(261)

would be! and what would she not deserve at his hands?

Nor would she communicate to Fred's mother, then in, or near, Boston. She would invent a pretext, and ask her to send her the requisite dates and names, places, and so forth, and she would at once enter personally upon the investigation. She was exhilarated at the thought of travelling, of going out and of attempting this adventure, and was amazed at the energy which the thought called up.

She wrote to Mrs. D'Arlon, and arranged to return home. On her arrival there, she found the desired answer. In substance, Mrs. D'Arlon stated that her husband, in the month of September of 1821, with their infant son, then about two years and a half old, left Charleston to go into Virginia. He travelled in his own carriage, with two servants, and had with him a large sum of money; that in the mountains of North Carolina, a few miles west of Linvill, in attempting to pass a swollen stream, his coachman was drowned, his baggage and money lost, and himself fatally hurt. His servant, with some assistance, rescued him and their son, and he was taken to a sort of tavern in that wild region, kept by a man of the name of Jarvis Bibb, where he soon after died. The son, Ethfred, was placed with a poor man in the neighborhood named Sam Warren, a cousin or nephew of Bibb's, but was taken sick soon after, and also died. The servant disappeared, and had never been heard of since. She, the writer, was absent in Cuba, prostrated with illness, and months elapsed before she, or any of her friends, had learned the fate of her husband. When she finally visited the region, to remove the remains of her dear ones, all these matters were fully confirmed to her. She had understood from her husband, that a little time before his marriage he had travelled over this road, and Bibb told her that he spent a few days at his place, hunting in the wild region, some three years before the fatal accident. In the face of this statement, Belle, woman-like, believed that Ethfred and Fred were the same; that possibly the money was not lost, and that it might furnish inducement to Bibb to change his name, and so forth. At any rate she would go to North Carolina, and if Bibb and Warren were there, she was mistaken, and would abandon the quest, unless, — well, she didn't carry out the chain. Her father was still absent, and she at once went to Philadelphia, and took Maud and her husband into her confidence.

"Oh, Belle! Belle! Belle!" exclaimed Maud, "what did I tell you? This is the disguised young prince, is it, who comes to break the spell and liberate the princess? What did I tell you?"

"Maud, you may shake your head, and look wise, and laugh as much as you please; I am decidedly in earnest in this."

"So I see; and as decidedly in love with this handsome young lawyer as any Miss of fifteen. How romantic! How exquisite it is! Ha! ha! ha!"

At first, Marbury and Maud were little inclined to give heed to her hypothesis, but soon found that she was inflexibly determined to pursue the enterprise. At Marbury's suggestion, an experienced detective was called, who, under the inspiration of a large fee for a not unpleasant service, did see much in the facts sub-

mitted, and declared that Belle was a born detective.
Belle determined to proceed at once to North Carolina
with the detective, and of course was attended by Marbury. They had little difficulty in finding the locality,
still wild and thinly inhabited. Some of the people
remembered the circumstances for which they inquired.
The sum of the information was, that D'Arlon died of
injuries occasioned by the upsetting of his carriage,
four or five days after that occurrence, at Bibb's, who
did not maintain a good reputation. That the child
(some thought that it was a girl, and some that it was
a boy) was taken to Warren's, as Bibb's wife was
dead, and died soon after; although there was a story
that it was Warren's little girl that died. Nobody
remembered the name of the child. Bibb had a sister,
named Sally, who was away at the time. The servant
disappeared the day after the accident, and there were
stories that Bibb made way with him, and some of the
money, and that the winter following he and his sister,
and the Warren's, packed off for Tennessee, and had
never been heard of since. All this strongly confirmed
the general outline of Belle's theory. Descriptions of
Bibb and his sister, and the Warrens, were taken with
as much accuracy as possible, and the party returned
directly to Ohio, where they found Belle's father, and
where they were soon joined by Maud and her children.
The next point was to identify Bibb with Green, or
Warren with Warden, and inquiries were quietly made
about Mantua, with no result save the confirmed mystery of Fred's birth and person, and something of a
paper executed before Esquire Ladd. Then it was
resolved to pursue Sam Warden, who was necessarily

Warren, and also trace out the fortunes and whereabouts of John Green and Sally. Soon after their return from North Carolina the murder of Olney was committed, followed by the arrest of Jake Green. The detective had an interview with Jake, who was reticent, but informed him that his father and aunt were at Nauvoo, and he believed Warden was with Jones in Missouri. Nothing could be got out of him, if he remembered anything, as to the matters of immediate inquiry; and yet it seemed, from what he did say, that his father had moved several times. Belle, herself, at her own suggestion, had written the note to Fred which called him to Jake's side, and Marbury copied and mailed it. The enthusiastic and romantic girl was full of the generous confidence that Fred at once, without fee or its hope, would magnanimously rush to the defence of his old enemy, and the son of the man who, as she believed, had done him the greatest wrong — had perhaps murdered his father — and how wonderful that would be! The inquiry in North Carolina had shown that her conjectures as to Fred might be possible, unless, indeed, he may have been Sally's son, which seemed improbable under the light of the ascertained facts. Warren had a child, which, with the Darlon or D'Arlon child, were the only ones known. If Sally had one, then there were three, and one only had died, which may have been Warren's; and there was no rumor in that neighborhood that Sally, whom her brother was said to have ill used in some matter of their father's property, had ever had a child. Yet this was possible, and it had been suggested, after inquiries in Mantua, that it was doubtful whether the Wardens had ever had a

child as old as Fred; they may have taken Sally's, and
the fact that Bibb sent the Darlon child to them,
seemed to furnish some shadow for this also.

In the latter part of March, Belle, now accompanied
by her father and the detective, started for St. Louis,
intending to go to Nauvoo, while a trusty man also
went with them, who was to hunt up Sam Warden, and
secure his return to Ohio if possible.

All that was learned at Nauvoo was the death of
John Green, and that Sally had a month before started
east, intending, it was said, to return to Mantua. She
was traced to the river; but whether she took a boat
down, or what became of her, they could not ascertain.
No result attended the inquiries of the detective con-
cerning the writing executed by Green in Mantua. He
found many old acquaintances at Nauvoo, prominent
men among the Mormons, but no one seemed to have
heard of it. A little depressed, but with her faith in
no wise shaken, Belle returned home, not without the
hope of finding Sally at Mantua, and to await news of
Sam Warden. All that was known and rumored about
Mantua had been carefully collected and collated; and
notwithstanding Sam Warden had bound Fred to John
Green as his son, Belle had contended that this was
more than met by Green's own assertion that he was
of his own blood, — Sally's child, in short; and that it
was very plain to her that Sally never had a child. It
was true, of course, that Sally had seemed very devoted
to Fred; but then, any woman would love him in a motherly way when he was small. Many of the Mormons
remembered Fred at Kirtland, where the impression
was that he was a son of Sally by some Southern gen-

tleman; and it was understood among them that Sally
was a party to his escape. which was inconsistent with
her being his mother. Why did she not keep him, or
why not go with him?

Esquire Ladd had told all he knew of the paper
acknowledged before him. It was a lengthy, closely-
written document of several pages, of which he knew
nothing, save that it bore the mark of Green and his
own signature as a witness and justice; he could not
remember that Smith or Rigdon signed it.

What was this writing? It undoubtedly was the
written history of Green's life, and as undoubtedly contained the story of Fred and his father's fate. So Belle
claimed. The descriptions of Green and Bibb coincided; Bibb's sister's name was Sally, and Warden's
name was Sam. Of course, if they removed from North
Carolina for any crime of Bibb's, their names would be
changed; they might go to many places and change
many times. Green had probably made a confession
to the Prophet, and this placed him and his money in
Smith's power. The Mormons would be likely to want
to keep and train Fred in their faith and ways, for fear
he might himself, in time, discover his birth and demand his rights. In this opinion the detectives and Mr.
Morris concurred. It was strengthened by the account
of the Mormons, that Green was very poor, became
crazy, and was kept in confinement, and died there.
From an examination of the land records of Portage
county, it was ascertained that at the time of his conversion he was an extensive landowner, and that soon after
he had sold all his real estate. Thus the case stood,
when Belle returned home. Not all at once, nor by any

continuous argumentation, had Belle's conclusions been
reached, nor could she tell how or where the various
elements and processes of it had taken form.   Nor had
she reached them unaided; numerous and repeated
discussions and arguments had been holden upon every
fact, incident, and rumor connected with the case,
from which her mind, and those of her assistants, had
outlined the final course of thought, till what seemed
likely and probable to others, were settled convictions·
with her.

She returned to hear the rumors of mysterious papers
found on the person of Jake, for which he had probably
murdered Olney, and which might prove to be the writ-
ings acknowledged by Green.   They all looked forward
to the trial of Jake as an event that might throw important light upon the mystery, perhaps clear it all up.
To Belle, there was beautiful and retributive justice in
Fred's being thrown into such an important position in
reference to the case; he was actually to defend Jake
as his counsel.   Vaguely, the dim and wondrously
fascinating outline of a dramatic, almost poetic romance was dawning upon her woman's vision, in which
she, too, was deeply involved.   Was she to unravel it, to
be in some way a sort of heroine in it?   How sweet and
entrancing the fancy was to her, — too exquisitely sweet
and delicious to ever be more than a dream.

Wansor, after ineffective pumpings of the truculent
and sealed-up Jake, now under the advice of counsel,
made advances to the prosecuting officer, who finally
found, as he thought, that the shrewd Wansor had
useful information for which he might exchange a secret
of State, not to be divulged till after the trial.

CHAPTER XLIII.

BELLE ARGUES HER CASE WITH MAUD, AND IS WORSTED.

OH, Belle, what a marvel you have become! I look upon you with perfect amazement! You, my dreamy, mystical, romantic sister, who looked upon all men as so many big brothers, to be believed in, with never a lover among them all, — here you are a perfect heroine, — making long and dangerous journeys in the winter, and leading and managing men as if they were so many little boys."

This conversation was had the first night after Belle's return from the West, and after she had recounted the particulars of her journey, and Maud was now sitting at her feet.

"And, Maudy dear, I'm a wonder to myself; I wonder at my strength and courage and energy. Oh, I've dreamed all my life till now, and how glad I am to wake up! You don't know the exhilaration and almost ecstasy of doing, or of trying to do things, to feel your faculties like new fountains stir, and hear their voices calling, like new sounds. How we women live out of the world! And to find these men out, to see what dear, delicious humbugs they really are. Just to sit and hear them argue, for instance, is too funny for anything in this world. Our father and Mr. Wansor

would not at first agree upon anything. Our dear
precious is more unworldly than even a woman;
and Wansor, in a small way, is shrewd and subtle.
He does everything indirectly. He'd rather not know
a thing unless he can draw it out in a cork-screwy
way. He always supposes men act from the basest
motives. Indeed, he don't believe that any others
exist; and he and our father argued and settled, and
unsettled everything; no matter whether it was of the
least importance or not, or whether they could connect
it with anything, it had to be settled, and then talked
over, and then set down for argument. And then,
Maud, if you could see how these Mormons live, poorer
than the whites among the mountains, so squalid, and
the women, poor things, so ignorant, and yet such
enthusiasts, that it was almost beautiful. But what a
horror Nauvoo is! What dreadful men must have
congregated there! And then, Maudy, men are coarse-
fibered. I suppose they have to be; one cannot associate two months with a detective and hear his unconscious talk without thinking less of the sex. They
make such innocent revelations of themselves. Of
course, dear, our father, and your James, and — "

"Your prince, Belle, are exceptions. Dear, I know
all that; let them go for the present. You are just a
shade thinner, — look a little worn, and yet, somehow,
you are lovelier, — have more character. I only fear
that this hero may not be worthy of you, after all.
Dear stupid! mooning around, unknowing, and you
worrying your brain and soul out for him! Oh, if he
don't worship you when he knows, — no matter how it
comes out! And, Belle, dear, I half suspect that this

letter is from him," — holding up Fred's note from
Mantua. "It has been here many days." As Belle's
eyes fell upon it, they filled with the old, marvellous
light, and just a bright suffusion kindled up lip and
cheek. She opened it with a hand that trembled, ran
her eye over it, and, with a cry of anguish, threw her
face down upon the bosom of her wondering sister, and,
for a moment, abandoned herself to tears.

"My poor, poor Belle! My precious one!" And
with tender words and gentle caresses from Maud, Belle
recovered, and, placing the letter in Maud's hands,
walked away to a window; then she came back, and,
kneeling by Maud, looked mutely up into her moved
face.

"Belle, Belle, do you not love this so sorely-stricken
and beautiful young man? Oh, I forgive him his innocent stupidity!"

"Oh, Maud! and you a woman, to ask me this!"

"And how do you love him?"

"With heart and soul and mind and strength, — as
a woman may worship her idol!" dropping her face
into Maud's lap. Maud's arms went about her sister's
waist.

"Why should you and he be longer unhappy, then?
Belle, I cannot understand you!"

"Am I not a wife, with a husband only just a
little away from me?" with a deep, earnest, hollow
voice. "Oh, Maud! If by any unheard-of evil miracle
a man, an ideal one, should love you, and your whole
self was drawn to him with more than answering love,
and he should ask for a token, no matter what or how
small, from you, what would you answer?"

" But he only asks for a sign that you forgive him — the good Lord knows what for ! — that he may be but your casual acquaintance."

" Maud, don't mistake, — the smallest, tiniest thing that is, would grow to be the largest in the world; it would be a token of love ! "

" And why shouldn't you give him a token of love, pray? and your full heart and whole self, — I beg to know ? "

" Because, — can't you understand, Maud ? "

" No, I cannot. Oh, my poor, precious Belle ! too pure and precious for earth ! Can't you see that this is a phantom? Don't you feel that it is, in your heart and soul ? "

" I begin to feel that it is, but I cannot so see it ; " with a lower and smaller voice.

Maud was too wise to press the question. She would leave it to the logic of love, — the only logic she had much faith in.

" And this Fred, this D'Arlon, — and what is to become of him, Belle? What if he comes, finally, and demands your love — demands you — comes and takes you? It is in his old Norman Norse berserker blood, perhaps."

" He will not, Maud, when he knows all."

" Don't delude yourself, Belle. Man is born to dominion. To covet, with him, is to acquire. When he woos, he will win ; and it is our poor nature, Belle, to be wooed and won. Where a woman's heart has gone, she is very apt to follow."

" Don't you believe, Maud, that there are men capable of loving women generously, purely, and self-sacrificingly? and that there are women who can be so loved, and who will not permit themselves to be loved in any other way?"

"I do believe both. But, Belle, if this youth is what you suppose, or if he is not — and it makes no difference, as I see — would you doom him to a solitary life, — a cold asceticism, without home, or wife and children?"

"Might he not finally marry; and would he not love his children?"

"And you hold the first place in his heart? What a wrong to some sweet, pure woman, and what an outrage to him!" And stepping to the nursery door, where her beautiful children were with an attendant, just being put to bed, — "James, come here!" In tripped a child of wondrous beauty, with cherub face and locks, and in an earthly night-dress, — "Jimmy, go and climb into Aunt Belle's lap, and put your arms about her neck, and call her mamma!" and the frolicksome boy obeyed. Springing to her lap, and throwing his arms about her neck, he nestled himself upon her bosom, with, "Mamma! oh, my beautiful mamma!" Then, releasing his arms, came back for his mother's kiss, and sprang to his bed.

"Belle," said the sweet and thoughtful mother, "suppose that Fred was the father of that child, — would it not be agony beyond endurance, the thought that another woman was his mother? Oh, Belle!"

"Maud!" — from the innermost depths of her being spoke the strongly-agitated girl — "the most sacred and the holiest thing in the world is to be a mother. The

18

mystery of the first creation is no greater miracle than this wondrous thing."

"And loving as you do, Belle, would you put all this from you?"

"Oh, Maud! Maud! Maud! Ask God to help me!"

CHAPTER XLIV.

MOSS-ROSES.

MARBURY'S trip South had given him new views
of slavery, which were largely sympathized in
by Mr. Morris; and the announcement that Mr. Giddings was to speak within two or three miles of them,
induced them to attend the meeting. On the morning
of the day, it was rumored that the eloquent young
Democrat mentioned on the placards was no other
than Fred, who was now an object of paramount interest to the Morris circle, and whose fortunes had for
the last two months been their one theme of thought,
labor, and anxiety. There was the greatest curiosity
to see and hear him.

To Belle, the news that Fred was in the neighborhood was peculiarly exciting. She determined at once
to attend the meeting, and induced her sister Maud,
who, next to Belle, took the largest interest in Fred,
to be of the party.

Before she left home, she selected a few half-opened
moss-roses, which she wore on her bosom, as may be
remembered, and which Maud observed seemed to be
adjusted in a manner that would admit of their being
easily removed. On consultation, the gentlemen were
decidedly of opinion that Fred should be invited to

spend the night at the Morris mansion; whether he should be let into the secret of his fortunes, should be afterwards determined.

Belle was decidedly opposed to this, — perhaps she could not tell why, had she tried. It may have been more a matter of womanly feeling and sentiment than of reason. When pressed for a reason, the miracle of coolness, and shrewdness, and practical sense which she had become, only pouted, and said very prettily, but very decidedly, that she was a woman, and not obliged to give a reason; and Maud instinctively adhered to Belle. Poor child! she must see Fred; she wanted to be near him and hear him, and she meant to carry that bunch of rose-buds, and if she gave them to him, then she wanted to go away from him for a little. She could not tell him about himself till she could make it certain. She had not yet heard from Warden or Sally. She would at least wait till after the trial. She wanted to hear again from his mother. She wanted to wait; she wanted time for herself. She knew she should tell him all her heart and self, and she wanted to know her full self. Somehow Edward had grown more shadowy, and her marriage to him had become shadowy too, and did not seem to rest on her conscience at all, but only as a phantom in her mind and memory.

They went and heard the speeches, and were all alike in ecstasies over Fred's. Mr. Morris and Marbury, as well as Maud, had seen the famous portrait in Florence, and at the owner's residence in Boston; they pronounced Fred its living counterpart, and had no lingering doubt of his being the son of its original.

As for Belle, Fred's speech was more than it could by possibility be to others. Through his eyes she could look into his soul, which she felt was pure and exalted as her own. How much he towered above all the men about him! and in his anger he was the retributive angel of wrath, beautiful and terrible. Even Maud could now forgive him for not reading the sealed book of his own history.

When the meeting was over, Belle insisted on going home, and for once did not have her way. Mr. Giddings's friend had, in advance, sent Mr. Morris and party an invitation to dinner, which had been accepted. Then Fred was brought in; all the glory of his face was gone, and he was cold, almost haughty. She could not wonder at it, but was hurt and pained more than she could express. She could not comprehend or make allowance for him. Why must he not know that he could not love any woman in vain? that there must be some reason for her silence and seeming coldness? Had he not, while on the stand, looked into her very heart, and when he took his seat, like a marble statue by her at the table, was he not a mere machine? Yet she could see that he had grown thin, and was now almost haggard. She felt that he was as wretched as he could be, and what a grieving joy that was to her. What a blessed thing to be near him, even in this mood. How madly and meaninglessly voices clamored and clangered about her! He spoke, but how cold and constrained; and was not she frigid and distant also? But then he would turn to her, and besides, all eyes were on him constantly. — and then he was called out, and in the little swirl and turn of heads to follow him, the moss-roses, in their greenish purple hoods from which they were just breaking, somehow reached the side of his plate, and he did not return. Poor roses!

Was it a providence that called him off? What if some accident should happen to him? But none would happen. God would restore him to his mother; that surely would happen. Then joy and hope sprang up in her heart, and light and warmth to her face; she heard so gladly the warm and just things spoken of Fred, and could have kissed Mr. Giddings for his beautiful and kindly words.

A more wretched young man did not breathe on the continent than the so loved, admired, praised, and gifted young orator, who rode out on his lonely way. He felt crushed, and, man-like, was taciturn and gloomy. The man who came for him, after two or three vain attempts at conversation, relapsed, through Yankee-doodle badly whistled, into silence, and devoted his energies to his horses on the home-stretch.

What was it after all to sway men, to stir up a mob, to win their admiration? Even now it was being whispered about the thing he was, and she would hear it. His heart was too utterly wretched to feel even this sting. Let it go: some cheer, some comfort, some light — at least rest — might come. Love, warmth, and gladness were not for him. Then with a determined effort he crushed his emotions and heart-throbs down in a mass, and placed his will upon them. No; these things were not for him; his way was to be solitary, — had always been. As they gained a hill under the rays of the falling day, far in the upper air, cold and thin, and where the light was still white, his eye caught the form of an eagle flying eastward, cleaving the air, as by an effort of will. in calm, proud, conscious might, sweeping from gathering night to meet the day that was to come, and alone. High up and solitary his eye followed it till the bow-like curve of the mighty wings melted, till, diminishing to a speck, the eagle disappeared in the darkening void, coming from mystery and lost in the unknown, flashing for a moment on the wondering gaze of men below, and passing beyond the reach of their feeble vision. This vaguely hinted to him of a career straight, high, proud, and alone. Lord! how his man's soul swelled and went upward, crushing its mist into his dimming eyes at the thought.

As he went on, he seemed to detach himself from the clinging, haunting presence of Belle; and as he receded from her radiance, if his shadow of intense darkness grew huge and shapeless, it also dissipated and grew less palpable and obscuring; and when he finally escaped to a sort of hazy twilight, and mentally turned backward, objects seemed again to fall under the law of perspective, and he determined that Belle should maintain her proper place. Other men had been slighted, scorned, and despised, and had lived, perhaps, improved and benefited. He knew he must live; but to what purpose? Pshaw! how weak and commonplace he was. And he closed his eyes to it all, and rode forward.

Twilight had come, and the fingers of the early night had shaken out upon the gathering dew the aroma of the flowers, and were closing their censers till another day.

Sleepy children subsiding from the long day's happy

play, and in whose swimming eyes the shadows of dreams were deepening, dropped on doorsteps, and nodded in forgetfulness. Lights came cheerily into darkening windows, and the contented voices of happy husbands and wives, and the laughter of girls, came out from many a wayside homestead. There came upon the consciousness of the burdened and weary. youth the vision of a rose-wreathed cottage, under frag- rant trees, in the twilight, and a white-robed form of wondrous loveliness tripping eagerly out, with red lips and white arms, to greet and welcome him. As the vision cheated him of pain, he did not banish it, though the form was that of Belle.

On his arrival he found that his associate had been notified that the prosecutors had determined to have the case set for Monday of the second week of the court instead of the third, which was to commence its session the next day. This arrangement would leave scant time to secure the witnesses for the defendant. The announcement was like a trumpet-call to Fred, who was prompt when challenged to labor on ordinary occasions, and now a summons to action was an abso- lute relief. The case was of the utmost gravity — the most important he had ever appeared in — he was to be the responsible counsel, and unembarrassed by the timid counsels of an older and more cautious leader. He believed Jake was entirely innocent. He thought he knew the whole ground, and had thoroughly culti- vated every inch of it; had examined all the books within reach, and taken all their hints.

He did not go the next day to Warren, and of course did not see Belle, who had become much interested in

Mr. Giddings's canvass, and induced her father to take Maud and herself over to town. In some way the meeting fell very flat to her, and she returned home grave and quiet.

Meantime, Fred reëxamined the whole case; made a very accurate list of the State's witnesses, with notes of their evidence, arranged his own, notified Dr. Ackly, and the witnesses from Ravenna and Warren, issued subpœnas for his witnesses, got a list of the proposed jurors, and ascertained all that could be known of them individually. When the day arrived he was ready. prepared, in the sense in which careful lawyers use that word. `

What motive induced a change in the programme of the State, Fred never knew, though he may have guessed; whether it was for the purpose of shortening his time for preparation, or for other cause, he did not trouble himself to ascertain, although he suspected the former.

CHAPTER XLV.

AN OLD TIME MURDER TRIAL.

CANFIELD was one of the oldest towns on the Reserve, in the midst of a rich and highly culti- vated country, and was noted as the residence of Elisha Whittlesy, Judge Newton, Judge Church, and other prominent men. It was a delightful little town of two or three hundred inhabitants, many of whom were wealthy and refined. The trial was an event of great moment, and although occurring at a very busy season for an agricultural community, was attended from the beginning to the end by an immense number of people, including many of the wives and daughters of the farmers, while many of the ladies of Warren, Youngstown, and other towns, accompanied their hus- bands and brothers, attending every day's session to the end of the trial.

Judge Newton presided, assisted by three associ- ates. He had been long and favorably known at the bar, had much reputation as an advocate, and as a judge presided with dignity and urbanity. By the laws of Ohio, thirty-six men were specially empanelled from which to select the jury, the defendant having twenty-three peremptory challenges, — a right to reject twenty-three without assigning any cause. The prosecuting attorney, on this occasion. was aided by two lawyers of local eminence. and perhaps they and the court were a little surprised — the latter unpleasantly so — that the prisoner should be represented by two mere youths at the bar, where a man is young at forty, one of whom was known to possess but moderate ability. The rumor of Fred's speech had reached Mahoning county, and many were in attendance who heard it. His youthfulness was a great point to him, after all, and with his rare personal advantages had made him a favorite at once, while the most extravagant stories of his powers as an advocate gained ready credence.

The ladies were captivated by his good looks, and began to look favorably on Jake ; while some men never knew a man whom ladies admired who knew anything, and as for Jake, — he'd be hanged anyhow. When the case was called, Fred promptly answered that he was ready ; which the State's attorney was a little surprised at, as he had counted on a motion to continue, or at least for a week's delay. and possibly for a change of venue. Young as he was, Fred knew the effect of a cheerful confidence on his part, upon others.

The jurors were called. and took their seats in a body. They had been selected with careful fairness from parts of the county remote from the scene of the murder, and underwent a close scrutiny by Fred, whose life and experience had made him a good student of men. The jury were sworn as to their qualifications, and examined by the counsel on either side, the State taking the initiative. — the court acting as the trier of the jurors. Fred conducted his side with great tact and judgment, and with a quiet, easy, grave manner that was quite charming and contrasted with that of the prosecuting attorney, who was sharp, and often rude, to his opponent. To the surprise of the court and bar, the twelve were secured from the first panel and sworn in an hour. Fred obviously looked for but one qualification — intelligence — and unhesitatingly accepted two or three who said that they had formed opinions. He knew enough of the workings of the human intellect to feel sure that when a man discovered that his opinion was based on an erroneous statement, he distrusted the whole theory upon which it was formed, and his judgment was apt at once to accept its opposite. Fred knew that it would be made to appear that the popular view of the homicide was very erroneous, and he counted on this law of mind.

The prisoner was arraigned, and the indictment solemnly read, the plea of Not Guilty entered, and the case was ready, when the district attorney suggested that the court take a recess for dinner. Those were the good old times of honest work in the country ; and after consultation with the counsel, Judge Newton announced that during the trial the court would assemble at eight, A.M., take a recess from twelve to one, and sit until six in the evening.

On resuming, the district attorney opened out his case in a written speech of much force of adjective and great clearness of denunciation. He said that the murdered man, Olney, had left the Mormons at Nauvoo, had visited his brethren at Kirtland, from which place he started two days before the murder, and passed along a well-known route, and was seen to enter the fatal woods just at dusk, and so forth. That he had been followed from Nauvoo by Green, himself the son of a murderer, as he was prepared to show, who arrived at Kirtland a day or two after Olney, and was seen on the same route following him. That he was traced into the woods and tracked out, and that when arrested there was found on him a remarkable document, which he presumed would amaze the counsel for the prisoner, which he had taken from the body of the murdered man, and which would furnish proof of motive, and so forth. It was to secure this that Olney was followed and assassinated.

When the witnesses were called for the State, Judge Newton asked Fred, in a suggestive tone, whether he would have them separated. Fred answered that he did not deem it necessary. He presumed the witnesses would do their best to tell the truth, and that in that rested the defendant's hope.

The State produced witnesses, proving the finding of the deceased, and the doctors, who swore that life was destroyed by a blow or blows on the head, fracturing the skull, and so forth. Fred, in a very quiet way, put these men under the gentle torture of a cross-examination such as the learned M.D.'s sometimes enjoy at the hands of their brethren of the bar. In this instance it was the more embarrassing, as the dreaded Ackly was observed to be a grim listener. When asked to explain how they knew that the man died of a blow on the head, their reasons were not satisfactory. They made no examination of any kind; did not deem it necessary. He was dead, his skull fractured, and most men would deem that sufficient. Of course it could be done by a blow, and in no other way. Had they removed the scalp? No. How did they know the skull was fractured? Did they know whether the neck or spine was injured? They made no examination. The questioning was cool, quiet, but long and exhaustive. It was evident that here lay one position of the defence, and the State's medical testimony left it dubious as to the means and cause of death. The quick, cool, shrewd spectators saw the weakness of the case. Some marks and bruises were found on other parts of the body, produced, as was said, by dragging the body after the murder; it was left quite doubtful whether they were not made before death, or might have been.

It appeared that it had snowed on the night of the murder, and the snow was two or three inches deep in the morning, covering the body of the slain man; and also that a watch and a small amount of money were found on him.

Proof was then made that he was at Kirtland; several saw him on the line of the road, and he was last seen, just at dark, entering the woods; that his horse was found nearly at the point of entering the wood, with one foot through the bridle rein, which had been loose, and which was now caught over a small stump or root, and thus tethered him. The saddle had turned, and was found partly under his belly. A small portmanteau which he had carried, was never found. Men swore to the presence of Jake in Kirtland; but the exact time was left in doubt. Many saw a person much like him along the route of travel pursued by Olney, and on the same days. The road traversing the woods, which were about a mile and a half in extent, ran easterly, and Olney was going east. At about midway of the woods a road running south terminated in this east and west road. Without doubt Jake had travelled this north and south road some time in the latter part of the same night, or early the following morning, for he stopped two miles south of it, where he took breakfast; and before the snow melted off he was tracked back to the east and west road; from the point where he had eaten breakfast he was traced to Coshocton and arrested. When arrested, he refused to tell his name, and denied having been in Mahoning county at all; and then he suddenly became silent, and refused to say anything more, and did not.

"What did you find on his person?" to the officer arresting him.

"A paper, or rather several papers, fastened together."

"Look at this;" handing him a closely-written document.

"That is it. He threw this from him, or from his clothes, where they lay in his sleeping-room, when we found him. I saw him throw it into the fire-place, in which was a little fire, and you see where it is scorched."

"You all see it, gentlemen," said the prosecuting attorney, with an air. "I propose," said he, rising, "to read this paper to the jury. It is a most remarkable document," glancing at Fred.

"Show it to Mr Warden," said the court.

"I presume he is familiar with it, or ought to be," remarked the lawyer, tossing it to him with an air of unconcern.

A thrill ran through the frame of Fred as he turned

over three or four closely-written pages to the end, and found, "John Green, his x mark," attested by "H. G. Ladd, Mantua, Jan. 10th, 1831."

"The gentleman is doubtless familiar with the signature?" meaningly.

"I've seen something like it; most men make marks alike."

"You'll find it an interesting document;" with indifference.

"That is very possible, though its interest does not shine out at once," with forced calmness, while a chill, like *a rigor mortis*, for an instant shivered through him, for his eye had caught his own name once or twice in running it over. It flashed across him that in this paper, Green, among other things, had set down his history, showing the details, probably, of his wretched birth, which could have no further bearing on the case than to show his personal relation to Jake, and create a prejudice against himself. His first and only thought was of the injury and mischief that such an *exposé* must work to the case. None but a lawyer can appreciate — possibly credit — this statement. To the true advocate, everything, and self more than all, is subordinated, sunk, for the client. Fred would oppose the introduction of this writing to the last, and with only this glance he arose with it in his hand.

"Do I understand that the prosecuting attorney proposes to read this thing in evidence?"

"Certainly."

"Your Honors, it purports to have been executed on the tenth of January, 1831, fourteen years ago, and can therefore by no possibility contain the slightest information as to the death of Olney in 1845. It was not made by the defendant, and its contents can by no rules of evidence be given against him. If I should be found with a book in my hands, you could not read it against me as evidence, unless you could show that I was its author."

" If the court please," answered the prosecuting attorney, " the paper was made by John Green, the father of the prisoner, as I will show, and as the gentleman very well knows, and contains statements of the most damning character," with a significant look at Fred; " and as I stated in my opening, it was in the possession of the deceased, and it was to get possession of this paper that this most bloody, atrocious, wicked, hellish and diabolical murder was committed. I hope the gentleman understands, and will interpose no further objection."

" I think I do," — very modestly. " It is offered for two purposes, I presume: to connect the defendant with the deceased by showing him in possession of the dead man's goods, and then to supply the motive by showing the quality or value of the thing taken."

" Exactly, — the gentleman states it exactly," in his seat.

" Before it can be admitted for either purpose," continued Fred, " it must be proven to have been in the possession of the deceased at the time of death; otherwise, the possession of it by the defendant raises no presumption against him. And as this is a paper writing, the contents of which alone give it value, proof of the execution of it, and the relation of the parties, must be first given."

" I will satisfy the captious gentleman ! " exclaimed
19

the prosecuting attorney. "Mr. Wansor, come forward;" and Belle's detective took the stand. A short, stoutish, sharp, but good-natured looking man, who said that he was a detective of Philadelphia, recently on professional business at Nauvoo, where he had occasion to inquire after John Green, and found that he had died the fifth of January before, and that his sister left, as was supposed, for Ohio some time after.

Fred, poor innocent, asked him, "What took him to Nauvoo?"

Wansor stared at him for a moment in bewildered amazement, that he, of all men, should ask that question: but recovering. "I went on professional business for Miss Belle Morris, as I understand it, and was accompanied by her and her father. I must refer you to her for the nature of our mission."

"Miss Belle Morris!" Fred's breath went, and her name escaped him involuntarily. Two or three minutes' pause, and then, in a softened voice. "Did you hear anything of Green's sister, the defendant's aunt, except what you have stated?"

"No; she was thought to have gone down the river."

"Perhaps the gentleman would like to inquire after some other of his old friends and relatives," with a meaning smile to the jury.

"I will — one other — if you please; Mr. Wansor, when were you in Nauvoo?"

"We came from there about two weeks ago."

"How long were you there?"

"Some two or three weeks."

"Did you make the acquaintance of many of the

saints. my old friends and relatives, as the gentleman calls them?"

"Well. I saw a good many."

"What was my old friend Oliver Olney doing when you last saw him?" Sensation.

"I saw Olney several times. He had just returned from Kirtland. as I understood. I saw him several times." Prodigious sensation, which reached the State's counsel and the court.

"That is all; many thanks," very quietly.

"Do you say that you saw Olney — Oliver Olney — at Nauvoo?" asked the prosecuting attorney.

"Oh, yes. I knew him before. Had seen him in Pittsburg. also in Philadelphia, and in 1836 at Kirtland:" and Wansor was dismissed.

There was a pause; the counsel overhauled the indictment with a nervous eagerness. followed by a blank dismay, and after some hurried consultation they went on.

They then called Ladd, of Mantua. who identified the paper; said that it was signed by John Green in his presence. and acknowledged before him in the presence of Jo Smith and Rigdon. on the day of its date. He knew nothing of the writing or contents of the papers. He understood that the defendant was a son of John Green.

Fred said that the defendant admitted the relationship.

"I suppose. now." said the prosecuting attorney. "that the gentleman is satisfied. and I may now read these papers;" with an injured air.

"One moment, if the court please," and Fred arose.

"The real difficulty in the way of the State is not removed, or even approached. Not a word of evidence has yet been given to show that this paper was ever, at any time, in the hands of the deceased. How, then, can it be claimed that the defendant murdered him to get possession of it? How does the possession of this document by the defendant, tend to show that he had ever even seen the deceased?"

One of the counsel for the State replied in a labored effort, and not without ingenuity. With no reply from Fred, the court unhesitatingly sustained the objection, and excluded the document wholly.

The State staggered on a little further, and in part met the blow it had received from its own witness, Wansor. A man who had known Olney in Ohio had seen the remains of the deceased, and recognized the body as that of Oliver Olney. He called him Olney, and so did others, and the body was spoken of as Olney's. In answer to Fred, he said that he believed that Oliver had a brother John, who resembled him, yet what became of him he never knew.

Others swore that the body was spoken of as that of Olney. It was further shown that the man had a small valise mailed on behind his saddle on the day preceding his death; but, as sworn to by others, no vestige of it had been discovered since his death. And the State closed.

It was somehow apparent to the spectators that the State had failed to make so strong a case as was supposed to exist, and, as often occurs, the outside opinion or impression was much changed, and was concentrating about the leading counsel for the prisoner, who was kindly looked upon, and sympathized with, as the defence. Nearly three days had passed in the trial. Numerous questions had arisen; a great many witnesses had been examined, and yet through all the struggle he had steadily gained on the crowd, court, and bar. Modest, quiet, cool, clear, ready, without having thus far exhibited brilliant qualities, with unceasing good-nature, and the bearing of a gentleman, he had all the time impressed them with the idea of any amount of power and energy in reserve, which they expected to see developed.

When the State closed, Fred drew a long breath of profound relief. He was still anxious, but without doubt of the result. He knew the proverbial uncertainty of juries, but had studied those before him, and had already received from two or three, unconscious glances of that intelligence which a look will flash from one mind to another. Without any opening statement, he called his witness.

When Dr. Ackly took the stand, there was a general movement to gain a good sight of the famous surgeon and somewhat distinguished scientific witness, certainly the most remarkable, of his day, in the West. Slightly above the medium height, and large, with a little stoop in the shoulders, a strong-marked face, dark, with black eyes that could flash out the original ingrained savage, or melt with the tenderness of the enthroned woman, who sometimes ruled them, which were overhung with heavy brows, while from his forehead was swept back heavy masses of coarse black hair. His manner was careless and free; a man of little culture, of commanding talents, iron nerve, and a cool, shrewd, artful, artless method of dealing and swearing, at once impressive, conclusive, and exceedingly dangerous. Like other distinguished medical experts, he was to be retained, and his evidence was an ingenuous argument under oath. Nothing was ever more simple and plain, and as to nothing did he ever seem so utterly indifferent as the wants or wishes of the side which called him; nothing was often so helpful as the seemingly unconscious blows that he appeared to give his own side. He was an intense hater, capable of narrow, mean, and cruel prejudices, and wielded a tongue sharp, bitter, and caustic, as well as soft, soothing, and seductive.

When called, he lazily arose, moved forward, and declined to be seated; stated his profession and residence; he had had some little experience in surgery; was a professor in the Ohio Medical College, etc.; saw the body of the deceased; it was disinterred, and found in a state of good preservation. He went on to say that, assisted by his distinguished friends Dr. Bond, of Warren, and Dr. Jones, of Ravenna, he had made a partial examination. They removed the entire scalp from the cranium, and dissected away the soft parts of the neck, so as to lay bare the spinal column; no injury of any kind had been sustained by the bones of the cranium; no fracture, and hardly an abrasion of the scalp; the skull was removed, and the condition of the brain demonstrated that no serious injury had fallen upon the head; the neck had been dislocated, broken, as people say, and that had caused death, which followed instantaneously; it was not produced by a blow on the head; could not have been by any possibility; it was undoubt-

edly occasioned by the man's being suddenly and vio-
lently thrown from his horse, so as to fall and receive
the whole weight of the body on the head and neck. A
horse suddenly rearing, so as to give an increase of
height, and throwing a man clear from the saddle,
would be equal to the injury. The man was found a
a little at the left of the road, through the woods; as
he was riding along cold and weary, something at the
right, and nearly in front of his horse, had frightened
the animal, when he reared, turned suddenly, partly on
his hind feet, to the left, throwing his rider helplessly
upon his head, and breaking his neck, and where he
fell, he was found. If care had been used, when the
snow melted, the tracks of the horse would have been
found where he turned and ran back; the imprint of
the man's head in the ground would have been discovered, and the profession would have lost the brilliant and useful example of its two members who swore
that the man was killed by blows on his head from a
bludgeon, in the hands of a man on the ground, which
had fractured his skull.

Dr. Ackly was put under a close cross-examination,
— as close as he ever permitted himself to endure; for
he had great power in good-naturedly holding his
cross-questioner at long range, just as suited the exigencies of his case.

He was asked whether he did not think that if a man,
the defendant for instance, had suddenly sprang at the
horse it might not have frightened him so as to have
produced the result named.

Fred asked " if that was a question for an expert."
Ackly turned and scanned Jake with apparent care for

a moment, and answered " that he thought that he might scare a horse, possibly. Horses had their own views of men " — a laugh ; but, lingering a moment, " he thought that if even Jake Green had been there to kill the man, he would not have commenced by trying to induce the horse to run away with him." This produced a sensation marked and distinct. When Ackly left the stand, the chances for the edification of the people, by a public execution, were much diminished. In his testimony as to the injuries to the deceased, he was fully sustained by the two doctors who assisted him.

Fred called several witnesses, who established the fact that the snow fell during the early part of the night in question, certainly before midnight ; that Jake had been about Mantua the latter part of February and March, and that no one had known of his having been in Kirtland ; that he had been into Middlefield and Parkman, in Geauga county, on business, and that late in the night of the homicide he had called at a small tavern, kept by one Blair, within four or five miles of the scene of the death, to inquire his way, going southerly, and was told that when he reached the east and west road so often named, he must turn, take it, and going east, take the first right-hand road ; that it was snowing then, — that he stopped long enough to get supper, when he went on, seeming to be in a hurry. Thus a considerable time was left, during which he was not accounted for. He had evidently traversed that right-hand road the next morning, and very early ; where he was during the intervening time, was not made very apparent.

Fred also called winesses who sustained the statement of Wansor, that Oliver Olney was still living, had been at Kirtland, and had, as was supposed, started west for Nauvoo; that he was a man five feet and about ten inches in height, and that the deceased, by measurement, was barely five feet seven. He also showed the distance from where the body was found, back to the corner, to be nearly a half mile, and that the track claimed to be Jake's came down from the west to the corner of the road in the woods, and then turned south. Then he rested his case confidently, but anxiously. Did mortal lawyer ever try a case that he was not anxious about, with an anxiety which nothing but the final verdict in his favor could relieve?

The counsel for the State had no idea of abandoning the case. They had commenced the trial with a flourish of the confidence which they really felt. Their experience in such trials had been small, and the preparation of the prosecuting attorney was very faulty. Their case had crumbled away in their hands, and had received two or three severe and perhaps fatal blows. They had also, as was natural, under-estimated their youthful opponents, and had suffered for it, as lawyers sometimes do. On the coming in of the court at one o'clock of the fourth day, their best advocate arose for the final argument to the jury.

Middle-aged, of fine person, good face, and not without skill as an advocate, with an ingenious way of grouping things, and a hard, dry way of making points, Mr. Mack arose to present the case for the State, and a hush came over the immense and expectant audience, which thronged the court-room of that warm, early June afternoon.

He began by amplifying the importance and gravity of the case. A murder had been committed in their midst. A young man arose early one morning, and on his way to his work had stumbled upon a corpse, stark, under the snow, — a man done to death by murderers, who had stolen upon, surrounded and murdered him in the woods, alone in the darkness ; and of this the jury were to inquire and judge. For the result they must be responsible. If it were of no moment, if life were of no consequence, the defendant could be acquitted, and the highways given over to bandits, to waylaying assassins.

A man, a stranger, had been slain, no matter by what immediate means, so long as it was made to appear that it was by violence, — whether the man was knocked off his horse or thrown off, if by the agency of the defendant, it was all the law required. He was a stranger, and men called him Olney, — Oliver Olney ; that was his name ; he was known by no other. And that was all that was necessary. No matter though there may have been fifty Oliver Olney's. Besides, it was a man, and not a name, that was slain.

Undoubtedly, several were concerned in the murder, all of whom had escaped but one ; and it was no matter what part he took, whether he struck, or watched, or merely bore away the plunder, he was guilty of the murder. That there were several, was proven by showing one man following on the track, while another was seen approaching the place of the final hunt, from one side, as unquestionably others did, though unseen from other sides. The defendant was proven, — it was admitted that he was within less than a half mile of where the body was found, and at a time awfully near the fatal hour. Nobody knows when the man met his murderers. It may have been early in the night, — suppose it was ; — the defendant was seen approaching the same place early enough to have met him. And if it is said that Jake Green never was east of the corner of the south road, what proof is there of that? Why, that he made tracks early the next morning in the road leading from that corner south. Where was he that night? and what was he doing? where did he stay? with whom? He was not all night walking from Blair's tavern to the corner, and where was Olney killed? He may have been killed west of the corner, and his body carried to the point where it was found, or Jake may have mounted his horse and ridden back, and ingeniously fastened it where it lay. He would know better than to escape on the horse of the man whom he had just murdered, and then he would have walked back to the corner on the new snow, all innocently, and take the road he had inquired for.

And what became of the portmanteau? Somebody stole and rifled that ; who was it? No man was known to be in those woods that night but Jake. If he did not take it, who did? It was not, after long search, found, and when Jake was arrested, he denied that he had been in that locality at all. If innocent, why make this denial? Then remembering all, he became dumb, could not speak, would not speak, and did not speak ; and then this fatal document, which he thrust so fearfully and foolishly from him ; we have not proved that it was ever in the hands of the murdered man, have we? Why, then, did Jake in mortal fear cast it from him? He knew what it was. He knew where he got it. He had murdered a man for it, and was fleeing with it. He knows where he got it, and can tell; and if he did not take it from the dead body of the murdered man, I demand that he tell us where he did get it. Of course he is silent. His act and conduct are a confession that he murdered the man and robbed his body, and then fled with his booty. And such a document! It has not been read; I may not read it; the confession of a crime, a murder and a robbery by his father, and he, the son, committing another murder and robbery to secure it, and of all the unheard-of marvels in courts of justice, that this young and accomplished lawyer should be here, his defender! I stand in the presence of these facts, and of this man so strangely brought together, in utter amazement, almost in awe, and I demand an explanation of him; this man is here defending his enemy — the son of his worst enemy, enemies alike of him and his race — of the human race. Then, with a happy and forcible peroration, he sat down.

The above shows the course of the argument, as well as its spirit. The speech was happy and forcible, and Fred felt that it had made a dangerous impression upon the jury, as it certainly had upon the crowd.

CHAPTER XLVI.

FRED'S ARGUMENT.

THE references to himself surprised Fred somewhat, and he did not know what to think of some of them; but looking at everything as an advocate during a trial, he supposed that they were made by counsel in the exaggerating heat of argument; not unwilling to produce an effect, and not scrupulous as to the means employed. He would, however, seek an explanation and an exploration of the Green paper after the trial, and dismissed both for a time.

The crowd in attendance had been constantly increasing, and on the day of final argument it had become dense almost beyond endurance. Great anxiety was felt to hear the speeches, and especially that of Fred. His reputation as a speaker, and the favor which his conduct of the case and manners had won him, made his speech the event of the trial to be looked forward to. There was a great influx of ladies. Several occupied the bench of the court; others sat on the clerk's table, and still others in two condensed rows between the bar-table and the raised jury-box, so as to be exactly between the speaker and jury.

In the moment's buzz that followed the speech of

Mr. Mack, and as the crowd was readjusting itself, a little movement, a rising and changing of seats, and a rustle of draperies by the ladies, who might be heard fanning and lisping from every part of the packed room, drew Fred's attention to the end of the table at his left; and there, within two yards of him, of all the mortals of the lower world, or immortals of the upper, sat Belle! His brain whirled, and he grasped the bar-table in a spasm. But there she was, — not cold, distant and repellant, as when he sat by her last, but radiant, triumphant and happy. There was the old light that flashed over the icy waters, that inspired him on the speaker's stand, and which now had something more, — something to assure, inspire, and, as it seemed, to reward. She was accompanied by Maud and a beautiful matronly woman, whom Fred did not remember ever to have seen before. A moment, — and he arose, calm, clear and strong, inspired and elevated, for his final effort. He stood for an instant under a weight of sensations, not favorable to rapid or even easy speech, and hesitated and faltered with emotions that interrupted the communication between thought and utterance. None but an advocate can understand the mingled feelings with which he arises in a momentous case, and no advocate has ever described or expressed them, and perhaps they cannot be expressed. Fred's voice was low, and a little plaintive, and hundreds of heads bent sidewise to catch his accents. He never, in after life, when famous as an advocate and orator, was a man of exordiums and perorations. Some simple preliminary matter, bearing directly upon the subject to be discussed, and then the case itself, and when that was presented, he usually stopped rather than closed.

When his voice was connectedly caught, he was saying something about law and its sacredness. "Both parties were struggling for its supremacy, the State appealing to it for punishment, and he for protection; and it was to be vindicated as an avenger or venerated as a protector, as the jury should find that certain facts existed or were doubtful. The most precious thing to the law was a human life; the thing it most abhorred, a murderer. The earth was of consequence because of human existence upon it, and things became property only because they were man's; and as the life of a man was approached, things grew sacred, and its citadel was inviolable. As it was the gravest known crime to take life without law, so when the law, which held life to be so holy, was through mistake or carelessness made the very means of violating, instead of protecting, it, the crime was immeasurably aggravated. The State demanded a punishment, and by the law was to establish with moral certainty that it was entitled to have it inflicted. The presumption that a man was innocent was not an idle formula, floating in the legal atmosphere, but an impregnable barrier, assuring safety, until it was swept away by evidence, and then the defendant only fell by having the ground cut from under his feet. He was not to be convicted of a crime because he failed to prove his innocence. That was the reverse of the rule. It was not sufficient to accuse of murder, and then hang him if he failed to show where he was on a given night. Nor could he be called upon to account for a given thing until it was

shown that at some time, somewhere, somebody else
had held the possession of it. A man, on sudden surprise, may equivocate, and not be guilty of murder;
and if folly is conclusive evidence of crime, how easy
to find a criminal!"—with a glance at the State's attorney. "It is a habit of the human mind, when aught
occurs that it cannot at once understand, to attribute
it to the supernatural, as it is its weakness to believe
the most heinous charge without proof. It is only
when it partly understands that it investigates, and
demands evidence only in trivial cases. If this Jake
was charged with a petty larceny from this man, still
living, even the prosecuting attorney would have ascertained his innocence. But when the man fell from his
horse in the night, he asks you to believe that Jake
Green killed him." These sentences, and many more
which at a grasp epitomized the case, were delivered in
a happy manner, and with great force and energy, and
shattered it ere the advocate had fully entered upon
its discussion.

"The grand jury, by this indictment, accuse Jacob
Green of killing Oliver Olney, in the county of Mahoning, and is to prove each allegation without doubt
or hesitation."

He then recalled the evidence, and said "he believed
that not a word of proof had been given to show that
the scene of the death was within the limits of the
county."

The prosecuting attorney started up, and said "he
was certainly mistaken. He had proved it."

"If you have, you can tell by whom. If the gentlemen, or the court, or any member of the jury, can

recall a word of proof bearing on this formal and also material point, he would thank them to remind him of it."

Then he sat down for a moment. A whispering of the State's counsel, and among the members of the court, with an overhauling of notes, was followed by silence.

By the Court. — "What do *you* propose, Mr. Warden?"

"Merely to show that there is not even the form of a case here. I do not wish it to go off on this point. I will presume or admit for the defendant that the *locus* is within the limits of your county, gentlemen, that you may have the genuine satisfaction of saying, upon your oaths, that the defendant is innocent. He is accused of the murder of Oliver Olney; not a man whose name is to the jurors unknown — any man who may go by any name — but Oliver Olney; not some man whose body after death was, in the absence of all knowledge of the name he bore while living, called Oliver Olney; but Oliver Olney himself, and not another, and no other was murdered.

"If the court please, I make this point here, and have the authorities which I will cite."

The Court. — "It is not necessary, Mr. Warden; the point is well taken, and so the court will rule."

Resuming, — "The theory of the State is that Oliver Olney, a native, and late a resident of this part of the State, was waylaid and murdered, and one man swears that he knew Olney in life; that he saw this body, and thinks it was Oliver Olney, but it may have been

20

his brother John; while others heard the body called Oliver Olney's body.

"We proved by the State's witness, Wanser, that *the* Oliver Olney was alive since this death occurred, and by half a dozen that he left Kirtland for Nauvoo. We prove him to have been five feet ten, while this body, by actual measurement, falls short of that by three inches, and the State three leagues of sustaining its case. This is not a formal matter, but one of vital substance. You are asked to say that this man was Oliver Olney, when not another man has said it, when six or seven say that he was not. You are asked to be certain in this point, when the one witness for the State is uncertain. You are asked to swear by your verdict that you know more than all the witnesses; not only that, but that they are all wrong. Otherwise, this defendant must go acquit. I might rest this defence here, but will not.

"How came this body to be nobody, but a body. The State says, in this indictment, that Jake killed him by fracturing his skull with a bludgeon; that he got himself suspended over the road with a war-club, and when the deceased rode along under him, he made a downward blow and crushed his skull. But my brother Mack, abandoning his two M.D.'s, assumes the equally plausible theory that the defendant scared him to death; that, wanting to kill him so as to rob him, he sprang up in his path and frightened his horse, so that mayhap he would turn and carry him out of his reach, but he happened to throw him and kill him; and that then, while he had every reason to suppose that the body's property was with or on it, he sprang into the vacant saddle, without touching the body, and rode off; and then having rode off, he prudently waited for a snow-storm, so that his tracks might certainly be seen, and then went tracking back, in the most sensible way in the world, to the very scene of his crime, for the very purpose, undoubtedly, of being suspected and detected. He has spoken of marvels, but failed to enumerate among them the most wonderful of all. We have proven that this man was not killed by a blow on the head; that he never received a blow on any part of his person; that he died of dislocation of the neck, which could be produced only by being thrown from his horse; that he died where he fell, and lay untouched, and that there, in the darkness of the night, the heavens kindly distilled over him their pall of beautiful snow, placing their pure white seal upon him, to attest that the cause of his death was innocent!"

This sentence was pronounced in a fervid manner, and produced a sensation. "Murdered? How? By whom? By a man who followed him on foot and would never have overtaken him, and would approach him from behind; by a man who intercepted him,— who knew that he would be there, and when. It was in a deep forest, ere the snow fell, and inky dark. Who would know him, or how would they know him? Oh, gentlemen, the darkness of this case is palpable! 'Mid uncertainty and doubt you are expected to grope about in it, and seize and strangle this unfortunate defendant. Murdered? for what? Why was not the body searched and robbed? For a paper? Who knew that he had a paper? You are asked to assume that he had a paper, and then to assume that some-

body knew that he had; that they knew he would
pass this place at that hour, that they would know
him, and that they could scare his horse, and that
he would throw him off, and that that would break
his neck.   Then after having performed all these probable things the murderer would run off without touching the body of his victim, on which the paper would
probably be.   A murderer would not have run the risk
of a failure in any of these.   He would have been
armed with a gun or pistol; he would have run no
risk, he would have shot him — shot him on his horse
— and then searched and robbed him.   There is no
pretence that he could have been robbed save by the
further pretence that he had a document; and in the
utter absence of evidence that he had this document,
you are to assume that he had it, that somebody knew
that he had it, and that they wanted it, and their want
was so imperious that they would commit a murder for it.

   " Who was this man? Nobody knows. Where did he
come from? Nobody knows. Where was he going to?
Nobody knows. Where did he get this paper? Nobody
knows. What was he to do with it? Nobody knows.
Does anybody know that this body ever had that paper?
No. What is this marvellous document, that anybody
should want it? We are not told even that. Had it
been of value, and pertinent to this case, the court
would have laid it before you. It was ruled out as
incompetent, irrelevant, impertinent, and yet it is the
only point in the case. The only material thing in
it was ruled out of it; and yet we are to deal with it,
and with nothing else. We are not to try this case on
the evidence that we have, but on that which we have

not heard. What is this thing, this marvel of marvels, that winds all about us, and enfolds even the counsel for the defendant? Oh, gentlemen, there are some things that I have so wanted to know—" This was a great cry of heart-anguish that uttered itself, that men who heard it never forgot. He rescued himself. "We are told that it is a confession of murder, made fourteen years ago by the defendant's father, and that the defendant murdered another man to get it! What did he want it for? Of what use could it be to him? What could he do with it? What harm could it do his father? His father was dead; the State has proven that, and he must have known it.

"But if it was of the fatal character claimed, then, indeed, the possession of it by Jake would of itself be sufficient, when surprised with it, to have caused him to speak in the suspicious manner that he did. But the gentleman demands that Jake be compelled to account for this, or that he go and hang for murder. Charge a man with murder, and, if he don't prove himself innocent, hang him! By all means, gentlemen! I would, were I you! If I must still treat this thing, which is not a thing, as in the case when it is out, may I not inquire that as between Jake and an utterly unknown stranger, who, while on his way from no place to nowhere, fell into nothing, which of them would be the most likely to have a paper made by the father of Jake?

"Once and again, as nobody knew this man, and as Jake cannot be presumed to have known more of him than did others, how could he have known that the unknown had this or any paper? or that he ever was alive, so that he could be murdered anywhere, at any time, by anybody?

"Your Honors, on the matter of this document, as it was excluded, I ask you to say to the jury in your final charge that it is not and cannot be an item of proof that can in any way, for any purpose, be considered by the jury in forming any opinion upon any part of this case. And I also ask pardon for asking this instruction."

By the Court. — "We will hear the other side on that proposition, if they think that they can combat your claim."

Resuming, — "It is the theory of the theoretical gentleman that Jake followed this man from Nauvoo. It is not proven that this man ever was in Nauvoo, while it was proven that Jake had not been there for years. There was proof that this man, or some one who resembled him, was seen near Kirtland, and travelled along, and entered the wood from the west, at about dark; but it is not proven that the man found was that man, or that the horse found was the horse which he rode; nor yet that the dead man rode any horse; nor that he was not travelling west, instead of east. But suppose he was the man, — if he was followed, who followed him? 'Jake Green,' answers the eloquent Mack, — but Jake Green came from the North, and could not have followed him. 'But it is the theory of the State,' cries the gentleman, 'that several were concerned in it, — and, like the other assumings of the same high authority, there is not a particle of proof to sustain it. What became of the following man? Jake was not seen with him; had no concert or connection with him; did not know the man who died, nor where he was, or would be. He had business, as was shown; was at Blair's, and left there while it was snowing. The man was found on the bare ground, covered with snow, — with snow as deep over him as on an adjoining log; so that he must have been killed before the snow began to fall, and when Jake was five miles away, at the shortest distance; and yet I am to argue that he did not kill this man, who was thrown from his horse several hours before Green, if he was driven forward by murderous malice, could by possibility have reached the place.

"When at Blair's, he inquired his way; and the roads he travelled were pointed out to him, and he pursued them. The elements prove this. The attesting snow fell to receive and retain his track; and it comes here a witness from the hand of God, an angel white-robed and pure, to declare that this charge is false and monstrous." A murmur, almost a break out of applause, followed these sentences.

"But we are told that Jake was somewhere that night, and was doing something. It did not take half his time to pass from Blair's to the turn in the road, and make that turn where he did make it; and you are asked to imagine that he filled the spare hours with wandering about that desolate and haunted wood, in the darkness of the night, a goblin damned, hunting up and wringing the necks of belated travellers, and galloping about stray horses with an extemporized troop of weird wizards, for the pure malice, the exquisite fun of the thing, and that, having gorged his maw with murder, he attaches his horse, elfin-like, to a root, a devil-snag from the world below, and resumed his man's shape and journey, after having conjured down a snow to hide his victim and his guilt.

" ' Where was he?' demands the gentleman. Sure enough, make the demand when you know that this indictment makes him a mute. Oh, gentlemen, in this rude wilderness world of uncharity and inhospitality — in our sparsely-populated forest country of straggling settlements and intervening wood — shall the belated, benighted traveller, whom weariness overwhelms, or sleep surprises, who sinks by the wayside, or slumbers under a tree, chilled, benumbed, and alone, while you, whom God blesses with hearths and homes, and whom He permits wives to love, and to whom He gives children to caress, lie secure in the circling arms of safety and peace, — shall the forlorn outcast be compelled to account for every moment of time so endured, at the peril of being hanged for any accidental death that may occur within five miles of him?" These sentences were delivered with intense warmth and force, and were greeted with sobs from the ladies. The words " whom he permits wives to love," was a wailing cry of a lonely heart coming out of stormy night.

" Here I leave this case. I have invoked the law for this man's protection. I have called time and space and the elements, and all declare his innocence, which your verdict will echo and record.

" Wonder and astonishment has been expressed that of all men I am here as this man's advocate. This man is my enemy, — the son of my oldest and bitterest enemy, you have been told. It is because he was my enemy that I am here. This message, holy as from

God, and mysterious, as if by inspiration came to me, in my far-off — not home, — I have none : ' Jake Green, your old enemy, is in jail for murder ; he is without money, without counsel, without friends.' Bless, a thousand times, the angel who sent me that message. I hope yet to kneel and kiss the hand that wrote it. It was a summons from Heaven, — the call of calls. He was mine enemy, of all mortals having the strongest claim upon me. And had his father murdered mine, and broken the heart of my mother, and cast me to die by the wayside, I would, as I did, have obeyed it. Through the rifts of eighteen hundred years of time, I heard the voice of the Beautiful One — the peasant-born, who walked the lovely valleys of far-off Galilee — commanding me to love this mine enemy. He was an hungered, with none to feed ; naked, with none to clothe ; sick, with none to minister ; in prison, and none to visit him. And I came ; and I come to you, and lay him and his case in the sustaining hands and charities of the law upon your consciences, my Countrymen, Gentlemen of the Jury." And he sat down.

Not a whisper save his voice, and the occasional signs of applause mentioned, had broken the rapt silence for the hour and a half he was speaking ; and when he ceased a low murmur arose, grew louder and louder, until the aroused court and sheriff united to quell and hush it, and save the propriety of the place. The above, extracted from the columns of a paper of that day, gives most of the argument, with some of the language employed, which is inserted at the hazard of producing an erroneous impression as to the speech, as a whole. Fred was then in the opening flush of his

rare powers as a speaker, and just awakening to the
consciousness of strength, without knowing its extent,
than which, in this world, nothing is more intoxicating.
He was perfect master of himself, and spoke in a
presence and under circumstances calculated to call
out his best. He arose with his audience in his hand,
and carried it whither he would; with his eyes never
from the jury, save when he addressed the court, he
seemed unconscious that another human being was
present. No attempt has been made to reproduce the
speech. It was a little marred by strokes of sarcasm,
but free from redundancy, with here and there a touch
of nature which was irresistible.

Fred closed at about five, and the court directed the
State to proceed with the reply. The original programme of that side was, that the prosecuting attorney
should open the case at the commencement, and that
Mack should open the argument, while Brown made
the final reply. For some reason this was abandoned,
and the prosecuting attorney undertook that rather
unpromising labor. It was the scattered pattering of
rain-drops, after the hurricane had swept the forest
and the bolts had fallen. As he went forward, many
went out. He became disconcerted, confused and ineffective. He finally fell back upon his written opening, under which he partly recovered, but closed before
the usual hour of adjourning, amid a thinning out, restless and weary audience.

The court held an evening session, when Judge Newton, in a clear, luminous, and decisive charge, sub-
stantially relieved the jury of the little labor which the
defence had left for them. They retired before eight,

and returned after an absence of twenty minutes; were called and counted, and when inquired of as to their verdict, shouted altogether, "Not Guilty!" A movement of the vast audience, and then a round of applause with clapping and cheers. Silence was restored, when the court ordered the prisoner to be discharged, and adjourned. While he still sat a moment, bewildered, an aged woman, who had for a day or two been observed about the court-house, and whom nobody knew, pushed through the noisy crowd, sprang to Jake, and threw her arms about his neck. It was Aunt Sally.

There was a general turning and movement towards the trial-table where Fred had sat, to congratulate him; but in some mysterious way he had disappeared.

CHAPTER XLVII.

AUNT SALLY.

ALONE, moneyless, with her bundle, and a little bent with years, but plenty of warmth in a heart early withered, but refreshed, Aunt Sally, unable to secure a passage down the river, turned from the chilly Mississippi to face a winter journey across Illinois, Indiana, and nearly the whole of Ohio, in the sole hope of again seeing Fred, and for the one purpose of aiding him, so far as she might, in penetrating the mystery of his birth and history. As stated, she was absent from her North Carolina home when the incidents of Fred's infancy occurred there, and it was only at the death of her brother that she reached a clear conception of the facts; and then he managed to escape out of the world, bearing with him the name of Fred's father, the importance of which the shrewd Sally quite appreciated, and which she hoped might be in the knowledge of Sam Warden. She had no very definite idea of the distance to be travelled, or of the difficulties, privations, and long-continued, wearing labor of the way. Fred was the one warmth, hope and cheer of her life. How large, and strong, and handsome he must be now! She could not think of him save as the tall, grave-faced, beautiful boy she had

(316)

parted with now so many years ago; and he must be a
man. She had once in a long while heard a word or
rumor of him, and he must be in Ohio, somewhere
about Mantua. Then she wondered what he would
say; wouldn't he be so glad to see her? He would
never forget her. Perhaps he was married. What an
idea, — little Fred with a wife! She did not at all
wonder that he had not come to see her. Of course, he
would never go near the saints; they might murder
him. So she thought, and mused, and croned over and
over, in her lonely old heart, her old woman's dreams,
memories and visions of Fred. The roads were deep
and soft, and often long stretches of desolate, inter-
minable, black, tenacious mud stretched over the
dreary, flat expanse of empty prairie which lay between the remote farm-houses. Sometimes she went
astray; some days she made not more than a mile or
two, and some, she was so weary, sick and sore, that
she could not move at all; and one night she spent on
the lonely, blank prairie. She was often hungry, many
times drenched with rains, — chilled and benumbed.
All along, at the farm-houses, she was kindly received,
warmed and fed, and cheered on her way. Men
wondered at her courage and hardihood; women, who
understood it, honored her devotion, and wept over her
sufferings, and little children gazed at the wrinkled
face and gray hair, lit up with the large bright eyes, as
something weird and uncanny. So across the muddy,
spongy Illinois, into and across fair wooded Indiana,
and over the intervening parts of beautiful and cultivated Ohio, the lonely old woman journeyed. Twice
she was detained by illness for two or three weeks,

and once by lameness, that threatened to prevent her journey. She traversed the southern sections of the States, and reached Cincinnati before mid May. The roads were now good and the weather fine, and hopefully she set her face to the North.

At near nightfall, on one of the afternoons of an early June day, Turner observed in front of his hotel an old woman, tall and gaunt, gray and grim, soiled and travel-stained, supporting herself on a long staff, with thin and tattered garments, and an old, worn, quilted hood, from which her long, gray elfin locks escaped in tangled rope-like masses. She stood in front of his house, looking about as if lost and bewildered. He approached, and kindly accosted her. She started a little at his voice, and looked sharply into his kindly blue eyes. "Is this the Corners? I otter know; but it's a long wile sin' I seen 'em."

"These are the Corners," replied Lewis.

"Are ye Lewis Turner? I tho't I knowd ye. I allow ye've forgot me?" turning full upon him. "I'm her as was Sally Green in these parts."

"Sally Green! Aunt Sally! I'm surprised. Why we thought you must be dead. Your brother's dead, ain't he?"

"Yes, and I've come back all the way ter find Fred. Ye knew Fred?"

"I guess I did. Come in, Aunt Sally, and let me care for you."

"I've got no money; nary cent."

"That makes no difference," said the kind-hearted landlord.

Washed cleanly, and decently clothed, Aunt Sally

learned with astonishment that Jake was then on his trial for murder, and that Fred was defending him.

"Wal! wal! wal! that beats all nater! Jake was allus a 'ard case. I'm not much 'stonished at it ; but Fred! An' Fred's a lawyer! an' a tall, 'ansom man, I know. Wal! wal! wal! Poor Jake! he was a purty baby ; an' his mother, 'ad she a' lived —" and a flood of old time memories of the life among the mountains came over her with a stir of tenderness for Jake, on trial for his life, and thought to be guilty, though the Mantua people had a strong faith that Fred would clear him. She found that it was thought strange that he had undertaken the defence. She was also told that Sam Warden had just returned from Missouri, and had been taken over to Canfield, and that many inquiries had been made about her. Some parties from Newton Falls or Warren had in some way been interested in making inquiries among some of the Mantua people about Fred and her brother, and about her, and they wanted her. On consultation between Turner and Uncle Bill, it was thought that Aunt Sally, who had at once determined to go to Canfield, should be sent over. Her fare was paid on the stage, and she was furnished with money and a few necessaries, and on the day after her arrival she was on her way to Canfield.

She reached there the next morning, with a letter from Turner to the landlord of the stage-house, who found her a place with a poor woman, and as soon as she received her breakfast, she hurried off to the crowded court-house. Accustomed to crowds of men, she pushed her way into the court-room, and caught a

momentary glimpse of Fred, as he arose to say a word
to the court. Before he sat down, he turned an instant
fully towards her, and that was Fred! How like a
beautiful angel he beamed upon her! All the misery
of her weary winter journey seemed a small price.
What a priceless boon to an aged and solitary crone is
a young man upon whom she can expend the hoarded
sweets of woman's measureless love for man — motherly, sisterly, womanly — a great stream mingled of
all, and pure in all!

At the recess of the court Aunt Sally remained inside, secured a more favorable position, and heard all
the argument. As the case was put together against
Jake, her attention was called to him, worn, pale,
sulky and cowering. He sat, enduring as he might,
and as she looked she pitied him — solitary, friendless, and poor, with her blood — a child of her girlish
friend. She found that she still had a place in her
heart for him.

When Fred arose, she knew that all that could be
said would be urged, and she somehow felt that Jake
would be saved. Her long sojourn among the Mormon
leaders had familiarized her with the idea of courts and
lawyers. Vaguely it came to her, the relation of these
parties to each other. This Fred, the cheated and out-
raged child, standing here and defending the son of
him who had so injured him for his life, and that son
his old malignant enemy!

As if, in some dark way, John Green had foreseen
the strait to which his own child would be brought, and
had taken this infant, and by black charm and spell had
bound him to a strange way and life, so that he should

finally serve Jake in his hour of need. She felt that
the over-ruling hand of God, or some nearly equal
power, that usually had its way, had shaped it all;
that Jake would be saved, and the glory should be
Fred's; and as something of this, shadowy and elfin-
like, passed darkly before her vision, Jake grew upon
her tenderness. How proud she was of Fred! What
a glory that he should come here, and push other men
out of the way, and command and subdue men and
women, judges and lawyers, rooted in no home, and
standing on no hearth! As she looked and listened, she
lost the meaning of his words; the sound of his rich
and full voice became a heavenly melody to her, and
his face and form expanded and towered up, and were
transfigured. Thus wrapt and enchanted, she watched
and worshipped till he sat down, and the enchantment
was broken. She watched him, and placed herself
anear as he passed out; but he did not turn toward
her, nor did she feel chilled that he did not. She knew
that he would turn to her, and perhaps let her kiss his
hand, when this was over, and she was content. She
went out and came in, and was there in her place and
waited; she saw the light and glory pass out from
Fred's face, and knew that he was weary and worn,
and needed rest and comfort. Then more and more
Jake grew on her kindness; and when the final words
of the jury were pronounced, and the whirlwind of
applause swept through the court-room and subsided,
she pushed forward, but Fred had disappeared. She
got near Jake, and when, in the hush that came, the
court announced his freedom, she called him by name;

21

he turned and recognized her, burst into tears, and was clasped in her arms.

After the disappearance of Fred. Jake was the principal object of interest. and the crowd and jury pressed about him eagerly. congratulating him upon his acquittal. and becoming immediately interested in Aunt Sally. whose sudden appearance upon the scene at this final moment had the charm of old romance about it, and invested her with much importance. She was at first supposed to be his mother, but when it became known that she was Aunt Sally. who had nursed and cared for Fred. the interest became warm and general, — for in some way the outline of Fred's history had become as well known in Canfield as in Mantua. Jake and his aunt were attended by a numerous procession to her humble quarters. after which the people proceeded to Fred's hotel, to call him out and cheer him.

CHAPTER XLVIII.

AFTER.

WERE it not often the cruelest, it would sometimes be the funniest thing in the world, could we see how blindly, and perhaps blissfully, men sport with their own fortunes, or the elements of their own fate; gayly and wantonly toying with, picking up and throwing down, running after and casting away as bubbles or trifles the factors of fates, the clews to fortunes, the keys to mysteries dearer to them than life.

Here was this youth, but a moment ago, holding in his hand, refusing to open and read it, strenuously struggling against its being read, arguing against and invoking authority to prevent his hearing what had shaped his life and pointed its destiny, and which would, at once and forever, have dissipated the nameless shadow in which he grew up. — have dissolved the invisible but potent chain that had so hopelessly bound him. Yet with what an air he cast the oracle down, never so glad as when it went back to silence and darkness, and left him to gnaw at his chain in the old shadow! Like Polyphemus, strong, but blind, he repelled it all for the sake of a sordid wretch, whose whole carcase, heart and soul thrown in, was not worth the idlest wish his advocate had ever breathed.

(323)

He had spoken in a sort of mental exaltation, such as usually accompanies the successful exercise of the best powers of a fine speaker of fervid feelings; quickened, as we have seen, by the inspiring presence of Belle, yet ballasted with the weight and gravity of the occasion; not strong and indignant, as when on the platform, but softened, elevated, exalted, with a little touch of pathos running through his tone, that went at once to the fountains of feeling and sympathy of his hearers.

When he sat down, he dropped from the upper atmosphere again to earth, and when, in the flattering elements of threatened applause, he ventured to look again to the place filled by Belle, it was empty; nor could he catch a flutter of the vanishing drapery. He avoided the press as much as he could, and came back to the evening session anxious for nothing but the termination of the case, the result of which no longer remained doubtful. If it did not run into the night, he had formed the purpose of leaving Canfield that evening, and escaping from a presence that had so haunted him. He took occasion, while the jury were out, to have a few words with Jake, to whom he also gave nearly all the small amount of money he had; and when the verdict was announced, after a word to his associate, he escaped, during the tumult that followed, by a near side-door, down a private stairway and out into the open air, with heart and brain, mind and soul, body and limbs crushed into a weary, broken mass, with the one relief, — escape.

It was a wondrous young summer night, with a full moon struggling with low, running clouds, and a lively air moving and rustling the maturing foliage of the numerous trees in little plashy waves about him. He hurried across a corner of the common to a narrow lane, which led to a beautiful maple wood, whose green tops had been beckoning to him ever since his arrival in the village. He walked rapidly, almost running, until he passed the straggling houses and cottages of the town, and found himself on the soft turf under the massive old trees, whose darkness promised a wood of some extent. The strain that had been on him was suddenly removed, and the burden which had weighted even his sleeping hours had dropped from him; he felt the relieving sense of work done, a task achieved, which is one of the rewards of labor. But as he fell back from the height of his great struggle to his old self, there were no sweet associations of tenderness and love to strew and brighten his triumph, or cheer and solace his weary spirit, or sustain an exhausted physical frame. What mattered it, save to the miserable Jake, of whom he could think of no commendatory word to say, even in his defence, whether he had failed or succeeded? What eye would grow bright, and what voice grow soft? And Belle — the inscrutable, mysterious Belle, who came to inspire and help — pshaw! not to help him, — at least, not for his sake, but only for the sake of the cause it was his fortune to advocate. But what under heavens was there in this case, the fortunes or fate of this Jake, to interest her? It must be something connected with her journey to Nauvoo, — and that journey might account for her absence from Martha's wedding.

How cool and sweet the shadow of the wood was;

how glad he was to get away from the crowd, and how
restful to throw himself upon the ground and kick his
limbs out! This Belle. — of course she knew her
power over him; perhaps it pleased her to exercise
it, and he hated and despised himself as a great feeble
mooing calf, that he had so abjectly abased himself in
the dust at her feet, and without daring to raise
his eyes to hers, had only asked that he need not be
compelled to avoid her, if accident threw him into her
presence. And he mentally swore, out there on the
ground under the trees, that he never would go into
her presence again: and he was glad that he had,
in the coldest way in the world, merely acknowledged
her presence when he last met her. He remembered
with pleasure that he had only stared at her once that
afternoon. Lord! what a look he received from her!
What an incorrigible fool he was — an ass, a very —
ass; and he smote the ground with his heel in self
scorn. "What ears I must have " — reaching out his
hands — " and there are other asses — hear them bray,"
as a shout like a cheer, and still another, reached him.
" Let them cheer, — the damned fools! Lord, how they
opened these same mouths to-day! What a contempt
a man feels for men, when he has seen them bobbing
and ducking about him. What are they worth? and
to think that this race should think that they were of
consequence enough to have God come down out of
heaven for them. — save them, as it is called, and
even He couldn't do it, so folks say. That was too
much for even omnipotence." There was a star, just
then, as the leaves flew aside. " Let me raise one of
my long ears and brush them out of the way, — make

them useful." Then he rose and followed the path deeper into the wood, trying now to collect and crystallize his thoughts, and ashamed of his own weakness. But he had been too profoundly stirred to recover himself, and finally the darkening sky, and rain pattering on the leaves, admonished him to make his way back. The crowd had dispersed, and most of the houses were darkened when he reached his hotel, which was still open, but quiet, and he went at once to his room.

He found it lighted, with Aunt Warren in it, anxiously waiting his return. She was an elderly spinster, almost criminally plain, whose unblessed, lonely life had been spent in other peoples' houses, and for their comfort and convenience. Not without character was she, and full of womanly kindness. She was a sort of cousin of the landlord, who gave her a home, and received in return the labor, care and fidelity of three or four servants. She had taken at once to Fred, and had made his comforts and wants her special care. The only fault she found with him was that he wanted too little — would not have much done for him — was not a man to be pampered and petted. So towards the close of his nearly two weeks' stay, they were very old and good friends. She was immensely relieved when he came in, but was struck with his worn and jaded air.

"Oh, I'm so glad you've come! Nobody knew what had become o' you. There's been everybody to inquire after you. The whole crowd came and called for you, and wanted you should make 'em a speech, and they give ye three cheers."

"I heard the noise," with the utmost indifference;

and seating himself by an open window, he thrust his feet and hands out into the falling rain.

"Oh, you mustn't!" exclaimed the alarmed Warren, "you'll ketch cold;" and fussing about until she got him to pull himself in, she closed the window.

"Do you know whether Jake — Jake Green — has been here this evening?"

"The man you cleared? Oh, he was here, and his aunt with him."

"How? What?" springing up; "his aunt? Aunt Sally?" with vivacity.

"Yes; that was her name, — an old, gray woman, come all the way from Nauvoo."

"When was she here? Where is she now? Oh, I must see her now, — at once!"

"You can't to-night; she's gone into the country somewhere, — she an' Jake. They came to see you, and she asked everything about you; said she hadn't seen ye for mor'n twelve year."

"It's strange!" said Fred, sitting down wearily. "Did they start back to Mantua?"

"No; somebody took 'em home with 'em. Jake is a great lion. I wish you'd been here."

"I'm glad I wasn't, — no, not glad, for I missed Aunt Sally. Old Aunt Sally, then, is alive, and came all the way — a thousand miles — to see me!" with a softened voice. "She must be quite old and poor. Aunt Warren, she is the only thing on this earth who ever loved me that was permitted to live, and it would have killed her if she hadn't been old and tough," — sharply and bitterly.

"Don't say that, — don't say that," — brightly and

gayly. "There is one of the sweetest and most beautiful young ladies in the world, who will give her eyes for you in a minute."

"Oh, Aunt Warren"—without the slightest lighting up of his face—"it's pleasant for you to banter me; but don't to-night."

"You'll see, you'll see! an' so 'll everybody."

"Aunt, I shall go in the morning, and I shall be really sorry to part with you. Have you any friends, relatives, or home, except this?"

"No. I've always been nobody. My father an' mother died before I can remember, and I had no brothers or sisters, uncles or aunts. I never had no chance in the world, and have always lived and worked for others." She said this uncomplainingly, but a little sadly.

Fred felt a pang of self-reproach at his unmanly repining. He, a healthy young man, full of strength, and, as he now knew, of power, to run off in a fit of spleen into the woods, and kick the ground in angry discontent, and curse men; and because—after all—because a woman scorned him, while here was this woman who had never known heart, home or love, and yet was toiling on cheerfully.

"Aunt Warren, I'm weary of boarding in a hotel,—of having no home. I will scrape together a little money and buy a little cottage, under some trees, and buy a cow, and you and Aunt Sally shall live with me. She is old, and shall milk the cow and feed the pigs, and you shall keep the house, and we'll have a very pleasant time of it."

"Yes, we will. Oh, if you'd seen and hearn what I

did, you'd never think of any old aunt again. I wish
I knew what had happened," — a pause; "you didn't
eat any supper, — let me bring you something."

"Not a thing."

"Not a glass of milk?"

"No, thank you."

"What will you have for breakfast?"

"Breakfast? Good Lord! I sha'n't want any."

"Then go to bed. Have sweet, sweet dreams, and
get up and feel better. Good-night."

The mind of the young man was healthy; only when it
was stirred up as it had recently been was it that he felt
to murmur, and now the thought of this faithful, patient
woman came in as the needed agent, that precipitated
the bitter and staining matter to the bottom. He sat
long by the window listening to the soothing plash of
the rain against the building, and raised the casement
to hear its patter and drip among the leaves; then
removing his clothes, laid himself down under its
drowsy influence. Wearied almost beyond endurance,
his benumbing memory could not retain the impressions of the liberated faculties, and oblivion finally
came. The last that he remembered, he was lying
under the trees on the grass, partly asleep, and was
aroused by a slight sensation about one ear, and turning his head, saw Belle sitting near him with a clover
blossom in her hand, and blushing with arch innocence.

He awoke in the morning to find himself really
down on the hard, bruising facts of life, with nothing to
buoy him up, or relieve the aches and miseries of his
position. On trying to arise, he discovered that he
was weak and sore. His right arm was almost immov-

able, stiffened by the force and energy of his gestures of the day before. He had been unable to eat his usual food, and had taken but little sustenance, and he was languid and dizzy. He approached the window, to find the rain still falling, and when he turned within, everything was dark and hopeless. Like a gallant bark, which, storm-tossed, had found shelter for the night in a land-locked bay, and whose mariners in the morning found while they slept the waters had subsided, and their ship lay broken and bruised upon the impaling points of rocks. He was obliged to exert himself, he dressed, and went down to breakfast. The hotel was still crowded, and men and ladies came admiringly about to congratulate him, and sympathize with his apparent illness. He answered gayly he knew not what, and what he said was almost cheered. He tried to eat, and could not. He drank a glass of water, and went back to his room to arrange for his departure. He wanted to go by private carriage to Warren, where he would take the stage. He made inquiries for Jake and Sally, and was told that they left the night before. He thought he would get over to Mantua, where he would find Aunt Sally; would go over to the Carmans and rest, and visit the Rapids, which somehow had a fascinating interest for him.

It still rained, and as he went back to his room he remembered that he had not more than ten dollars of money, not half enough to pay his bill, to say nothing of hiring a carriage. Strange to say, he had not yet learned the value of money, and knew no mortal of whom he could borrow a dollar. He sat down in a listless way, staring out into the still falling rain, without the power of being soothed by it, and worse beaten than he ever remembered to have been.

How long he sat he did not know or care; it was so much of time to be gotten over. He was in a sort of cold, aching stupor. At some time came a little knock, and the patter of Aunt Warren's feet. She came immediately up to him, and handed him an envelope, addressed in a lady's hand, wholly unknown to him. He took it listlessly, and looked at it with the utmost indifference.

"Open it," said Aunt Warren. He did so, and read:

" DEAR FRED, —

"Will you come to me at once?

" BELLE."

One moment of stupid surprise, when the light and hope of heaven came into his heart and flashed through his frame; he sprang to his feet, and turned to Aunt Warren with a great, eager interrogation in his eyes.

"There is a gentleman below wants to see — oh, I'm so glad!"

Half dazed, and as if in a dream, Fred followed Aunt Warren below, and was met by Mr. Marbury, whom he remembered to have seen each day about the court-house, and seemingly with Wansor, on the other side of the case. He came forward with the most cordial warmth to Fred, and held out both his hands. "Let me congratulate you, which I do with my whole heart and soul. I have a carriage here, and trust I am to carry you to Mr. Morris's, where your presence will give the greatest pleasure, and a good deal more, — I think I ought to say!"

"Mr. Marbury, this unexpected kindness takes me by surprise, and I have no pleasure in the world but to go with you."

"My dear sir, surprises rule these days, and I trust that none but pleasant ones await you."

Fred packed his valise — punched things into it — found his bill paid, gave his last ten dollars to Aunt Warren, entered the carriage, and was driven rapidly towards Newton Falls. The clouds had broken, — laughing fields of glorious sky appeared 'mid the clearing heavens, and looked down with, "Dear Fred, will you come to me? Belle." "Dear Fred, will you come to me?" sparkled in the sun; "will you come to me?" glittered in the bright drops; "will you come to me?" from the birds, the grass and the trees, from everything and everywhere.

What was it, — what could it — could it — mean? And for a moment the impossible seemed plausible and probable. But his mind soon returned to its healthier tone of the real and possible. Marbury was at first disposed to be conversational. He soon found that the young man, however brilliant as an orator, and logical and eloquent as an advocate, was neither a happy conversationalist, nor, although silent, a very brilliant listener, as with a bright smile he treasured up some of his wildest answers, possibly for Belle's delectation. It seemed to him that whatever was his usual frame of mind, — that of a sparkling June morning, after a rain, and the day after the close of an important trial, and while going to meet his possible lady-love, alone with another, a middle-aged man, he was slightly preoccupied; and he found abundant employment in furtive glances at his companion's face, and guessing at his probable thoughts.   But we'll leave the speculative Marbury the full monopoly of his gatherings, and if he should happen to get off a noticeable thing, we will give him the benefit of our circulation.

CHAPTER XLIX.

THE PORTRAIT AGAIN.

OVER the Morris mansion, somehow, was an air of
rather anxious expectation. Belle arose quite
early. I'm sorry to say, that this had been the prevailing tone for some time. Her face had a sweet look
of exultation. She did not sit much, or stand at ease,
or busy herself with any particular thing ; nor did she
talk, or seem anxious for the society of others. But
something like being in readiness for some very unusual
and grave thing which was approaching ; something
that had been labored for, longed for, — that might
have never happened, but which seemed certainly approaching, — the present was already tremulous with its
vibratory nearness. She was not at all serene ; many
long breaths, not to say sighs, would come, and would
not bring relief; and once or twice she clasped her
hands as in deep mental prayer. It rained, and would
rain. She finally, very quietly, but decidedly, ordered
the carriage to move off for Canfield, and pretty soon
wondered whether it had reached the hotel, and had
Fred received her note, and how did he look, and what
would he say. — would he come ? " Dear Fred, will you
come?" " Dear Fred ! " surely she might say that to

(335)

him. Didn't he deserve that? She had hesitated over it — that "dear" — and now she thought of it without a blush. Then she went to her marvellous room, half drawing-room, half boudoir, and several other sweet places all on the ground-floor, in a wing, among the three rooms devoted to her use. There she changed the position of a full-length portrait, with reference to the light, and had a hurried conversation with Maud; and stepped to one of her inner rooms and talked with some one, a lady — the voice indicated — there, and as she came out, the voice said, " Don't fear me, I saw him yesterday, and neither fainted nor shrieked." Then she went out and looked ; then the rain ceased and the clouds parted and began to clear, and she looked again. It grew toward noon; something had happened, and then over the rise of ground came the little fast-stepping " post-boys," their bay coats steaming ; the top of the carriage was thrown back, and two gentlemen were on the cushions. They turned in at the gate and swept around the circling drive to the front piazza ; the world turned also, and more rapidly, and the next moment the most charming, self-collected, perfect woman of society stood cool and alone, as if to receive an ordinary morning caller. She did not mean to meet him as an ordinary morning caller, by any means ; and when he sprang with his wondering face from the carriage — which drove off — she stepped eagerly forward ,and extended her hands to him. He took them, and could not utter a word.

"I'm so glad you've come !" in the sweetest of little voices.

"Oh, Belle, — Mrs. Williams !"

"Belle, — call me Belle ; all who love me call me Belle," in the same sweet voice.

" Love you, —I adore you !   I — "

" Hush ! " in a lower voice.   " You have already told me that, and I believe it," with a wondrous sweet suffusion on her face.   " Let us speak of some other things," and she led him forward along the veranda, towards her domain.   " You look thin and worn.   I hope you've not suffered, and you will rest now.   Oh, Fred ! do you know we were in raptures with you yesterday ? " — what a change in the subject !   Her arm was in his, although she had withdrawn her hands after the first pressure.   " Dear Fred " was only a dear friend, after all, as he knew the moment his thoughts came back to him.   " Let me invite you to my parlor. I left Maud there a moment ago," and Maud left it the moment after, as she was told to do.   They entered, and Belle motioned him to a seat which happened to command, in an admirable light, the portrait she had adjusted just before.

As Fred paused, bewildered with everything, and especially bewildered with the supreme loveliness of Belle, never so ethereally and spiritually beautiful as now, he saw the portrait.   His eyes dilated, amazement came into his face.   He lifted his hands, recoiled, as if from a blow, took a step forward, and stood speechless ; for there, complete and perfect in form, face, color, air, and feature, looking him mockingly in the eye, was his exact image, his counterfeit very self, and he thought it would speak.   The color left his face, a tremor shook his frame, and clasping his hands, with a

22

low crushed out voice, " My God, my God, who is this, Belle?" with an imploring look.

She came to his side, and laid her hand on his arm.

" Dont you know? Does not something tell you who this was?"

" My father! My father! God in heaven! My father!" and clasping his hands, he dropped on his knees before it, while a great rush of feeling swept over and through him. " I see here " — with a voice gradually sinking to a whisper — " the form and face of my father." Sobs shook him convulsively; and rising and stepping nearer, he reverently bent his head and placed his lips upon one of the hands; then turning to the sobbing girl at his side, " And he is dead?"

" He died in your infancy."

A pause.

" Belle, Belle, I implore you, — can you tell me of my mother? can you show me her image?"

" I can." She pushed open a door, and there walked into the presence of the more amazed Fred the beautiful, but now fearfully agitated matron who had attended Belle in the court-room. Had a spirit risen at the invocation of Belle, and assumed flesh and raiment, Fred could not have been more amazed. " Are — are you my mother?"

" I am your mother!" with a look and voice of intensest love. She wavered as she spoke, and was caught in the blessed and blessing arms of her son. A mother's form was never sustained by purer hands or truer son. She did not faint, or lose consciousness. She had the day before managed to see him at his hotel, and had found self-control afterwards to hear his speech, and had been taken away without being entirely overcome. Now with a flood of tears, with which his as freely mingled, she recovered herself. " Mother! mother! my mother! I have a mother, my beautiful mother! and I'm a happy little boy, with somebody so dear and sacred to love, who will let me love her. Oh, my mother! and you thought I was dead — and this — my father?"

" Ethfred," recovering. " I've heard what you've suffered. That was my husband, my — "

" Don't, don't, mother! you need not say that to me, your son; I know — I know — that must have been — 'Ethfred'! That is the name, and you are the mother of my dreams in some far tropical land. How came all this, Belle? Who made these discoveries? Who brought my mother here, whose name I don't even know?"

" She did!" cried his mother; " this precious, precious Belle. No love and devotion can reward her."

" You — Belle? Is this work yours?"

" Well," said the happy girl, dropping her head, and in a low voice, " I had seen and — and studied this portrait a great many times — I was a little taken with it. Well, one day, over to dear Uncle Seth Carman's, this portrait came through the little arbor, and walked around into the house. Then I knew you were his son. I had heard the story of your father's death, and of your history, and I knew that that was a mistake; so I wrote letters, and did things," very demurely.

" You, your very self, you, Belle?" — silence.

"She herself, Belle, employed detectives, made a long winter journey to North Carolina, and another to Nauvoo; she conducted it in person."

"Oh, Belle! There is nothing in the world I can offer that you will accept," — sadly. A pause, and sadder still, "You could not trust me with my own secret?"

"It might not be so. Are you unwilling to owe it to me, Fred?" reproachfully.

"Gladly, — oh, gladly!"

"She did not let me know it until after I came. I knew something was going on, for she sent to have me come and bring this precious portrait. What an exact likeness! How handsome he is, isn't he, Belle?" No answer to this.

Then came a little knock, and Maud came in and gave her congratulations. Then Mr. Morris, who declared that he had always liked Fred; then Marbury, and then in one way and another, by littles, from each of them, except from Belle, Fred came to know all that is known to the reader.

He was ever returning, with the fondness of a lover, to his newly-found mother, studying the form and features of his father, asking questions of his mother, and looking at the now demure and shy Belle with a wondering love; and all the time the idea was repeating itself: "Dear Fred" is "dear friend," — only that.

Curiously enough, in all the discussion among this happy group, on that long June day, not a word save that of his mother in any way escaped from any one, that this discovery and restoration relieved Fred from the prejudice attendant upon his supposed birth.

Indeed, in that party that matter never could have arisen, even in thought, for none of them had ever shared in it.

Belle suddenly asked Fred if he "had seen Aunt Sally? That was the most of a miracle after all, — her coming in, as in a story."

Fred had not. He understood that she and Jake had left. "I will call her," said Belle, and Aunt Sally came, fairly beaming with joy. Fred sprang to her, and pressed her in his arms, when she was too happy to speak. "And so, Aunt Sally, you came all the way from Illinois to tell me what you knew of me, and to love me, you dear old auntie!"

Then, turning to his mother: "Mother, she is the only woman who has ever loved me all these years, — indeed, the only human being."

"Do you really think so, Fred?" asked Maud, with a meaning glance at Belle; "well, we are all going to love you enough now, to make that all up."

"I've learned all your sad story from Aunt Sally," said his mother, scarcely restraining her tears, "and I know what a precious friend she has been to you, and to me as well."

Then Sam Warden and Jake came in. Jake tried to thank Fred, and told him "he allus thought suthin' was wrong about 'im, but never knowed wat." Sam Warden came in for his say, and it was explained to Fred how he came to be there. Marbury spoke of the way that the Green confession was treated by Fred in court, and that they never could get a sight of it, in the hands of the prosecuting attorney, until at the close of the third day of the trial; they had thought that they must rely on Sam, the portrait, and Fred's mother, for the last scene. Fred was asked if he would like to see that document.

"Not just now; when I am more myself. My mother's story has not been told me yet. You all know more of me than I do. I feel as awkward and stupid as if I was just made. I'll find time for that paper soon enough."

In answer to Marbury, Fred afterwards said that the document was actually in the possession of the deceased man, whose name he presumed was White, and who was accompanied by Olney to Kirtland; that White was supposed to be an adherent of Rigdon's, who was said to have established himself near Pittsburg, and he may have been on his way there from Kirtland. This paper was undoubtedly in the valise, which was said to have been carried by the man, and probably, when the horse ran back, as it must, with the saddle partly under him, the valise opened, and this paper fell out, as Jake solemnly declared that in walking along the road his foot struck the package, and knocked it out of the snow; that he picked it up and carried it on, and never knew what it was, fully, as he could not read much; he first examined it the evening after, and the wrapper then bore appearances of the water-stains made by the damp snow. Jake was following as fast as he could a debtor of his father, in the hope of recovering a debt; but no proof of this could be made at the trial, and he thought that it would be dangerous to attempt to give to the jury Jake's version of how he came by the papers. Some one, in passing along that morning, had undoubtedly picked up the valise, but dared not make it known, for fear of being implicated in a supposed murder.

CHAPTER L.

THE STORY.

WHAT strange sensations, what a new atmosphere sprang up within and about Fred! Here was a mother, his mother, this noble and handsome woman, with her hair silvered, and the lines of suffering drawn on her softened face. How lovely she was to him, and how natural and instinctive his love for her! There always was a place for her in his heart, and she stepped at once and fully into it. "Mother — my mother!" he was saying to her and to himself. This father he could see, — but then he could see himself in him, and was not vain, and he wouldn't let his notions run into form, much less expression; but he found himself with all the voices about him, wondering what was the feeling of a man towards his father. Father and mother, — but who and what were they? Where did they come from? When and where did they meet? How new and strange it all was! Then the cloud and shadow of his life were at once and forever dispelled. Now he could love this peerless Belle. who had done all this. The benefaction she had conferred gave him the right to kneel and adore her. This, at least, he could do, and he looked very much as if he would do it literally. Curious and expectant eyes were

(344)

on these two, — Maud's, in triumph, with a shade of anxiety; the mother's, with love and certainty; Belle's father's, with gratified complacency; while Marbury was treasuring with suppressed enjoyment two or three things which occurred on the homeward drive that morning. The time for them would come, and he could wait; as for Belle, she went around, not yet wholly at peace, though wonderfully collected and composed, innocently avoiding everybody's eyes, especially those of Fred. Thus happy, pleasant talk ran on until somehow Fred and his mother found themselves with Belle, alone, in her apartment. Then Fred's mother told her story to the living son, whom she remembered as lying amid the flowers, under the palms, surrounded with fragrance and the loveliness of that tropical clime, and who now sprang to her arms a grown man, full of intellect and fervor, gentle and tender as when she nursed him; and it was not a dream. But all the cruel past had arisen with him, fresh and torturing, and she told the story with much agitation and many tears. Some passages of it drove Fred almost mad; and once or twice Belle interposed to recall him to himself.

This, in substance, was what she told: Her name was Mary Sewall. Her father, in a right line, descended from the old Sewall; was born and educated near Boston. She had one brother George, three or four years her senior. Her parents died early, after which she resided with an uncle and aunt, on her mother's side. When George was sixteen or seventeen, he entered the navy as a midshipman, and remained in the service until his death, which occurred while he was abroad in 1830. A far-off cousin on her mother's side, with whom she in a way grew up, early became her lover, and when she was not more than fifteen, they became engaged. He grew up idle and dependent upon her uncle, and possibly the fact that she inherited a fortune had much to do with his pursuit of her. It was understood that the marriage should not take place until she was eighteen, the age when she would, by her father's will, become mistress of a certain portion of her property. She did not know, at the time, what were her feelings toward her lover; she only knew that as she grew older, the idea of marriage with him became unpleasant. But as the time was remote, she did not trouble her mind much with it. Her cousin became very irregular in his habits, and negligent of attentions to herself. She, to a certain extent, repelled him; without ever formally putting an end to her nominal engagement, she had determined that marriage should never take place between them, and treated him with distance and coldness. He was a favorite of her aunt's, who did what she could to maintain harmony between them. Her brother was expected home in the autumn, when she would be seventeen, and she intended, with his aid, to have the affair with her cousin ended. Her brother had, during the summer, written to her glowingly of a young South Carolinian, who had spent the summer, much of it, on shipboard, as a guest of the captain, while cruising in the Mediterranean. His name was James D'Arlon, or Darlon, a descendant of an old Huguenot emigrant, and the last of the line in the United States. They came; and — pointing to the portrait — Mrs. D'Arlon said, "That was painted two years later; yet, save that he was more youthful, you see how he appeared to me." After a pause, "We became lovers at once, — you know what that means." A pause. "My brother was almost in ecstacies over this. We were young; but there seemed no good reason for delay, and the following spring we were married" — a pause. "No young girl loved more fondly and devotedly, and no man was ever more deserving. After marriage we went abroad; my brother to rejoin his ship, and your father and I to travel, and visit the different cities in Europe, to love each other. Oh, what days those were! On the fifteenth of May, 1819, at Florence, you were born." Long sobbings, and Fred knelt at her feet, and laid his head against her bosom. "Your father had an English friend, who had died while they were travelling in Egypt, and whose name was Ethwold Alfred Bramler; it was his wish that you should bear the names of his dead friend in full. I consented to the two first; you were named Ethwold Alfred, and in a short time the two were contracted to Ethfred, and finally to Fred, which you still bear. Of all bestowed upon you by your father, this alone adhered to you."

"That is the name — Ethfred — that I have dreamed of, or remembered, and I must have remembered you. And I now remember that Belle, the first night of our meeting, told me of this name, — Ethfred."

"And you remembered it, and I was certain that I was right about you," she answered.

Mrs. D'Arlon resumed her narrative: — Her husband had an uncle on his mother's side, a rich Cuban planter, who owned sugar and coffee estates on the island, and the winter before Fred was a year old they spent with him, on his estate on the Canema River, not far from Matanzas. In the spring they came home, spending a few weeks among D'Arlon's relatives at Charleston; the summer and autumn they were in Boston, and other places in the north. Her husband's uncle dying suddenly in the autumn of that year, D'Arlon went at once to Cuba, followed, soon after, by his wife and child.

As she approached this point, she became much agitated, and then hurried forward. She went on to say, " That the nominal engagement between herself and her former suitor was not by express terms broken off, — that her brother did not deem it necessary, nor did she acquaint her husband with it, — that the man had rapidly descended, until he was almost disreputable; was a gambler, at times an inebriate, and familiar with all the worst vices. He followed her to Europe, was constantly thrusting himself upon her, and in unusual ways, and at times and under circumstances that occasioned her embarrassment, and that might attract the attention of others.

" Everywhere we went, sooner or later, he appeared. At first, I did not understand his object. He soon demanded money of me, and as an inducement threatened to make known our former relations."

" Mother, how dared he so follow you?"

" Patience! such a man dare do anything. I several times gave him considerable sums, which only gave him a hold upon me. I was young and ignorant. I was free from him in the United States. On my last visit to Cuba, I found him on board the ship which took me out, and in spite of his promise, he appeared at my uncle's estate. Your father was never jealous —"

" Jealous, mother? Good God!"

" But the dishonorable course of this wretched man must in some way, unknown to me, have excited his suspicions."

" His suspicions, mother! Of what?"

" You shall hear. If I had had the courage to go to him, and tell him the little that there was to tell. — In some way he found out that this man had sailed from Boston in the same ship, and I knew it displeased him very much.

" One day, late in March, I had taken you and your nurse down an avenue of palms, and near a grove of the native orange-trees, and had laid you down upon the carpet of Bermuda grass, where you were rolling and throwing out your limbs, and calling me pet names, when this man came down the avenue, much excited, and said he must see me a moment, — that he was going out of the island forever. He looked much distressed. Without a moment's thought, not knowing what to do, I accompanied him a few steps among the orange-trees, when, turning and seizing my hand, he began in a vehement manner to address some incoherent words to me. At that instant my husband dashed upon him like a tiger, and gave him a powerful thrust, which sent him several yards from me ; when he recovered himself, he turned white with rage, and I saw a pistol in his hand. I heard two reports, and nothing more." Fred was almost in a frenzy. " When I came to consciousness I was in my own room, with none but my uncle's servants about me, none of whom spoke anything but Spanish, and I could understand but little of that. By degrees the memory of the awful occurrences came to my recollection, and I called for my husband and child. Nobody answered me save by shakes of the head. A physician from the city had been sent for, and I had, it seems, been bled. In a frenzy of fear I demanded to know if my husband was hurt, and to my great relief I understood, by what was said, that he was not. The administrator came — an Englishman — and brought me an envelope, addressed in my husband's hand, which I tore open. In it was a folded letter from your father, and a small slip, on which was written, in the hand of the wretch who had pursued me, an appointment to meet him in the orange grove, and at about the hour that my husband found us. I had not seen it before." A pause. " Your father's letter — you may see if you wish " — her face was pale, its muscles rigid, and lips tightly drawn, while her eyes were cold and stony. " It accused me — of — of — oh, Fred ! " —

"God of heaven, mother ! Did this man dare" — leaping to the portrait with a menace. Belle sprang before him. " Fred, he was your father ! "

" It went on to say that this wretch had openly boasted of this in the city of Matanzas."

" Mother, does that wretch still live ? " hissing out the words.

" He died by the hand of your father."

" Thank God ! " with great fervor from Fred.

" Fred ! Fred ! for God's dear sake, spare him," cried Belle to the mother ; " spare yourself these horrible details."

The almost moveless lips continued: "It said that the amplest provision had been made for me, but that I would never see him or our boy again." Each word was pronounced by a distinct effort, and followed by a pause. Fred had returned, and knelt by her side, with his hands tenderly upon her waist. "And," going on in the same way, " I never saw him again ; nor you, till yesterday." These words came in hard, dry gasps, and with the last she threw her arms upon the shoulders of her son, and fell forward against him.

"Oh, Fred!" said Belle, going to them and laying her cheek among his black curls, with a hand on either, "I would have brought you joy and happiness and hope ; and you have only anguish and horror and pain."

"Bless you, Belle!" said Fred. "She has had to carry these awful burdens alone all her life; while I, poor wretch, have been unhappy because I've had no griefs, after all."

"I have little more to say. I fell into a brain fever, and was only returning back to life amid the heat and vapor of the rainy season. I always wondered why I did not die, — I know now. In October. I returned to Charleston, only to learn that my husband and child were both dead. The news again prostrated me ; and it was not till December that, accompanied by one of your father's friends, I went to the scene of the final catastrophe. About a month before my arrival in Charleston, he had started with a carriage, a servant, and coachman, and taking you and your nurse, to make a journey into Virginia. What his ultimate purpose was did not fully appear. He had converted

nearly all of his effects out of Cuba into money, which
he carried with him, — over an hundred and fifty thousand dollars.   Your nurse was taken sick, and left on
the road, and while attempting to ford a swollen stream,
in the mountains of the Western part of North Carolina, his coachman missed the ford, overturned the
carriage, and your father, with a fatal injury, received
probably from one of the horses, yourself and his servant escaped.   The horses were drowned ; and most
of his baggage, with the trunk that contained his
money and papers, were swept away, as was told me.
He died two days after" — with the old, hard gasp —
"of his injuries.   In his last moments, a sense of his
fatal injustice to me seemed to have been permitted to
come to him, and I was told that his last words were a
message to me, imploring my pardon for his rash mistake."   Once again her head went down.

   "Thank God for those words !   Oh, my poor, poor
mother !"

   "A day or two after, his servant, with some effects,
which he is supposed to have saved, disappeared, and
was never heard of ; and you, my precious child, was
left alone.   Bibb — Jarvis Bibb, who kept a kind of a
wild place near the ford, where your father was taken
and died — placed you in the house of a poor man by
the name of Samuel Warren, where, within a few days,
you were said to have died also.   You must read this
awful Bibb's confession for the actual facts.   When I
reached Bibb, in December, all these matters were told
to me as I give them to you.   With barely life and
strength to drag myself to the graves of my husband
and child, and without question of the truth of what

was told me, I could, in my short-sighted grief, only kneel by them and ask to die. As soon as possible I had their remains removed to Charleston, and interred with his ancestors. Thus, Fred, I have hurriedly given you this hard skeleton of our wretched, wretched history ; some time I will give you many details that I feel myself incapable of now. Don't, don't think hardly of your father. He was one of the noblest and truest-hearted men who ever lived ! " And she laid her head upon his shoulder.

" My poor, dear mother ! How impossible to console you for these heart and soul stabs and losses ! Only let me love and comfort you, as God will permit me to now ; He permitted it to happen."

" God did finally send me surcease of pain and anguish, and the hope of reunion in His heaven brought endurance of life. Time benumbs the power to feel sorrow, and God comforts as He will."

So, with many words of mutual comfort, and gentle, assuring caresses, the strong, brave son took up the burden of his mother's griefs, and bore it and her from that moment onward. As the story ended, Belle left them to their sacred communings. Ere long they, too, escaped into the glad sunshine, and amid the gush of the outer life of the young, warm summer.

23

CHAPTER LI.

A S Fred went out, he took in his hand the Green document, determined to master all the remaining facts of this tragic story, the substance of which he supposed he already possessed.

In a quiet nook, he opened the paper, and recognized the hand of Cowdry. Although purporting to give the language of John Green, it was rendered in tolerable English, and ran thus:

"Being moved by the spirit, and admonished by the most holy Prophet of Almighty God, I, Jarvis Bibb, called here John Green, and once known as William Evans, to the end of promised pardon, and the peace and comfort of the Holy Spirit, that passeth understanding, make this my solemn confession:

"I was born about ten miles west of Linville, Birch County, N.C. My father left to my sister Sally and myself a place called Bibb's Tavern, sometimes known as Bibb's Hole, and often called Bibb's Hell. To prevent my sister Sally's marrying, and thus to secure the whole of this property to myself, I induced the young man to whom she was engaged to believe that she had criminal connections with young Phil Coney and others, and did induce her to join in a sale of the

(354)

property, and never paid her for her share until this past year.

"In the year 1821, about the twentieth of September, there had been a freshet, so that Devil's Creek, which ran near my house, was dangerous to pass. Just at night of that day, James D'Arlon, of Charleston, S. C., attempted to pass the ford, which he missed. The carriage was overturned, the coachman and horses drowned, and most of the baggage was swept away. Mr. D'Arlon was badly hurt; but owing partly to the exertions of his servant Dick, and by my help, he and his little son, called Fred, were got out and taken to my house, where, on the next day, he died of his hurts. As God is my judge, I never thought of injuring him. He talked a good deal of his wife, and said he had been cruel to her, and left word for her to forgive him. The boy Dick said that his master had a large sum of money, in gold and bank-notes, in a small iron trunk, which would, of course, sink. Just before Mr. D'Arlon died, we found this trunk, and got it out. The trunk was very heavy, and Dick said there was half a million of dollars in it. My place is among the mountains, with few living near it, and the devil entered into my wicked heart to make way with the boy Dick, and keep the money. It was a dark, rainy night; and having given him something in his liquor, when he was stupid and asleep I strangled and carried him down just below my house, and pitched him into the 'Devil's Hole,' in the creek, and told that he had robbed his master, and ran away. I got the key, and, on opening the trunk, I found there the bank-notes, mostly on New York and Boston banks, as I learned afterwards, had been rolled in oil-skin, and were not wet. I don't know how much there was — I never could count it rightly — more than I ever saw before or since. When Mr. D'Arlon died, I sent down to Linville, about fifteen miles, and got a coffin and a notary and a preacher, and Mr. D'Arlon was buried. The notary took an inventory of what he had — his watch and chain, and what money was in his purse, and some papers — paid my bills, and took them with him to Linville. He also wrote to a man in Charleston to hunt up and tell Mr. D'Arlon's friends. I never touched a thing but what was in the trunk, which I hid.

"What to do with the boy, about two or three years old, I did not know. Sally was away all this time, and I got Samuel Warren, a sort of a relative who was at my place, to take him till his friends should come for him. About ten days after that, Sam's child died, and I then thought that this boy might pass as his, as there was nobody that knew which child died; accordingly it was given out that the boy had died also, as was reasonable. I was afraid that if the boy grew up among his father's friends, or with his mother, when he was old enough something would happen, and he would find everthing out. So I paid Sam fifty dollars and the run of drink, to take the boy as his own. When the boy's mother came, Sam's wife went up into the mountains to a place I knew, and took this boy with her. I told them all about it, and finally they had the bodies removed.

"After this I did not feel safe; I could not use the money, and in the spring I sold the place, and Sally signed the deed. I took Sam and his wife, and the boy, and Sally, and went across the mountains, into Tennessee, where I was known as William Evans. Sally was my widowed sister, and kept her name. We stayed there and cropped one season, and then moved to Western Virginia, where I met a man from the Western Reserve, who owned land in the town of Mantua. I found there was no communication between that region and the South, and that no man from the South ever moved on to the Reserve; so I bought his land, and took the deed in the name of John Green, my wife's brother; buying up a good many cattle and horses and things, I moved here, and came in the spring of 1824. Here I took the name of John Green, and Sally, my sister, though called a widow, came to be known as Sally Green. We brought the boy Fred, and I bought a piece of land on the river in the woods, so that nobody might ever see the boy, for he was not like common boys; and Sam, whose name here was Warden, built a log house and lived there. When his wife died, I had him bind the boy to me, and when the fight came off, and Jake killed his dog, I told the selectmen that, after all, he was Sally's boy. She had suspected something all the time, and always declared that this was not Betsey's, — Sam's wife's child. We had an awful quarrel, and to quiet her, I gave her a deed of the Jim Frost farm, and five hundred dollars in gold.

"The older this boy grew, the more anxious I was to keep him. Something has told me, that if he goes away, he will hunt up harm to me.

"Sally don't know how it got out that the boy is hers, and as she has taken such a liking to him, she seems not to care about it. I never really thought of putting

this boy out of the way, though I did not know what
to do with him. I never murdered any man; I only
killed the nigger boy Dick.

"In the name of God, Amen.

"JOHN GREEN, his ⋈ mark.

"In presence of H. D. LADD.

"MANTUA, January, 1831.   *Acknowledged, etc.*"

Fred had read in the law-books the digest of singular and vulgar crimes, and the uninstructed rude
and simple details of them, in the naive confessions of
low-bred villains; but for straightforward, hard, dry,
unrelieved, undressed narration of murder and robbery,
nothing that he had ever met in downright honesty of
statement equalled this. The grim *naiveté* of the declaration, that he had never murdered a man, had only
killed a nigger, and chucked him into the "Devil's
Hole" of a dark night, was not wholly lost on Fred,
even now. And this was John Green's secret, and it
was by means of reaching his superstitious fears that
this paper was extorted; this placed him with his
uncounted plunder in the hands of the Prophet; made
him and his, the bound thrall of Jo Smith; compelled
him to submit to an instantaneous sequestration of everything he claimed, and closed his mouth against outcry
or complaint. In the dark and mysterious courses of
permitted and punished crime, what surpassed this?

This was his story. The child of these beautiful,
loving, and unfortunate parents, born in Florence,
snatched by his father from his mother, and hurried off on a mysterous journey, and substituted for
another, and hid from his mother in the mountains; his

pilgrimage through Tennessee and Virginia, and strange
wild life in the Ohio woods; twice bound, and always
kept under the eye and shadow of this murderer; his
life warped and darkened by him in his unsleeping
fear; led by Green on a circuitous, obscure road,
running through all the slow-moving years of infancy,
boyhood, and early youth, until, when he had matured
into the image of his father, he was thus brought
under eyes that recognized him at a glance, and that
penetrated the hidings and frauds of these fears and arti-
fices, in a moment. How shallow and futile the strat-
agems of the most cunning criminal always are, always
leaving a clew dangling in the eyes and within the
reach of the hands of men, could they only see it. How
strange and mysterious the way in which this document
came to his hand, to finally tell the story, thrust upon
him, while he was defending the son of this man!
Nay, that son was the messenger who bore it to him!
His mind, trained to acuteness, could rapidly run over
and through the links; yet the why and wherefore was
as inscrutable to him as to the thrush that piped the day
through from the forest thicket. not remote. And how
darkly he had been closed in and circled about by the
lines of all these tragic years! Suffering. and helping
to pay the penalty of his innocent mother's ignorance,
and of his maddened father's rashness. He was at the
end of it now, and how diminutive seemed Jake, and
his petty trial and final acquittal. He, too, was caught
and nearly crushed in the recoil of the acts of his father,
committed in his infancy. And on his trial the bare
possession of this writing might have been fatal to him,

could the fact have been established, that it was in the possession of the dead man. But how far off now in remote perspective lay the trial which had but just closed, clear away at the other end of the dark history, so suddenly unrolled between it and the triumphant advocate.

In the midst and through the mist of it all, and up over it all, floated the form of Belle. Her eye had detected the likeness; her hand had clutched the, to others, unseen clew, which, with her undreamed of energies, she followed up. True, the slow-growing fruits were ripening in their bitterness, and a catastrophe of some kind would have precipitated itself. Green's confession was on its mysterious way East; its messenger was to be slain; the paper was to fall into Jake's hands; — had it fallen into any others, or lain on the ground, no trial for murder would ever been had. But it was Belle, as he had learned, who had dictated to him the message that put him in connection with the case. To him, how wonderful it all seemed. And it was wonderful.

And did none or all of these things presage that the history of Belle and his own were finally to unite in one sweet story of old time romance? Thus he mused and wandered in the shrubbery, midst opening roses in the declining afternoon. Others were coming and going in the walks, and the eyes of two were specially on him — his proud and almost happy mother—who was not remote, and shy and innocent Belle, who was remote, and who yet, curiously enough, did not long have him out of the range of her downcast eyes.

Soon came the call for dinner, when Fred and his mother met, and he took her arm, and as they walked toward the house, somehow Belle was standing in their course, and took her other arm, and the three found Maud and her father and husband awaiting them.

CHAPTER LII.

THE LOVERS.

IT would have been curious to an observer — the tacit concert of those who gathered around the dinner-table — by which no reference was made to any of the late exciting events, or the incidents of the tragic history, which all knew was now common property. Maud, in her graceful and ripened beauty, presided at the head, while the manly face of her husband, rich with the play of genial humor, looked back to her from the other end of the table. Fred, with his mother on one side, and Belle and her father on the other, with the beautiful children, one by the mother and the other by the father, made up the party. Mr. Morris, in his soft, low voice, said a short grace. No one was much inclined to conversation. Mrs. D'Arlon had recovered her wonted serenity, and peace was in her eyes. Fred's face was grave and thoughtful, with an occasional lifting of his eyes to the demure face of Belle, opposite him, who did not meet them at all, as the observant Maud noticed, from which she augured favorably. She thought that this matter would be left to the silent workings of Belle's own heart and soul, with Fred standing by in reverent silence. That was, of course, all very high, and sacred, and sublimated.

(362)

She doubted if she could quite appreciate it; and as she met the frank, loving glance of her husband, with their beautiful children in her eyes, she realized that husband and children were preferable to mere soul-love above the clouds. As she looked at the kindling face of Fred, she doubted whether ambrosia and nectar would always sustain him, and whether he would not at some time dash his arms impetuously about Belle's waist, and assert the rights of his man's love. She was much inclined to rely on these reserved forces if need be. Yet on the whole she doubted whether they would ever be called into action. Her sister had so suddenly developed the strong and deep qualities of her real nature, that she had become inscrutable to Maud; yet she fancied that, like many a maiden wondering over the opening secrets of her own heart and its needs, she was even now trembling with running over its hoarded sweets and wealths, and that it would ere long make its voice heard on Belle's mooted question. Much as a fond mother who is intensely interested in the varying phenomena of a daughter the worshipped of a true and noble man, toward whom every element of her nature was drawn, watches her every movement in a charmed atmosphere, colored with his presence, she closely observed her sister. As the afternoon lapsed into twilight, and the softened breeze in dying whispers was taking tender leave of the closing flowers, and the full moon was shooting its silvery darts aslant under the trees, she missed the forms of both. They were not on any of the verandahs, nor in the parlors, or library — not in Belle's boudoir — and she thought that she had once caught the gleam of a white dress in the famous

grape arbor, a little remote, and which terminated one
of the walks. As the twilight deepened, and the night
air grew damp and chill, she remembered Belle's light-
robed shoulders, and knew she would not come in—
that girls were never known to—and taking a light,
warm wrap, she went toward the arbor, along the
gravelled walk. Like the considerate Mrs. Nickleby,
she signalled her approach, and looked away from the
arbor. As she stood in the leaf-surrounded entrance
with the proffered wrap, Fred arose from a low seat at
Belle's feet, came forward, and took the shawl with a
low "thanks," and she turned away.

Not all the possible nameless details that may have
hovered in the atmosphere of Maud's fancy—perhaps
none of them—had marked the interview. Fred had
fallen on his knees on the low seat at Belle's feet as
she sat down, and in a very compelling way she bade
him assume a more ordinary, if, under the circumstances, a less lover-like attitude. But his impetuous,
heartful and soulful voice would not at first be quenched.
"Oh, Belle! my heart and soul will speak; will be
heard—not in little paper parcels—but at your feet I
will say, that with every power of heart, soul, and
brain, with every emotion and fibre of my being, I
love you; not with a love that would command or
compel; not a love that will implore or supplicate,
but a man's love, to reverence and worship; a love
that you may smite and reject, if you will, and it will
not murmur." Once, as he spoke, she extended her
hand, and then snatched it from him. In the already
twilight arbor, he could not see her face, but her form
shook as if with a suppressed emotion. She removed

her hand from her face, — "Fred, Fred!" in a deep, earnest voice, "I am a woman; I cannot bear to have you think that I am less than a woman; a woman to be loved; a woman to be glorified and crowned with with such love as yours; one who would above earth gladly give back all she is and has!" — a pause, and lower and deeper. — "Listen! I am a wife now."

"A wife! You a wife!" starting up in amazement, almost in horror. "How? I don't understand. I thought your boy-husband died years ago. Is there? can there — ?"

"There cannot be; there is no other. Oh, no other, Fred!"

"Did not his death dissolve this marriage? Are you still bound to a phantom — a shade — a memory?" with astonishment in his voice.

"Were I free as you are free, to give you myself, as I would give; and should it please God to separate us for a little, would you, in my absence, woo, love, win, and wed another?"

"Oh, Belle! how you torture me. In my heart and soul I reverence a true marriage as eternal."

"Would you take another's wife in adultery?"

He dropped his face and groaned. "It was not so much to hear you, or to argue this matter with you, that I came with you here, as to tell you my own little story." Then without hesitation, in her unconscious innocence, she told him the story of her married life. And if there was ever lover worthy of such a confidence, it was he who reverently listened to her on that June night. When she finished, a silence ensued, and it was during this silence that the thoughtful Maud brought the needed wrap. As Fred received, he laid it with a tender reverence about her shoulders, and still remained standing, as if she would terminate the interview then. She evinced no such purpose, and Fred resumed his seat.

"Fred," speaking again, "this has been the subject of thought and prayer and of some conversation with Maud; and I say frankly, that lately, when I've tried in my own soul to meet it, I am in doubt. I think I can see where my duty lies, but I don't feel it so strongly —" with a sweet sincerity — "and, Fred, knowing this —"

"Belle, Belle, don't let me be tempted to assail, to throw my arms of passion about the soul's wings, when it would arise white and spotless to God's throne for light. God, with your soul, must decide this!" with a sad earnestness.

With a wonderful sweetness and trust, she now placed her hand in his. "Oh, my soul's lover and brother, — now indeed can I trust you! Do you not feel it possible, that out of the atmosphere of earth and above its clouds and gross perfumes, souls may meet and commune?"

"Belle, I distrust this. The most elevated and exalted soul is only strong as its temple is pure and sacred. For one, I dare not hope that such a union can ever become purified and sublimated, and beside, is not your marriage one of soul and spirit, purely! and will your wedded spirit admit another to communion with it?" Was there a little of sarcasm in this? or was it the recoil — the revolt of the instinctive man from the only hope she proffered?

" Fred," a little coldly, " there can be but one marriage of soul as of body. The chaste and pure may have friendships, may they not? "

" Friendships! friendships! and friendships of the soul! What empty, meaningless words! I am but a man, and never less a man than now; " with a sad bitterness.

" Fred," solemnly, " would you wed with me, take me as your wife, if I, consenting, should still see this other tie lying between us? "

" Belle, though I would compass earth and compel all its impossibilities to reach you, yet you must come to me without the shadow of doubt or distrust, — with your whole self."

She extended to him her other hand, and they arose, passed out under the moon, and without another word returned to the house, and, at the door of Belle's apartments, they silently took leave of each other for the night.

CHAPTER LIII.

BELLE SENDS ANOTHER MESSAGE.

LATER, Belle emerged from the charmed mysteries of her sleeping-room, with hair looped up in beautiful hanging festoons, with light rippling through its wavelets, in a simple robe of white, that just gave freedom and air to the shoulders, and fastened in front, so as to permit a little auroral white to radiate up through its openings. Lightly her graceful folding robe of white silent stuff, gathered about her waist, under the easy restraint of woven silk cords tied at the left side; and as she came forward and reclined upon a spacious sofa-like lounge, with rich silken cushions, the snowy slipper which stole so innocently and unconsciously into the light, betrayed that it alone covered, without hiding, a foot that had but one peer in the world. Her face was never so serenely lovely as now; not the warm sensuous loveliness of a promised bride, half conscious that sense united to form its glow; but the celestial and serene loveliness of the affianced of Heaven, in which the vague and far-off emotion of earth was still present, but purified until it took the color and hue of heaven.

The face was grave, too, almost to solemnity, for she felt that the hour of final ordeal had come. She had

(368)

shrunk from this love that had so enfolded her, and would not let her escape, and in which she could hardly have breathed had she not compelled it to color and shape itself in the grasp of her high ideal. She had shrunk from herself, would not be with herself, would not know herself, and as constantly rushed out of and away from herself; now for this day she had been compelled to reoccupy her inner self. And Fred, — she was not now compelled to avoid him. He had been the one subject of thought, action and being; but it was in the deceptive character of an object to help, toil, scheme, and plan for, not in the guise of a lover, who was some time to know and reward with a life of devotion. Now this delusion had vanished, and he was before her with his great unselfish love, tested by her two or three questions, and she knew that it could be trusted. All the time, the two or three cries of anguish which had escaped him in his moments of heat in his speech for Jake, were haunting her memory. Now she must answer to herself, to the memory of Edward, to her soul, and to God, and that she might answer the final question to Fred.

So, alone in the cold, white, colorless chamber of her undraped, ungarnished soul, she knelt, not to argue, not to question, not to yearn, or implore, or supplicate, but by the mighty power of silent, undoubting, unhesitating faith, to draw herself into the serene presence of her highest conception of God, and lay herself hopefully and confidingly at His feet, in silent, receptive communion. A sweet and blessed peace seemed to steal upon and pervade her heart, and to her closed eyes appeared to come a pure, colorless light, gradually in-

24

creasing until the apartment was luminous with it.
Radiating from no centre, it cast no shadows, but grew
brighter and more effulgent until every surface was
tremulous with its undazzling brillancy. Then slowly
it receded and faded out, and the white rays of the
moon fell through the uncurtained window, visible in
the dim light of the lamp, and the rustle of the silken
curtain answered back to the whispering zephyr.

Had she slept, — had she dreamed? What mattered
it? Light and rest had certainly come in that hour,
and drawing a covering over her, she passed from waking to sleeping consciousness.

Fred, though blessed, and for him happy, like most
mortals, found great incompleteness — something wanting, — and that something was, after all, the only thing
in the world. He had Belle's love, — he knew that
he wanted her. He had never really hoped for her
love. He knew he had it now, and this knowledge
brought a great, but at best a pained exaltation. Now
he understood it all. She had loved him ; her love had
inspired her, in the great labor, and with a great sagacity, to catch at clews, and follow them through lab-
yrinths with confidence, where others could not see, and
followed in blind distrust and uncertainty. And after
all, was she not too beautiful and good, too high and
sacred, for any man's wife? So he could but canonize
her, and surround her with a halo of saintship, and set
her apart for worship. But it brought no peace, did in
no way meet a great want. She would not change.
She had set herself apart, and would remain conse-
crated, and it was not for him to throw his earthy
shadow over the stainlessness of her soul.

The awful strain which for many days had been upon
his strength and energies, in actual and long labor, and
the fearful excitement that involved the deepest and
strongest emotions of his heart during the day, and
for many days, had at last completely exhausted him;
and he was soon overwhelmed in profound and dream-
less sleep, which differed from death only, in the vague,
far-off, feeble consciousness of continuing life. When
he awoke, he awoke from a deep sleep, almost as
profound as that from which it is said the dead may
finally spring. It was well in the morning as he
arose, with all the recent events throbbing back upon
him. Belle was the first, and then his mother, and
these brought all the rest back. He was a little languid and a little sore, and found that his eyelids looked
heavy, as if oversteeped with sleep. He dressed himself slowly, and stepped out. Just outside stood a
young girl, a maid of Belle's, who approached him with
a blush and courtesy:

"Please, sir — Miss Belle said will you come to her,
please?"

"Certainly;" and by a way new to him, he was conducted down and through a passage to the door of her
boudoir, which was slightly ajar. His attendant pushed
it open, and he entered. Belle, without raising her
eyes to his, met him and held out both her hands, with
a conscious flush deepening on lip and cheek. Wondering, he took her hands, which were not quite steady,
and in his confusion he stooped and kissed them, and
as they were not withdrawn, he lifted his face towards
hers; there were her rich red lips, very near, and to
these he placed his own; one arm clasped that little,

yielding waist, as a lover clasps ; and their warm, glad, happy tears united and fell. A moment, — "Belle — this means love and hope and life?" — in breathless ecstacy.

"Love and hope and life, Fred!" — just raising her eyes and dropping them again.

"And wifehood, and all it means?" eagerly.

"And wifehood, and all it means," with sweet firmness.

"Freely?" — a little anxiously.

"Freely, — and oh, so gladly!"

And they knelt together, and united in blessed thanks, that brought new blessings.

In the capacious library adjoining the breakfast-room were assembled the other members of the party, awaiting the arrival of our principal personages. The mother had not seen the newly-found son that morning, nor had Mr. Morris seen Belle ; yet if one might judge by the countenance, Maud was more anxious for their appearance than any of the party. So intensely and so hopefully had she sympathized with Belle's love for Fred, and quite as much with him, and so little had she appreciated what appeared to her as the shadowiest of shadows, which Belle permitted to interpose between her and Fred, that she was impatient for the conclusion which to her clear-seeing and practical mind was at some time soon, inevitable. The grape-arbor interview she highly approved of ; but she had observed that they returned from it early, and she had seen nothing of either since. After all, was this son of a fiery Southern, with his French blood, to prove a sort of a 'Miss Nancy in love'? or had he, too, been infected with some of Belle's ecstatic notions of shadowy marriages in heaven? She thought that he would be very likely to have healthy views, and on the whole she was hopeful. Then the door was pushed open, and Belle and Fred entered and paused a moment, beautiful in the light and glow of their perfect happiness.

"Oh, Belle! Belle!" exclaimed the excited and now satisfied Maud, springing forward, and throwing her arms about her sister's neck. "Oh, I am so glad!" In a moment it flashed upon the rest; and father and mother, with tears and happy words, embraced, blessed, and congratulated the lovers, while Marbury, who had a profound admiration for Fred's talent, and who had a real liking for him, assured him, with tears in his eyes, that this alone was needed to complete the happiest circle.

A moment after, Maud, who had disappeared from the room, returned with a small morocco case in her hand, and going to Fred, she said: "I never was so near having a brother before; let me contribute something to make this new relation seem more real. I knew this would happen, and so I provided for this blessed hour!" She opened the case, and, producing a beautiful solitaire. Fred took the ring, mid the silence of the approving throng, and placed it upon the finger of the blushing Belle; then raising the jewelled hand, pressed it to his lips, leaving tears upon it. Then, with joined hands, the two received the blessings of the father and mother.

The housekeeper, who had taken special care of Aunt Sally, brought that personage forward, who had already learned what Belle had done for her favorite, and she stood now a little abashed in presence of Fred's mother and Belle and Maud, glad beyond expression at his wonderful restoration, yet sad, as she felt that he would now be shut away from her forever. As she entered and paused, Fred seemed to comprehend what was passing in her mind, and going forward to her, took her hands, and cried : " No, no, Aunt Sally! You are always to live with me, and be my Aunt Sally."

" With us ! " cried Belle, coming up and kissing her ; " and be our Aunt Sally. Next to his mother, you have the oldest claim upon him, and we will make you blessed and happy ! " When Fred's mother joined in this assurance, the old woman seemed supremely blessed.

Sam Warden and Jake, who were discovered at the door, were brought in, Fred saying, pleasantly, " that as Sam was a sort of foster-father, and had always been kind to him, he thought he, too, had a right to know of the marvellous good fortune that had finally overtaken him." It lost him not a bit in the love of Belle, that in this moment he should recall even the little that he owed to Sam. Jake, who would have been embarrassed by the presence in which he found himself, had also the grace to feel the position he occupied towards Fred, whom he had met but once since they parted, the night of his acquittal. He stood hesitating and crying. As Fred approached him, his face grew first sad, as the memories and sufferings of his life thronged through his mind, and tears, too, came into his eyes. " Jake," he said, in a softened voice, " we are finally friends, are we not? Not a word of the past years, Jake. In a way, we were involved in a common misfortune, and thankful are we that we have escaped." Jake would have spoken, but could only raise Fred's hand to his lips, and sob over it. There was nature even in him; and it had at last been touched, and at that moment he looked almost good in Belle's tear-blinded eyes.

And all this time the breakfast cools, — and let it cool!

All that happened, — oh, ever and ever so long ago! Twenty-eight years, on this last day of May, 1873, as the vision fades from my regretful memory, and dwindles to a tale that brings a blinding mist to my eyes.

Just before the war, which has antiquated everything that preceded it, I stopped at the Mantua Station, on the Mahoning Railroad, after long, long years of absence. There was the old Judge Atwater mansion turned into a tavern, and save the Cuyahoga, a diminished but still a beautiful stream, my eye saw no familiar thing. In a heavy but bent form, I finally recognized Darwin. It was a pilgrimage for me; and, as I stood about the depot, curious strangers looked at me, and queried of my name, and when they heard it, no man could identify me, and I knew none of them. I wandered up the banks of the river, recalling all the past. In a bayou overhung with willows was the remains of a little dug-out, covered with the still water, and nearly buried with drift. Somehow it reminded me of Fred's little canoe, cast adrift so long ago. Farther up, in a lonely mullen and thistle-grown field, remote from any dwelling, I recognized the deserted heap of stones, and the solitary apple-tree, that marked the site of the rude hut that sheltered his child-

ish years. Melancholy beyond expression, I returned
to the Station, and wandered up the old State road,
towards the Corners. The old brick tavern had disappeared, and no vestige of the old South School-
house remained. Chapman, an elderly man, had turned
farmer, and grown weighty. Turner had been for years
out of the hotel, and was also a thriving farmer.
Nothing at the Corners remained. Young Foster had
built a new store, where the old Maryfield house once
stood, and a stranger was in the old tavern-house. In
the kitchen-garden, under the barberry bushes, was a
small marble pillar, with the name " Sir Walter." In
the now populous cemetery, over west, by the side
of Elias's grave, stood another stone, sacred to the
memory of Mary Carman, and still another to the
memory of Sarah. Uncle Bill Skinner slept near by,
and a neat stone marked the resting-place of Betsey
Warden, having " Fred " on its base. Fenton had
moved away.

My friend George Sheldon took me up the State
road, just beyond where the Fenton place was, and
there in a little cottage, presided over by a beautiful
daughter of Sarah, we found Uncle Seth, still serene
and cheerful; although, save this young maiden and
her sisters, nobody was left to him. Martha had died
years before, in her distant home, and slept in other
earth.

We went along up to the next corners, from which a
mile east could be seen the upper story of the Carman
farm-house, to which we drove. The old pear-tree was
dead, but still standing, a monument of the blight and
decay that had fallen on the once beautiful homestead.

The farm-house was shabby and neglected, weeds and burdock were in the yard; Sarah's flower-garden had been turned into a pig-yard, and neglect and ruin brooded over all the old home. A coarse, common man had purchased the property, and cut down a part of the old orchards, and left the fallen trees to decay where they fell. The fences were rotting, and falling down; the "Springs" were choked up, producing bogs and small swamps.

We drove over to the Rapids. The magnificent chestnut forests had been cut away, and rude, stumpy fields and sordid farm-houses gleamed and glinted in the late August sun. The Furmans had moved away. All the forests had vanished from the now tame and shrunken Cuyahoga. A flouring-mill and machine-shop employed the water, and the already dilapidated little wooden town of Harrison disfigured the eastern bank of the river.

We talked over the old time exploit of Fred; the rescue of the drowning maiden — whom we also saw, a comely matron with her children — and recalled the fortunes of some who had been connected with his earlier years.

Jake Green had accompanied Warden back to Missouri, and had not been heard of for years.

Father Henry had lost his voice in the dark waters. He "assisted" at the wedding of Fred and Belle; and the quaint and tender things said to have been uttered by him on that occasion were still remembered and repeated with variations and additions.

And Belle and Fred, — what of them? — whose real lives were about to commence so brightly, beautifully, and hopefully? Would you know? They had a history, and if the world evinces an interest in these preliminary chapters, that history, much of which the world knows, may be indicted more completely.

DATE DUE